MAN IN THE STRUGGLE FOR PEACE

MAN
IN THE STRUGGLE
FOR PEACE

By

CHARLES MALIK

HARPER & ROW, PUBLISHERS
NEW YORK, EVANSTON, AND LONDON

This book issues from the lectures by Charles Malik at the Twentieth
Annual Lecture Series of The Claremont Colleges, Claremont, California
Claremont Graduate School and University Center
Pomona College
Scripps College
Claremont Men's College
Harvey Mudd College

341/3
M29

FIRST EDITION

B-N

LIBRARY OF CONGRESS CATALOG CARD NUMBER: 63-8007

Dedicated to
the loving memory of
My Father and Mother

HABIB and ZAREEFI

for whom life was a perpetual struggle
for Being and Peace
and who were granted in this life of struggle
a glimpse of the Peace Beyond
which shed its wonderful light
not only upon their thankful children
but upon all those who knew them

CONTENTS

INTRODUCTION

I

WE ARE THROWN into this world of struggle and care. We made neither our world nor ourselves: we *find* ourselves in this state. Before we can even ask the question "Why?" we must first exist, and, existing, we must recognize our condition such as it is: we are beings of care, beings who have our mind on all sorts of problems and concerns. Only such an existing being can "recognize" his state, and, in recognizing it, can ask the question "Why?" about it or about any other thing. The man who is not struggling or the man who is completely care-free does not exist. This is our human condition, this is what it means *to be* a man, this is our fate. Here the word "fate" has nothing to do with chance or fatalism, with predestination or the necessity of nature, if by any of these terms is meant that in struggling and caring we are not essentially free and accountable. Any notion that for anything involving our caring decision we can invoke some *kismet,* some *deus ex machina,* to relieve us of responsibility for that decision is utterly foreign to our mind. Man is as *fated* and *doomed* to be free and responsible as to struggle and care. He is thrown into this world and left to struggle and swim on his own. In fact, it is precisely because his possibilities are never completely closed before him, but he can always throw himself upon any one of them (at least he can be silly or he can be true), that his life is ever a life of struggling care. He cares and struggles *because* he is free; because, that is, he can always be one of a number of possibilities, and in being one, he has thereby for that occasion categorically excluded all the rest. This natural tragedy (the hallmark of his human limitation) whereby there is ruthless *destruction* of possibilities in every decision and choice is the ultimate ground of his anguish. His heart aches because he *must* destroy. But *what* he must destroy, *that* is left to his freedom. When we say, "this is our fate," we mean this is our essential nature, this is the sort of being we are. And this being originally and inalienably includes our freedom.

All this is part, indeed it is but the elementary part, of the teaching of Heidegger.* But regardless of Heidegger's ultimate motives in not wanting explicitly to ground this fundamental insight in the Judaeo-Christian tradition (it is quite reasonable to suppose that, personally-existentially, he himself owes it to this tradition), but choosing instead to invoke a fable from outside this tradition, a fable "which is pre-ontological in character" and whose "demonstrative force is 'merely historical,' "† this insight is absolutely integral to the Judaeo-Christian tradition. The Old Testament begins with this judgment upon man, which appears essentially to have stamped his being for all time:

And the Lord God called unto Adam, and said unto him, Where art thou? And he said, I heard thy voice in the garden, and I was afraid, because I was naked; and I hid myself. . . . And unto Adam [the Lord God] said, Because thou hast . . . eaten of the tree . . . cursed is the ground for thy sake; in sorrow shalt thou eat of it all the days of thy life. . . . In the sweat of thy face shalt thou eat, till thou return unto the ground; for out of it wast thou taken: for dust thou art, and unto dust shalt thou return.‡

---

* *Ibid.,* pp. 241–243.

† The publication in 1962 of the translation into English of Heidegger's *Sein und Zeit* (*Being and Time,* translated by John Macquarrie and Edward Robinson, New York: Harper & Row, 1962) is for the English-speaking world a philosophical event of the first order.

‡ Genesis 3.

This passage is full of suggestions precisely for the sort of ontological analytic of man that Heidegger would delight in. The passage can be easily purged of any special mythological-theological overtones or interpretations arising from the "cursing" of "the ground" and the "eating in sorrow" and "in the sweat of thy face," as well as from the other imagery used; when thus purged, the passage would clearly reveal the pure phenomenological notion of care (Sorge) in the Heideggerian sense. Although the Psalms do not purport to be a systematic-philosophical treatise on the ontology of man, and although David was not trained in the techniques of descriptive phenomenology nor steeped in the Kantian critical-transcendental method of uncovering the *a priori* "conditions of the possibility of a thing," still the Psalms, rightly and correctly understood, are the greatest fundamental ontological-existential work ever written. They portray in the clearest and most authentic manner every possible existential mood and state of being into which man can fall. They provide all the necessary material for a complete ontological system. And not only this: if philosophical ontology, by its very nature and claims, is able to reveal, through the systematic disclosure of phenomenology, only those structures which belong "by nature" to human existence, and if, side by side with this disclosure, there is also at least an intimation of a genuine realm of transcendence, a realm whch can only be pointed to from a distance but can never be penetrated by any ontology or any human reason, then the Psalms supply, not only material for a complete "natural" ontology, but much positive information about that realm of transcendence itself.

The Book of Job is another great ontological storehouse within the Western tradition; the material it yields on "the human condition," not only for the special interpretation of Christian theology, but precisely for the requirements of philosophical ontology, is virtually inexhaustible. The Books of

Ecclesiastes and of the Proverbs contain marvelous ontological disclosures about man and his state. One may say that the basic theme of the New Testament is the conquest of death through death, the redemption of the finite by the infinite taking on the form of the finite, the overcoming of essential human limitation and corruption* by the perfect and incorruptible deigning to become and converse with man. But no themes are more ontological-existential than these.

In fact, what does the whole Bible purport itself to be? It purports itself to be the Word of God, in a sense to be responsibly determined by theology. But the God of the Bible is the *creator* of heaven and earth, of everything visible and invisible, and therefore certainly of man, whom, the Bible affirms, God created in a very deep sense in "his own likeness and image." Now a whole tome, composed of scores of books, worked out by innumerable minds over the span of some twenty centuries; a tome whose explicit theme throughout is the ground of all existence, including above all human existence; a tome, moreover, written, not about "ideas" or "structures" or "phenomena" of existence, nor about the direct, immediate, personal existence of some philosopher, but about actual, existing, historical men and peoples, in their *actual, historical dealings* with the ground of their existence: such a book must obviously occupy a unique position in all the annals of ontology; it must serve as the fountainhead *par excellence* of all existential-ontological material.†

* On the point that Heidegger's analytic makes no "ontical assertion about the 'corruption of human nature,' " see Heidegger, *op. cit.,* p. 224. But our reference to the New Testament need not involve any "special theology" or doctrine of "sin and corruption"; we are here only saying that genuine ontological structures can be culled in abundance there.

† Consider further the following passages from the Bible. These were certainly not written expressly to meet the needs of some speculative existential philosopher. They contain more material than what is "conceptually" proper only for ontology. But they help, together with hundreds of other passages that could also be cited, to exhibit the Bible as a fundamental mine of ontological suggestion:

II

Nothing would appear more incongruous than to introduce this book with this strange meditation on the human condition and the relations between Heidegger and the Bible. But apparent incongruity here is not the last word. We will therefore proceed to dispel it.

In Heideggerian terms, man is a struggling-caring being. In Biblical terms, man is a being estranged from the ground of his being; and because he is thus estranged, and he knows it, he desperately seeks that ground again. Put in better terms still, man is a creature; but whereas all other visible creatures just obey and raise no fuss about it whatever, this particular creature, man, has developed a sort of misunderstanding, even a sort of quarrel, between himself and his creator; he therefore seeks to "settle" this quarrel, or, better, his creator himself has sought to "settle" it for him. While this quarrel, this "enmity," lasts, he can never have peace; and so long as he exists, it will last. The struggle for peace, then, is grounded in a much deeper and more original struggle. Man struggles for peace because he *is essentially* a struggling being. But for this original ontological-existential struggling, there would be peace; his struggling essence makes possible his struggle for peace. It is not that he is all happy and peaceful to start with,

---

"And God said unto Moses, I AM THAT I AM." Exodus 3:14.

"Yet man is born unto trouble, as the sparks fly upward." Job 5:7.

"Man that is born of a woman is of few days, and full of trouble." Job 14:1.

"For what hath man of all his labour, and of the vexation of his heart, wherein he hath laboured under the sun? For all his days are sorrows, and his travail grief; yea, his heart taketh not rest in the night." Ecclesiastes 2:22–23.

"That which hath been is named already, and it is known that it is man." Ecclesiastes 6:10.

"Man is like to vanity: his days are as a shadow that passeth away." Psalm 144:4.

"For we know that the whole creation groaneth and travaileth in pain together until now." Romans 8:22.

and then, turning around, he *finds*, as it were casually, that
there is something the matter with the world (in his family, in
his immediate environment, in his country, between the nations); and so he sets about reforming the world. It is not that
he is descending from the peace of Mount Olympus to dis-
tribute peace upon the world. To start with, man exists in such
a fashion that he *is not* at peace either with himself or with
the ground of his being. Man struggles for peace, and for other
things too, because he is essentially a struggling-caring being
—struggling and caring, above everything else, for the integrity of his being. He is struggling for outward peace because,
and at the same time as, he is struggling for the peace of his
own soul. In all such struggles there is an aspect of "the blind
leading the blind," of "physician heal thyself." Man in the
struggle for peace, if he is serious about it, if he really knows
what it is all about, can only take his task with a sense of
humor, even with a certain measure of cynicism. That is why
most diplomats smile: it is not hypocrisy—it is a sort of meta-
physical awareness of the human impossibility of their task.
Man must first put his own spiritual house in order before he
can help to establish peace in the world; or, at least, he must
struggle for both ends at the same time. It never follows from
this that man must fold his arms and do nothing until he is
completely reconciled to God. There is a fundamental Christian dogma which, if he is a Christian, can help him immensely
in this regard: the dogma that the reconciliation is *already
vicariously accomplished* for him. That ought, to some extent,
to put his mind "at peace"; at least to the extent of releasing
him to struggle, in all humility, as best he can, and with such
means and material as he may command, for the peace of the
world. The struggle for peace cannot be understood exactly
for what it is until it is viewed as an aspect of a much deeper
struggle in the very being of man.

Now, some of the most creative minds of the West are trying to think out their ontology independently of the fountain-head of all ontology, a fountainhead which is at the base of all Western existence. This is a most significant phenomenon. These minds appear to be ashamed to face their existence; they seem embarrassed by it; somehow, they do not feel "free" in its presence. In the name of the autonomy of reason, they develop a view of human existence which is quite divorced from the actual, historical ground of that existence. There is something artificial, something even superficial and pathetic, in this attempt. It seeks existence and integrality with passion and singleness of mind, but there is about it a shying from, a disowning, even an ingratitude for, the ground of all existence. What is the ultimate reason for this secularizing and humanizing, this de-theologizing, de-spiritualizing and de-Christianizing, tendency? May it not have something to do with the sort of being that man is—a being who does get ashamed of his cause and ground, a being who recognizes his ground by rebelling against it, or even by maintaining a golden silence about it? Why this shame? Why this ingratitude? Why this disowning? Why this silence? It could have arisen from the sufferings of two wars. A deeper struggle than any that has been noted so far appears to be called for here to overcome this disowning shame, and therewith to try to re-establish harmony and peace between man and his ground. Whether in this deeper struggle man can re-establish this harmony and peace on his own is of course the perennial question.

This phenomenon extends far beyond the confines of contemporary existential philosophy; in fact, this philosophy itself is rooted in the radical existential estrangement pervading the spirit of this age. Atheism is fundamentally only a rebellion against the real, living, historical "ground." The entire tone, the fundamental orientation, of present-day existence—political, social, literary, artistic, scientific, philosophical, cultural—is secular, nonreligious, even anti-religious and atheistic.

"There is" the material world with its vast resources; "there is" man, however his existence is conceived; and "there is" reason, however its powers are interpreted: *that is all*. Man and the world between themselves are absolutely self-sufficient; man needs absolutely nothing outside his possibilities to master the world, including of course himself and others. No wonder people talk of a "post-Christian" age, although their spirit is more to welcome and confirm than to regret and combat this tendency. We face therefore the phenomenon, in the practical-historical-cultural sphere, of the pride of existence and of human self-sufficiency. Man proudly refuses to acknowledge his ground, his origin, his dependence, and to draw the shattering consequences that that acknowledgment entails. So long as this radical existential pride holds sway, not only in individuals here and there, but in the fundamental direction and tone of a whole epoch, can any thinking man, with a broken and contrite heart, really expect any peace on earth?

We thus raise the question as to whether the peace that is sought after and struggled for under such conditions is not elusive; whether man is not only deluding himself when he thinks that through pride, cleverness, and self-sufficiency he can attain peace; whether on the pure presuppositions of reason, nature, man, and existence, peace is possible; whether under such conditions even the best will in the world avails; whether the struggle then is not in the end blind and hopeless; and whether, therefore, all that one is hoping to achieve is simply not to let the peace be disturbed through him and in his time. He says in his heart: The thing is hopeless, so let me at least not be responsible myself; let whoever comes after me take responsibility for *the thing* himself. In all diplomatic, political, and international existence, there is a point at which the phenomenon of "passing the buck" is bound to manifest itself. How can man, forsaking his origin, disowning his ground, hugging himself alone, ever attain peace? Peace is some kind of harmony and order, a species of equilibrium and tranquillity, a form of justice; but when man, either willfully or misguidedly, turns his back on his creative origin, is he any longer sure that there is much harmony and order, much equilibrium, tranquillity and justice, left in him?

Let there be no misunderstanding on one point: Man will certainly keep on struggling—struggling for the highest prize, which is certainly peace. Man will struggle with the utmost sincerity and good faith, and with everything he has and is. He will achieve whatever measure of peace is humanly possible. No war at any time is altogether inevitable; something could always happen—and through human agency it could be made to happen—that could prevent, or at least that could postpone, any war. Thus, one will never relent in working day and night for the cause of peace. Nothing could be more noble. But let the slightest germ of doubt enter his head that on account of his pride, his self-sufficiency, his willful disowning of his origin and his ground, and his self-congratulation and self-satisfaction he has at last "caught" his existence and displayed it all by himself, the peace he seeks with such a spirit and under such an aegis is altogether false and illusory, and the deepest sadness will overtake his heart. He is no longer sure of himself. His whole attempt is vitiated at the core. He appears to himself beaten in advance. The greatest goal in the world—peace—is then revealed a veritable mirage, resting on insecure foundations. He appears silly in his own eyes. His self-respect and his sense of seriousness become undermined. A dislocation assails his being. The "struggle" appears quite hypocritical—in the final analysis, without hope. One indulges in it as a game, really sporting with destiny; it is not the real thing. Although you will never fail an occasion when it presents itself, you somehow know that you are engaged in a patching-up operation. You may have helped in averting this war, and you may with justice feel profound satisfaction, saying to yourself: That is all I can do, let others now do their part. But you know that that is not enough; for you are not seeking only your own glory, or that the world should applaud you for having "saved the peace," or that you should then merit the Nobel Prize. You are interested in something much more profound and much more serious. You really want to know whether lasting peace is possible; for a non-lasting peace is clearly not peace. You are asking about the nature and essence and possibility of peace. For although you have done your best and saved it this time, how can it last if human passion continues to take its own course, unpurged and uncontrolled? How can it last if man is such that self-love (Augustine) is the ultimate principle by which he is governed? Must you not then leave aside all your hypocrisy, all your sporting, all your patching up, all your struggling for peace, in order to enter into a new sphere of struggle altogether— the struggle for coming to terms with, and getting hold of, the mystery of your own nature and being and ground?

There is something at once necessary and noble, and false and sad, about the struggle for peace: necessary, because caring-free man must struggle; noble, because the struggle here is for the greatest prize; but false, because man is struggling in his own power; and, therefore, sad, because he knows that such a struggle, for all its heroic and noble necessity, is doomed in the end to tragic failure.

"The peacemakers shall be called the children of God." Nothing from the point of view of our discussion could be more strange and significant than this statement. It is full of ontological meat. It affirms that there is a direct relationship between peacemaking and having the right relationship to God —the ground of being and existence. It implies that you cannot make peace if you violate this right relationship. All struggling for peace where this relationship is broken is therefore false and futile. A proud and self-sufficient being, turning his

back on his ground and origin, can never make peace. Western
civilization, in dislocating itself from its source and creator, is
not in the best position to make and secure peace.

III

Men struggle for peace on a thousand fronts. One such
arena is the United Nations. Here the peace meant is "international peace and security": the absence of armed conflict
between the nations as well as "the development of friendly
relations" among them. From the moment Secretary Stettinius
banged the gavel on April 25, 1945, opening the San Francisco
Conference on International Organization, to the moment almost exactly fourteen years later when I, in my capacity then
as President of the General Assembly of the United Nations,
banged the gavel in New York closing the Assembly's Thir-
teenth Session, I had close and almost uninterrupted relations,
in one form or another, with the United Nations. It was my
privilege during this period, in addition to doing many other
things, both to represent the Republic of Lebanon on delegations to many United Nations organs and to serve as an elected
officer of many of its bodies. Besides being continuous, my
experience at the United Nations was most inner, intimate,
and intense. The first part of this book contains but the barest
and most preliminary sketch of some of my existential conclusions from this experience. The individual human person
here is struggling always with a view to bringing about some
understanding, some concord, some "relaxation of tensions,"
some positive agreement between nations; not indeed at any
price, but under the guidance and with the determination of
some notion of justice, as embodied principally in recognized
international law and in the Charter of the United Nations.
But above both Charter and law, the most decisive element is
the living agreement of free agents. When there is a dispute

or a conflict or even war, and when the parties concerned freely agree to some settlement, the agreement is itself the law and the charter of that situation. Once an agreement is reached, and however it is reached, nobody thinks any more of the United Nations, of international law, or even of justice. The parties concerned are now quite satisfied, and that is the end of the matter so far as "international peace and security" are concerned. There is no law or power above the will of the parties concerned; this is another way of saying that they enjoy the status of "sovereign equality." International law and the Charter of the United Nations serve only as general frameworks for promoting and inducing that agreement. *Peace* in the international field is in the end nothing but agreement. The ultimate regulative idea of everything that happens at the United Nations is therefore *how to bring about agreement.* Man in the struggle for peace at the United Nations is precisely a slave of this regulative idea.

What happens now to this poor or happy man? How does he give effect to this regulative idea? What modes of being does he get himself into? What does he concretely go through? What does he "come up against," both in himself and in the world? Through what passions, what tendencies, what forces, what actual organized movements, must he thread his path? How much is he personally "compromised" in the process? He is at once a representative of a certain national interest and a responsible member of the world body; how do these two loyalties, his national citizenship and his world citizenship, interact? When he is elated, what elates him? When he is depressed and disgusted, what depresses and disgusts him? What is the rock on which he rests in his darkest and loneliest moments?

What is it that keeps him going? Ambition? Vanity? Flattery? Glory? Pure chance? Sheer doggedness? The glamour of the show? The simple fact that he has a good "job"? The service he is rendering his nation? The love of international concord? The lure of justice? The wonderful experiences he undergoes? The fact that others "need" him and have entrusted him with important responsibilities? The compelling nature of the prospect of peace? The pure inner satisfaction that he is a faithful soldier in the battle for peace? What is it in "the constitution of his personal human existence" that makes possible his international role? His rational being? His sense of human brotherhood? A certain cosmopolitan-international background in his education and upbringing? His fear that war would destroy him and his loved ones? The thrill of taking risks and of danger and adventure? A special weakness for the material, social, and political benefits enjoyed? An original, inexplicable, irreducible, special, personal interest in matters international? A special devil (*daimon*) dogging him on?

Does man in his international struggling today differ existentially from man struggling internationally at any time in history, when, for instance, the Spartans sent embassies to the Athenians, or the Athenians to the Romans, or the Byzantines to the Arab caliphs, or when statesmen forgathered at the Congress of Vienna or at the Paris Peace Conference of 1919? What does this constancy of human nature mean? Is not the doctrine of progress, then, a sort of escape from this constancy, a sort of childish wishfulness that it did not exist?

IV

These are all perhaps interesting questions, but there are much deeper themes still. The United Nations sharpens the sense of history. It reveals to man struggling in it the phenomenon, in all its awful concreteness and complexity, of historical decision. Some such decisions are taken at or by the United Nations, but the more important ones are taken outside its pale. Wherever history is decided, a ripple of varying intensity reaches the United Nations, and you decidedly feel it. The constancies of history and man are important, but what is historically more important are the decisions of history. It is the unique in history that matters most, and therefore the struggle for peace always takes on the tragic character of the unique.

Concrete responsibility and decision are indispensable for the proper understanding of history, and one wonders if the historians, and *a fortiori* "the philosophers of history," would not significantly change their interpretations if they had been entrusted with concrete historical responsibility, or if they came in direct contact with the actual process of historical decision. Had Hegel, or Nietzsche, or Dilthey, for instance, known personally and intensively what it meant to be responsible for actual historical-political decisions affecting the fate of a nation or a people or a culture, would they still have conceived history in the manner they did? The absorption of things in general ideas is not history: it is the unique decisions that count. You are a philosopher of history; but history is primarily responsibility and decision, and you have had no part in any responsible, historical decision; how, then, can you philosophize about that which, in a sense, you really know nothing about? It is not enough to be responsible for decisions affecting your ideas or your writings, your personal existence, your family or your immediate circle of friends, or even some institution of which you may be the head. All of this is not history, except in a very derivative sense. History is constituted primarily by responsible decisions affecting the fate of peoples, nations, and cultures. Philosophers who have not staked their life and reputation on concrete, responsible, historical decision; who have always lived, protected and sheltered, in their "ivory towers," viewing the world safely at a

distance from their monadic windows; who have never allowed
their aesthetic integrity to be soiled and smeared by the dirt
and corruption of the world: such philosophers can perhaps
philosophize about all sorts of things, but not about history.
History is a different beast altogether from your feelings and
sensations, your concepts and categories, your ideas and experiences, the logical forms of your thought, the beautiful
systems which you playfully construct, and what other philosophers, with whom you are arguing or against whom you are
reacting, have said or opined. Responsible experience at the
United Nations sharpens the sense and reality of history as
nothing else does.

What is history up to today? How is it being decided? This
craze for international organization—what does it mean historically?

What is the historical-existential significance of the challenge of communism? What does "ideological peace" mean?
How does "international peace and security" depend on "ideological peace"?

What is the historical-existential significance of the rise of
Asia and Africa? How much myth and how much reality is
there in the whole theory and practice of "independence"?
What is the ultimate meaning of development and under-
development? What is the principle of development? What is
the end of development? What are the agencies of development?

How do the principal cultures, civilizations, systems of valuation, fundamental outlooks on life, mutually challenge, judge,
test, and exasperate one another today? Who is learning from
whom, who is influencing whom? What values are historically
at stake today? How are the authentic Western values faring
in the historical-existential "struggle for existence"? When the
values that you love and that you wish to bequeath indefinitely

to your children and children's children suffer a setback, what do you do? What are you doing, both personally and in historical decision, to strengthen and deepen and extend these values? How do science and technology today enter into the determination of history? In the onrush of technology and materialism, are the tested human and spiritual values of the past doomed to extinction?

Since history must pass through, and since it is uniquely constituted by, the decisions of the men and women who are historically responsible today, how is this generation acquitting itself historically? Is there real historical greatness today, so that epochs will be named after this or that event, this or that decision, this or that man? What constitutes historical greatness?

When peoples suddenly "take up" their history, what does that mean? Can history be "suddenly" taken up? What is the difference between a history that has never been broken to be taken up again, and a history that has been broken and is now taken up again, or that is suddenly taken up "for the first time"? How did the whole notion of history historically arise in the first place? Who first created this notion?

What does the absolute loneliness that characterizes every truly historical decision mean existentially? What is the place of morals in historical decision? What is the role of the accidental in historical decision? What is the exact balance between the so-called "personal-subjective" and the so-called "social-objective" in the decisions of history? Since every historical decision involves the destruction of innumerable possibilities, how do these destroyed possibilities nevertheless continue to live? In the actual, historical, concrete clash of cultures and civilizations, is the agent who carries the brunt of decision really free? What is the secret of the strange phenomenon of "secrecy" in all historical decision?

In what concrete sense is the future dependent on the past,

and in what concrete sense is the past dependent on the future? How is history created by the future?

Who really writes history? If history is created by decision and responsibility, who decides responsibly the writing of history? How much "truth" is there in written history? What is "historical truth"? Can history ever be really written? What is it that can never be written or known in history? How important for history, and for "the truth of history," is this thing that can never be written or known?

It is relatively easy to ask these questions, although the very asking of them can never be excogitated *a priori*. It is likewise easy to answer them by constructing a special theory of man, time, and history. How "true" this theory is remains the great question. What is not so easy, what is *the problem* for any philosophy of history, is to try to answer these questions *in terms of specific, responsible decisions, known firsthand, which have actually made history*. The published memoirs of statesmen, politicians, and diplomats, and the archives of governments supply original material in this field. But usually what is unpublished and inaccessible is the decisive thing; and if the philosopher himself is not the responsible statesman or politician or diplomat in question, he again receives his material *secondhand*; he was not existentially involved and implicated; and, therefore, he will never be able to know, he will only be able to guess (and some guesses are pretty shrewd), what was really decisive. Some of these questions are raised in this book, principally in the first and third parts. Apart from certain obscure intimations here and there, no actual, historical *demonstration* is given. Such a demonstration would be a work of intensive research. It would constitute an attempt at a new philosophy of history grounded integrally and radically in the fundamental ontology of man, where *firsthand* "experience" supplies all the material, where decision, responsibility, and the historically unique are the determining phenomena, where death is ever hovering on the horizon, and where something even beyond that, something true and radiant and wonderful, keeps hovering too.

V

Actual, human, personal existence struggles for peace at the United Nations. In this struggle everything about existing man is put to the test; his whole ontological apparatus is brought into action. Always and everywhere, in the case of the simplest peasant woman and in the case of the most responsible statesman, man's whole ontological apparatus is in action; but at the United Nations it is in action for international peace and security. This is the object, and not any special "existential experience" or any particular existential sharpening of the sense of history. "Existential experience" and the sharpening of the sense of history are accidental to the main business of the United Nations. The United Nations is not intended to be a staging ground where philosophers are jolted out of their dreams and biases (one would hope that life in her munificence would not have denied them this corrective jolt even if the United Nations never existed); nor is it intended to provide them with an intensive course in what I have just called "existential experience," including the intimate knowledge of how history is a matter of decision and responsibility. If a man happens profoundly to "wonder about" and "care for" these things *for their own sake,* then his experience at the United Nations could serve as a most wonderful opportunity for clarifying, deepening, and rendering absolutely concrete his view of man (meaning, always, his view of himself) and his view of history (meaning, always, what decides and makes history). But this "happening" is altogether accidental.

In fact, if philosophers can learn much philosophically from and at the United Nations, there are limits to how much philosophers *qua* philosophers can serve the United Nations. Too many philosophers there could ruin the place. Lostness in words and ideas, in arguments, and even in "the truth" could do much harm where living historical issues of destiny and decision were at stake. Philosophers must first become sensitive "men of the world," in the most exalted sense of the term, before they can do much good politically, whether nationally or internationally. There are inherent limitations, which can be ascertained philosophically, to the ability of Plato's philosopher to be a king. There is no rule, no formula, no short cut in all this: there is only suffering (and it belongs to the essence of suffering that it cannot be known in advance nor fully expressed even after it is known), experience, and a certain transcendent grace.

The substantive business transacted at the United Nations consists of the items discussed and decided by its diverse organs, and of the vast amount of extra-official diplomatic activity transpiring all the time among the delegations, through intercourse, intrigue, and maneuver, and through informal sounding and negotiating. The United Nations does not justify itself because philosophers learn anything from it, although there would be virtually no limit to what they could *philosophically* learn and profit from the world body if they should happen to be responsible actors in it for any length of time. The United Nations is justified by how successful it has been in fulfilling its fundamental purposes, which are: "to maintain international peace and security"; "to develop friendly relations among nations"; "to achieve international cooperation in solving international problems of an economic, social, cultural, or humanitarian character, and in promoting and encouraging respect for human rights and fundamental freedoms for all";

and "to be a center for harmonizing the actions of nations in the attainment of these common ends" (Article 1 of the Charter).

The second part of this work is a sort of *apologia* for the world organization. It is an expression of positive faith in the necessity and usefulness of this body. Nothing is easier than to criticize the United Nations, except perhaps to close one's eyes and softly dream of it as a *catholicon* for the ills of the world, as "the last best hope" of mankind. What is to be determined here is the simple question whether a world with the United Nations is better than a world without it, and how much better. My answer is that, for all the defects of the United Nations, a world without it would be, not just poorer, but much poorer than the present world. This is not a general, "internationalistic," "optimistic," sentimental conclusion; it is a judgment argued soberly, somewhat exhaustively, and, I trust, solidly in the second part. Considering existing world conditions which have developed and ripened completely independently of the United Nations, and considering the moral-cultural-spiritual situation of the Western world, the United Nations, as an international-political body, is fairly satisfactorily fulfilling its ends. The simple proof is that it has not gone to pieces, and nobody, not even South Africa which received endless defeats and censures in it, would dare leave it. As a mechanism, it can certainly be improved in a number of ways, although how practicable it is even to try to bring about the desirable improvements is a great question. I have not suggested a list of "amendments" to the Charter on such questions as the method of voting, the composition and functions of the various organs, the procedure of debate, the structure and functioning of the Secretariat, etc. Good ideas on these and other matters have been offered by many sources. The trouble, where it exists, is not with the mechanism, but with the independent, political, international, and intercultural conditions prevailing in the world, conditions that would have tended to vitiate even the best mechanism. To expect these independent world conditions to improve through the mere improvement of United Nations machinery is a relapse into superstition and magic.

The Western world, and especially Western Europe, have had much to complain of at the United Nations lately, but this is only an aspect, and a very minor aspect at that, of the world position of the West in this age. The West should thank the United Nations for having helped to shock it into an awareness of its real position. If you are driving an old-fashioned car that is nevertheless in fairly good order, and if you experience some difficulty on your journey, either because you have taken on too many passengers with many conflicting opinions as to where you should go, or because you are running a fever yourself, or because you do not even know yourself where you want to go, then you are not likely to get there faster and safer in a brand-new model. First, get rid of your fever, make up your own mind, and see to it that some consensus has developed among your fellow passengers, and then you will start making progress whatever the state of the vehicle. You might even then reach your destination on foot. If the West were not in the state in which it is—divided, infiltrated, softened, unsure of itself, morally weakened, congratulating itself over veritable crumbs, repeating the wonderful slogans of "man," "freedom," "truth," without, however, filling them with full-blooded content, apparently unwilling ascetically to pay the price of rising to the spiritual heights of which it is certainly capable—the whole situation, not only at the United Nations, but in the whole world, would have been different. The United Nations sinks into insignificance when it comes to the ultimate questions of war and peace today, and of the fate of Western civilization. An independent, original inquiry into the cold war, its nature and its prospects, has therefore to be attempted. This is the burden of the third part of this work.

VI

It is always a question of peace, and of the kind of peace. This question today takes the form of whether communism can live at peace with the non-Communist world. The Communist version of the question is whether the non-Communist world, now ripe for communization, will allow itself to be communized without resistance involving war. Resistance there will be, but let it not lead to war, since the end is inevitable—this is how communism interprets this moment of history. In either form, the question is whether communism and the rest of mankind can live together at peace in one world.

What do we mean by communism? The *total phenomenal fact of communism* is presented in Chapter 13. To understand this moment of history, and to be clear in one's own mind about the question of peace and of the kind of peace, one must absolutely face these twelve items which together constitute, each in its own way, and all in the complex manner in which they variously articulate into a whole, the total phenomenal fact of communism. When one fully, absolutely, and unescapingly faces them, then the question is: *What do you think of this most arresting fact?*

To the question, What do you make of the total phenomenal fact of communism? there are four answers: (1) Communism deserves to win and will eventually conquer the whole world. (2) Well, the peoples themselves will try it, discover that it is false, and then reject it; so, do not be too obsessed by the thing: nationalism will take care of the matter. (3) Well, the Communists themselves will mellow and change, and we, too, will change (in fact, both of us are changing and have already changed considerably), and thus approaching each other, one day we will meet and live together in peace; so, do not be too obsessed by the thing: time and change will take care of the matter. (4) We know the thing is hopeless, and so we are preparing to settle our accounts with them through war. Before the total phenomenal fact of communism, one rests existentially either in communism itself, or in nationalism, or in change, or in war.

The first answer cannot be held by Western leaders and thinkers except if they are already "won over." Man is such that this "being-won-over" can be so subtle and unconscious that he who *is* "won over" will fiercely resent any suggestion of the kind. Thus, the first answer is but a repetition of the challenge of communism to those who have not been "won over." That leaves us only with nationalism, change, and war as the saviors of the world from communism.

We demonstrated in Chapter 15 that all three hopes are empty. The native forces, otherwise called nationalism, do not command sufficient vitality and resources to resist successfully an eventual Communist take-over: the Communist onslaught is too much for them. The hope that salvation comes from the processes of change and mellowing is superficial and wishful. And as to war, it has been virtually abolished as a deliberate instrument of national policy; it has become obsolete, irrational, and impossible as a way out of the challenge of communism.

If these three hopes are false, and if the West does not propose to surrender, then we are faced with an unprecedented situation jolting the West out of any sense of existence-as-usual and catapulting it into a real revolutionary mood. For that which is neither war, nor surrender, nor change, nor nationalism, can only be revolution; namely, something which (1) will, in the *peaceful* competition with communism before nationalism everywhere, especially in Asia and Africa, prove to be far more attractive and irresistible than the assault of communism; (2) will not wait passively and hopefully upon communism to change according to its own inscrutable natural laws, but will confront it with such a powerful challenge—economically, politically, intellectually, morally, and spiritually—that communism will have to respond (and, we must remember, war is out of the question for it too), either by disintegrating from within, or by "changing" itself, peacefully or through revolution, in the image of the irresistible challenge; and (3) will attain the ends of war (war being no longer possible, even if in the past war—I mean preventive or aggressive war—was ever justifiable) without firing a shot, namely, the reduction and transformation of the enemy, in this case, communism. A thing of this order of magnitude can only be fundamental revolution, and I believe nothing short of this is adequate to the historical moment. Any hankering after existence-as-usual is a nostalgia for the impossible today.

Our argument is with the thinkers and leaders of the West. How do they understand the present moment of history? What do they make of the total phenomenal fact of communism? Some of them at least appear quite satisfied with "keeping the peace" and "maintaining a steadily rising standard of living." Is this enough? But they may be preparing something in secret, something of a profoundly spiritual order, with which they will surprise us later on. What is it, beyond peace and security, that they are preparing in secret? Are we living in a period of great, expectant gestation from which tremendous new spiritual energies are going to be released? Perhaps we are, but the question is always the *type of man* who will emerge, and not the speed with which he will circle the earth or reach the planets, or the state of impeccable health and mind at which he will be when he will die from some accident or from a sudden heart attack at the age of 230. Will he be applauded and admired by the deepest men in history? And who precisely are these deepest men who are competent to judge us all? Who are still regarded as the deepest men of history? Who is the judge and who is the deepest?—this is the ultimate question of Western existence today.

VII

There is a sort of conspiracy of silence about communism. People appear to be no longer appalled by the total fact of this phenomenon; they are getting "used" or "adjusted" to it; it no longer shocks them. The possession of atomic and nuclear weapons, and the means to deliver them, by the Communist world appear to have overawed people into silence. Thus, a real "evolution" in the thinking of people appears to have occurred. This is part of the general atmosphere of "peaceful coexistence." One gets the distinct impression that, if only people were assured that they would be permitted to hold their own, they would be happy and satisfied. They do not seem to want anything more. If this "adjustment" means the banishing of the thought of war (except, of course, taking every precaution for self-defense), then it is all to the good. But if it means that the total phenomenal fact of communism no longer demands a radical answer, then a most dangerous softening has set in.

There are some analogies between the present struggle and past ideological-political struggles on a world scale. But these analogies are superficial and misleading. Today, the struggle is as much internal as external; Western values in the past were not infiltrated and undermined from within; there were no representatives of the alien ideology active and boring from within, either through political parties or through books and the radio, in Rome and Paris, in Oxford and New York. This is the radically new situation. In the past, there were physical and psychological barriers safely protecting Western civilization; when the enemy bodily reached the frontiers, he was unmistakable—politically, culturally, militarily, radically; and the defenders of that civilization rose up and defeated him. Today, the enemy is as much internal as external; in his internal guise, he belongs to the same race, language, culture, civilization, body politic; he cannot be automatically identified as an "alien." Existentially, the enemy now is hidden; he has gone underground—so much so that he no longer appears as enemy; and the very word "enemy" has now become objectionable. And yet he is as bent on destroying the ultimate values of man, truth, God, and freedom as any enemy in the past. Where the foe is no longer sharply marked off from the friend, the struggle is more dangerous. One can write a whole book on the many ambiguous alliances that have developed all over the world, with their endless complications, obstructions, and confusions.

Darwin was not an accidental product of the Anglo-Saxon mind: he expressed one of the deepest aspects of its nature. For centuries that mind has felt itself oceanically protected, secure, apart, and imperturbable: nothing could reach its citadel without adequate advance notice. In this "fortunate" state, which was denied others, it could take time, both in changing itself and in adjusting to the changes of the world. Nothing it hated more than upheaval, cataclysm, sudden change, revolution: all this was horrible; besides, it was unnecessary.

The law of existence, then, was evolution, not revolution. Today, however, there is an equalization of danger and insecurity. Cultures obey their inner laws of development, some possessing in their very nature vital ideas with almost unlimited creative possibilities, some soon brought to a halt because of the narrowness and rigidity of their vision. But so far as the dependence of cultures, in their being and not-being, upon inscrutable external forces is concerned, there is today virtual equality, at least among the major cultures of the world. None enjoys greater external immunity than others, none can talk "from above," is though it were not subject, like others, to the law of profound modification and even of sudden death. In this *external* respect, "fortune" no longer favors one more than others; "justice" has spread its wings equally over all; with a most exhilarating sense of freedom as the result. This has not yet seeped into the creative conscience of the Anglo-Saxon mind. In this discrepancy between the new truth which disturbs and the lingering tradition which tranquillizes lies hidden part of the meaning of the present crisis. This is a revolutionary situation; it is yet another reason why the old horror of revolution must itself go overboard.

As soon as you mention the topic of the cold war, people demur and appear offended. It is as though you were meaning them in person. But the issues transcend every person and every regime. The thirty-three criteria of Chapter 16 must be faced in all honesty. They measure accurately the performance of Western civilization over a span of about two generations. Above every irritability and personal ambition, leaders and thinkers must make the coldest possible assessment of where their civilization is, at its deepest, and where it is tending at the present rate. They stand before the tribunal of history and the truth; they cannot take refuge in diversions and dreams.

VIII

Some will say: Let us then support revolutions wherever they occur. In the less developed countries, conditions cannot go on as they have been since time immemorial; a change is long overdue. When the change comes, and regardless of the modality it takes, let us make sure that we do not stand in its way. Let us help the wave of the future wherever we can peer into it. But three questions arise: (1) Since no change ever comes about spontaneously, who is going to start and who is going to direct or influence the coming change? (2) Are these revolutions which are now taking place all over the globe learning—economically, socially, politically, ideologically— more from the West or from the Communists? (3) What about the strange phenomenon of the West ending, virtually invariably, by supporting totalitarian regimes? Does it accept the verdict that its forms of government and of social and economic organization are unexportable, whereas those of the Communists are? This is most disturbing to one who cares in the slightest degree about whether his values are true and universal. It is the initiative of the change, the spirit and direction of the change, and the outlook on man and destiny and history that emerges from the change, that the West must first weigh and consider. If the change means the inevitable sprouting of totalitarian regimes which drive out every fundamental Western value; and if the West's only interest in these regimes is the political one of making sure that they do not ally themselves (or do not ally themselves too much) with Moscow and Peiping; then the West, by thus writing off its deepest values as of no importance, or of no universal validity, in this moment of history, has thereby doomed itself. In the end, not form but spirit determines everything.

Another notion has gained currency in high places. These peoples (the underdeveloped, the unaligned, the neutral) are in a hurry to "modernize"; so let us carry the banner of modernization for them and help them to modernize fast. With our resources, we can do it better than the Communists; here, then, is a field in which we can excel—*the modernizing of the world*. But this is sheer empty formalism again. Poor man has sunk into the background: only roads and instruments and standards of living and stages of development are meant. It is good to wave the slogan of "modernizing" if this is the language these peoples understand; but it is one thing to use their term, and it is another thing altogether to be clear in your own mind as to what content you wish to pour into it. The merry modernizers must face these questions: Modernize *from what?* Modernize *into what?* How different is my concept of modernizing from that of the Communists or of those who do not care for my fundamental values? If by their culture they are neutral or indifferent or even hostile to me, am I allowed by my culture to be neutral or indifferent or hostile to them? If they cannot include me in an all-encompassing idea, if they can only "use" me, do I have an all-encompassing idea myself under which, far from just "using" them, I can creatively include them as ends in themselves? What kind of humanity do I wish to see them develop into, what kind of fundamental values do I hope to see them realize and love, after they have become, through my help, thoroughly "modern"? What may I, from my resources, from my background, from my heritage, from my civilization, hold out to them as a fundamental message? The gay modernizers will become the laughingstock of the world if all they know is how to modernize.

IX

In many respects China appears to be the ultimate problem. We can speak of China *and* the world as we can of no other agglomeration of people. Culturally, the Chinese are a world "walled" apart. India has always interacted vitally with the rest of the world; it exported Buddhism northward and eastward; it had throughout all history intimate cultural relations with the Middle East; the most important linguistic family of the globe, the Indo-European, proves the existence of deep common historical-cultural roots between India and the West; British rule has made a deep mark upon the mind and life of India. Persian history is bound up with the history of peoples east and west. The Arabs through Islam established the most intimate spiritual relations with peoples throughout Asia, Africa, and the Mediterranean. The peoples of Africa have always had more or less close relations with the Mediterranean world, with Europe, with the peoples of South Asia and the Middle East, and with the Western Hemisphere. Greece is the mother of Europe, including Rome. The Russians are only the eastern Slavic segment of Europe, with a predominant Byzantine fundamental outlook. Western Europe is one family, and between this family and its two daughters, Russia and America, subsists the closest kinship. None of this is true of China. How China, whatever its ideology, can be peacefully and creatively integrated with the rest of the world appears to be the long-range problem of the future.

It follows that the relations between the Soviet Union and the non-Communist world are generically different from those between Communist China and the non-Communist world, not because Marxism-Leninism in the one case is different in spirit and intention from Marxism-Leninism in the other, but because Marxism-Leninism is overlaid, in the one case on a Russian, in the other on a Chinese, basis. The Russian basis could conceivably throw off this yoke and reassert its spiritual unity with the West; the Chinese basis, even if it threw off Marxism-Leninism, has no original spiritual unity with the rest of the world to reassert. With Marxism-Leninism-International-Communism anywhere there can be no peace, but the prospects of peace with the Soviet Union, owing to the Western-Russian-humane ingredient in the Russian soul, are decidedly greater than with Communist China. This circumstance introduces modal differences of the utmost importance in the elaboration of policy towards these two Communist giants.

It follows further that the relations between Russia and China could not be watched too closely, nor could people be too discreet in watching them. The developing rift between these two countries furnishes a welcome respite to the non-Communist world, provided it does not lead to falling back into the mood of existence-as-usual. One of the failings of the West has been that, while it had for more than a hundred years every opportunity to penetrate and transform China, it was only the Western aberration of Marxism-Leninism that finally succeeded in penetrating that land. Whatever happens to the present apparent alienation between Russia and China, whether it should blow over in time or deepen even to the point of open war, Marxism-Leninism will continue to mean the hatred of the ultimate values of the West and the determined drive to destroy them.

Thus the yawning questions persist: What is your attitude towards Marxism-Leninism, whether of the Russian or of the Chinese type? Are your relations to the outside world, to the Chinese and Russians as well as to the awakened peoples of Asia and Africa, going to be only political (the control and domination of imperialism; the "independence" theory of the present era; the "war" theory with respect to communism)? Are they going to be only external (through trade and commerce)? Or do you have something deeper than politics and externalism that you feel called upon to give, something cultural-existential-spiritual of which you are sure and conscious; and how do you consciously and responsibly propose to give it? How do you propose to reconstitute yourself spiritually? How are you going to relate yourself to your own history? The respite of the rift, while most important, should not be allowed tragically to cause people to relax in the historical-existential duty of facing these decisive questions. The challenge today is far more cultural, civilizational, spiritual, than military and political.

X

An authentic Western revolution is absolutely necessary. This is the crying demand of the moment. It will brush aside all superficial thinking and all existence-as-usual. It will deal with fundamentals. Putting behind all timidity and all bourgeois complacency, it will ascetically dare to face the ultimate issues of existence. It will not be ashamed to identify itself with the deepest in the four thousand years of Mediterranean-Western history. It will develop a tragic-ecstatic sense. It will know that there is no thickness of history anywhere comparable to this one, with its wonderful values, tested and confirmed again and again. Such a revolution cannot be synthetically improvised; in a sense, it cannot be even planned; it can only be called for, yearned for, prayed for, expected. It will only come in "the fullness of the time." A revolution means first of all *revolutionaries,* not ideas, not hopes, not plans. Whoever thinks there is such a revolution, let him point out his revolutionaries. When the revolution comes, *it* will determine its ideas and its ends. But in the last chapter of this book I ventured to suggest a few *notes about the revolution.* The moment *calls* for a revolution; the present situation *is* revolutionary; and these "notes" determine, not the revolution, but the historical-spiritual-existential character of the "revolutionary situation." I am convinced there can be no authentic Western revolution adequate to the tremendous demands and opportunities of the moment without taking full account of the considerations I have urged.

This age is perfectly cut for the highest heroism of the spirit. Every aspect of human existence—material, social, political, international, intellectual, spiritual—is in the grip of some revolutionary ferment. We live in some sort of a day of judgment. Eschatology is of the essence of existence today, a passing to the limit and a peering beyond. One is constantly reminded of Berdyaev's expectation, in one phase of his thinking, of a new age of the Holy Spirit, an expectation that goes back to St. Seraphim.

The heroes called for will outgrow by a million degrees all

mediocrity and shallowness, all pettiness and narrowness of vision, all littleness and shortness of breath, every softness, unworthiness, cleverness, ungenuineness, subjectivism, sentimentalism, bravado, and personal ambition. Every word they utter will weigh a world. They live and move and have their being in directness and silence, in certainty and truth, in depth, rapture, and triumph, and in utter simplicity. In the solitude of their being, they are always transfigured and transformed in the presence of the ground of all being. Nietzsche was quite right in calling for such men, and much of his prophetic description of their character is true. A Nietzschean determination is of the essence of this moment of history. But in the name of what are Nietzsche's men to exist and yearn and create? Obviously, having, at least on the surface, no truck with God, Nietzsche's men can only exist, yearn, and create in the name of nothing. But what is needed is not nothing, but Being. This can only be the Living God, the creator of heaven and earth, and of everything visible and invisible, the God of Abraham, Isaac, and Jacob, the God who has been concretely known and loved for four thousand years. While he has showered special blessings upon the West, he is the God of the whole world. Nietzscheans humbly grounding themselves in God is what this moment of history really needs. Let the West grope and fumble as much as it pleases: it can never meet the enormous demands of the moment without this requirement.

XI

Having begun this Introduction with Heidegger, I wish to end it with Jaspers. In quoting the following passage, I am committing myself to nothing in it. In fact, I have strong reservations about many of the ideas expressed, especially about Jaspers' over-confidence with regard to existential philosophy. But it appears to me to bring together within one compass, in a special sort of way, the many themes and threads that have been touched upon in this Introduction. It serves only as a compendium of the topics that should be critically and much more profoundly gone into.

But if the question is put what, if anything, Europe could make of its pre-Biblical and pre-Greek origins, without the Bible, then it must be said again and again that we are what we are in virtue of Biblical religion and the secularisations which have sprung from this religion from the basic principles of humanity to the motives of modern science and the impulses of our great philosophies. It is a simple fact that without the Bible we pass into nothing. We cannot abandon our historical origin. The nihilist way as the product of Christian development, and thus as itself conditioned by Christianity, was Nietzsche's great theme. But nihilism can only be transitory and momentary. For in itself it is nothing, it lives only by opposition. . . .

No one can imagine what will be. To outline it would mean to create it. Only in indefinite terms is it possible to say that the Bible and the classical heritage are not sufficient in the form we have known them till now. Both must be transformed in a new appropriation. The vital problem for the coming age is how Biblical religion is to be metamorphosed.

What can bring the transformation about? Only the primal faith out of which the Bible arose, the source which never *was* at any time but always *is*—the eternal truth of man and God, existence and transcendence. Everything else appears as a foreground to this, which is fundamental in Biblical religion for Jew and Christian, and also for Islam.

Biblical religion has in fact continually changed its appearance, as it were its clothes. What is the basic unchanging factor? The answer can only be given in the abstract as "the one God; the transcendence of God the Creator; man's meeting with God; God's Law of the choice between good and evil as absolutely valid for man; consciousness of historicity; the meaning and the dignity of suffering; openness to insoluble problems". . . .

We dare not forget the dead, the millions of the slain, and how they had to suffer death or how they sought it. We must regard all suffering, including that which did not touch us, as something which ought to touch us, and from which we are saved without our deserving it. Indifference is all the more untrue in face of the terrible evil which can strike us all, and of which indeed men speak, but without its becoming a reality in their souls. Was Kierkegaard right when he said, "All the frightfulness of war will not suffice; only when the eternal pains of hell become a reality again will man be shaken into seriousness"?

I dare to believe that this is not so, and that the pains of hell are not the only way by which man can reach seriousness in humanity and truth.

Alongside the religions in their church forms and in polarity to them, philosophy, as in the ancient world, will be a form in which men will discover, in stillness and without noise, absolute seriousness for themselves. In more than one European country to-day, under the name of existential philosophy, the thought is growing of a common practice of life—different in form, it is true, to the point of alienation, but perhaps arising from related impulses. . . .

The philosophically serious European is faced to-day with the choice between opposed philosophical possibilities. Will he enter the limited field of fixed truth which in the end has only to be obeyed; or will he go into the limitless open truth? That is, will he submit to a dogmatic form of total knowledge; or will he hold in balance, as the means of his existence, all possibilities of thinking and knowing? Will he solidify his independence till it petrifies—as the Stoic philosophy was a refuge when the world failed—content in the peace of apathy and in the solitude of a rational attitude (dogmatic or sceptical); or will he win this inner independence in perilous openness, as in existential philosophy, the philosophy of communication, in which the individual becomes himself on condition that others become themselves, in which there is no solitary peace but constant dissatisfaction, and in which a man exposes his soul to suffering?

No valid image of man faces us, as in the deceitful Stoic ideal; but man's way. We trust our direction when we hold to three claims: (1) Limitless communication between man and man, from the depth of the existential, loving struggle, in which truth arises, up to honourable dealings in the compromises of existence. (2) To become master of our thoughts, to submit to no form of exclusive knowledge, to bind ourselves to no standpoint and no -ism. (3) To acknowledge love as the final guide, but under certain conditions to nourish an unavoidable hate and as soon as possible to let it die down again.*

C.H.M.

Beirut, Lebanon
November 1962

---

* Karl Jaspers, *The European Spirit* (London: SCM Press, 1948), pp. 60–64.

ACKNOWLEDGMENTS

A preliminary sketch of the first five chapters of this book was first used before private audiences at Dartmouth College in the spring of 1960, and then before a public audience at Harvard University in the summer of the same year. A primitive outline of the argument of Part III (not including Chapter 16) was presented to private and public audiences in Washington, D.C. during 1961. Both of these preliminary sketches were then revised and delivered, as thus revised, in November 1961, as two lectures under the auspices of Claremont University College in California, one at Los Angeles and one on the college grounds. Some of the ideas contained in Part II were used in addresses delivered throughout the United States during the last few years. All this material was then thoroughly gone over and rewritten, and substantially modified and expanded, expressly for this book. None of it was published before. Added to this material are the last three chapters of Part I, the last chapter of Part II, Chapter 16 of Part III, and this Introduction, all of which have been written only with this book in view.

The arrangements for the publication of this book were first made by Claremont University College under the lectureship undertaken in November 1961. I was honored to be asked by the College to lecture to its friends, faculty, and students, and I wish to record my appreciation of President Bernard's unfailing courtesy and encouragement. I am also grateful to Willard Hunter of Claremont who was always understanding and helpful. To Harper & Brothers (now Harper & Row), and especially to Richard B. McAdoo and his colleagues, go my thanks for their cooperation and their many helpful ideas. Much of this material was first articulated in my mind always of course on the basis of previous knowledge and experience while I was associated with Dartmouth College and with The American University in Washington, D.C. I am permanently and gratefully indebted to these two great institutions.

PART I

The United Nations:
An Existential Interpretation

CHAPTER

1

EXISTENCE AT

THE UNITED NATIONS

I

IF YOU SERVE at the United Nations for ten or more years, and if you are entrusted with positions of responsibility in the hierarchy at once of your government and the United Nations, so that you cease to be a mere sentimental or ineffectual outsider, or a well-meaning armchair thinker, extolling or criticizing the United Nations in the abstract; if you not only observe, no matter how closely, the functionings of the world body at the highest level, but actually participate in its decisions, no matter how humbly, and take responsibility for them; if you come from a fairly sensitive and central region of the world whose problems are constantly under review and debate at the United Nations, and, as a result, you and your country and region are for the greater part of that period more or less constantly in the limelight, defending or attacking, parrying or thrusting; and if, after and despite all this, you manage to remain alive, not only physically, but above all spiritually—

3

then you have been afforded one of the richest and most rewarding experiences of your life.

You represent your government and you speak in its name. Depending on your relation to your government and on the relative degree of unimportance of the issue under consideration, you may indeed be given considerable latitude in your judgment, but on the whole you must conform at least to the general framework of the instructions under which you operate. The distinction between individual judgment and governmental policy becomes one of the sharpest distinctions in your mind, and the independent reality of your nation, your state, your government, assumes almost crushing proportions. The best cure for any form of idealism, whether Kantian or Hegelian or Berkeleyan or Humean or Platonic or Marxist or nationalistic, the best method of awakening the mind to the sober and sobering realities of realism, is to be entrusted over some years, away from all thought and all books, with governmental representative responsibility abroad, especially at the United Nations: you soon discover that there is no doubt whatsoever that there are active realities, active centers of will, beyond you—your government as well as all those other governments—forming themselves and coming to their own conclusions completely independently of you, according to a will and a law of their own; and you soon settle in the conviction that whoever of the philosophers was so wrapped up in himself (regardless of the "causes" of this self-wrapped-up-ness, whether it was his "fate" or the result of his own responsible personal choice) as to seriously doubt this primary fact was a bit touched in the head. You soon find out that these individual centers of self-will, far from just providing you with "food for thought," actually require you to adjust to their independent and often unpredictable ways. You do not just "live on" them, the way the philosophers for the most part "live on" what they are talking about: you have to "live with" them, if you are to live at all. Far from the real being only that which fits into your mind, that which you notice, that which you understand, the real appears to be precisely that which does not fit your mind, that which is beyond your understanding, *that which leaves you yourself completely unnoticed*. He who haughtily notices must here struggle to become noticed himself, and such struggle, with all its dirt and danger, the idealists, in their morbid fear of being contaminated, either disdain or know nothing about. This radical awareness of and radical "existence with" others, where, to be at all, is to be one among many—and you are fortunate if you attain even that—is the characteristic lack in all idealism; and political-international existence, especially at the United Nations, is the perfect remedy for this lack. Nothing is healthier in philosophy than for the philosopher to realize—morally, existentially, personally, actually—that, far from being himself the center of the world—as Hegel, for instance, managed to persuade himself—he is not even at the periphery: he hardly counts at all. The importance of philosophy is never better revealed than after its self-importance has been completely exploded. The spiritual adjustment in the soul of the philosopher consequent upon this shock is the real conversion to which Plato should have called attention in the allegory of the cave, although his meaning was the exact opposite.

II

It is a common experience at the United Nations for one delegate to tell another, especially if they are otherwise on friendly terms: "You have completely convinced me personally, but I am under orders to vote against you"; or, "You are a very nice fellow and I love you and we are friends and all that, but unfortunately such are my instructions." It cannot be stressed too often or too much that the United Nations is an organization, not of individuals nor certainly of philosophers, but of sovereign states which have freely and sovereignly agreed among themselves to bring to the conference table only certain clearly defined questions, to discuss them according to an agreed procedure, and to place on the results of this discussion clearly agreed juridical values. The Charter and the Rules of Procedure cannot in theory be infringed upon, because they are of the nature of international treaties: in the full freedom of their sovereignty the member states have agreed upon them and the United Nations is constituted precisely by this agreement; and when you become a member, you have thereby accepted to be bound by them. I say "in theory" the Charter and the Rules of Procedure cannot be infringed upon, but in practice there is scarcely a session of the principal organs of the United Nations and scarcely a meeting in each such session in which the Charter and the Rules of Procedure are not more or less seriously violated. The United Nations *in session* is its own master—even the master of its own interpretation of the Charter and the Rules of Procedure.

III

This illustrates a fundamental principle in human life, namely, existence is superior to its laws and rules; life is prior to and indeed makes fun of all legalism; corporate being has a life and a soul and a substance transcending all its inner regulations and operations and contradictions and inconsistencies; and once you are integrated in an organism, once you are really "in" it, you will put up with every trial, every frustration, every discomfort, every annoyance, every defeat, every blemish in the functioning of the organism, rather than allow the organism to disintegrate or allow yourself to break away from it. Nihilism is essentially limited; and no matter how critical or rebellious or revolutionary or nihilistic you might be, you could never aim at the complete destruction of that to which you "belong"; for if you should chance *to be still there,* after your revolution had taken its maximum toll, and if you should be told then, "All right now, come along and take over and let us see what you can do"—or if you did not wait to be told that, but simply stepped in and seized power yourself—then you would find yourself necessarily proceeding to build on the basis of the old, conserving all that you could conserve from the wreckage. There is a great mystery here. Life moves on despite any revolution, and the continuity of existence is seamless.

Nothing is more instructive and sobering at the United Nations than the experience of seeing people utterly exasperated at each other, even to the point of calling each other all kinds of names, because the Charter and the Rules of Procedure are broken on every turn, and yet nobody daring either to withdraw from the Organization or to do something that will cause it to disintegrate. I believe the Soviet Union regretted its policy whereby it chose to be absent from the Security Council on June 25, 1950, when the Council took a decision to intervene in Korea without the possibility of the Soviet Union casting its veto. Of one thing you can be absolutely sure: It is exceedingly unlikely that either the Soviet Union or the United States will ever withdraw from the United Nations. They will put up with every disappointment and every defeat, rather than have it said of them that they sulkingly quit the assembly of nations.

THE CHARACTER OF

REPRESENTATIVE RESPONSIBILITY:

YOUR GOVERNMENT

I

I SAID THE REPRESENTATIVE acts under instructions; the instructions are formulated by a sovereign state; and the sovereignty of the member state is guaranteed by the Charter. In short, *the representative must be responsible.* I now ask: *What is this representative responsibility? What does this responsible representation mean?*

It means, in the first place, that you are actively conscious of the principal to whom you are responsible. You thus abstract from yourself—your whims, your interests, your opinions, your ideas, your likes and dislikes. You speak only in the name of that which you represent; certainly not in your own personal name. In fact you soon acquire the strange ability— so unphilosophical!—of identifying yourself with your principal, and the world takes that identification for granted. You *become* in a sense that which you *represent,* and when you are called upon to speak, you are never called upon by name, but always by the name of your country. If you attend a meeting, then it is your country that is present; and if you are away, then it is your country that is absent. Wherever you go and whatever you do, it is your country that is acting through you.

II

It means, in the second place, that you keep many things to yourself and your immediate associates and only release in your speeches and your contacts so much of what you are charged with as the immediate occasion demands. If you judge what goes on at the United Nations only by what is publicly said, or even by what privately transpires between delegate and delegate, you form the most superficial view of United Nations politics. The truth is hidden in what people withhold, in the national archives of member governments, in the secret records and diaries of those who keep them. Representative responsibility includes the by no means simple art of knowing precisely what to withhold—and when to withhold it—and precisely what to reveal—and when to reveal it. If your squeamish soul is tortured because you feel you must shout everything you know from the housetops, then you are not fit to represent your country responsibly. Opportuneness, judiciousness, selectiveness, self-control, the sense of relevance, infinite sensitivity to situations, a searing sense of humor with respect to what you must keep to yourself, the wonderful grace of silence—all these virtues the genuinely responsible representative must soon perfect. Representative responsibility has nothing to do with open agreements openly arrived at.

III

It means, in the third place, that you are the eye and the ear of your government at the United Nations, that you cannot therefore shut yourself up within your private shell, that you cannot excogitate the world *a priori,* that you must enter deeply and understandingly into the movements and trends of the moment as they reflect or unfold themselves at the United Nations, that you appreciate the issues and interests involved, that you report on these movements and trends and interests and issues faithfully, continuingly, interpretively, to your government. The ability to enter into and fully appreciate and therefore authoritatively interpret what is going on at the United Nations and—what is far more important—in the world at large (which the United Nations in the end only reflects) presupposes profound spiritual culture. This raises the searching question: Which culture really understands what is going on? Which has the original, creative, interpretive norms? It may be that some "understand more" than others. It may also be that the understanding is "more free and more potent and more the master" than the understood. To say that "highly educated people alone" can adequately represent their countries at the United Nations (and the level of education among representatives at the United Nations is very high indeed) leaves this question unanswered: Educated where? Educated in what? Thus, types of education, types of spiritual culture are of the essence in all responsible representation. Now because upon your interpretation depends to a large extent the formulation and prosecution of policy by your government, you cannot feel too responsible in the discharge of this important task. It is quite true that a representative, once he is handed down a policy decision, must mediate it in all fidelity, no matter what strange modalities this mediation may take at times, but prior to the moment of decision the representative, if he is worth his salt and if he is alive to the issues and to his possibilities, can make a significant difference, sometimes a decisive difference, in the formation of the decision itself. You have failed in your duty as a responsible representative if your views are not taken into account, and from this failure you must draw your own conclusions.

IV

Representative responsibility means, in the fourth place, that just as you cannot remain aloof from the world and its issues, but must enter into them, understand them, and interpret them, so you must not lose yourself in them. You must always remember that you represent, you are an emissary of, a center of will quite independent of these issues into which you are entering, and that the interests of this central will may sometimes clash with these issues. Your primary identification is with your government and not with the movements and issues at the United Nations, and only with these to the extent that your government has identified itself with them. A denatured, self-lost, confused representative not knowing where to call a halt to his contacts and commitments and sympathies and entanglements is simply irresponsible. How to know without becoming engaged, how to enter into a matter without losing yourself in it, how to identify yourself without losing your identity, how to reach forth outwardly without losing your grip inwardly, how to eat into the world without allowing the world to eat you or at least to eat into you, how to be open to everything without "the thing" that is you becoming thereby overwhelmed, how to be exposed to the four winds without forgetting or losing your bearings, how to listen and wonder and take in all that is said to you while reserving your ultimate freedom of judgment, how to be a sympathizing and understanding subject without becoming a pathetic and compromised object, how *to be* amidst the terrible flux of *becoming* —in short, how to maintain an independent dignity of your own amid the infinite waves that heave and splash about you and upon you from all directions, and that must be allowed to heave and splash if you are to be and remain a responsible representative: being all this involves a power and a virtue that you are not born with, that you do not once and for all pick up from your environment or tradition or culture or background, that you do not learn from books or speeches or lectures, that you never simply acquire from association with even the best of men, that you never attain by prayer or fasting or by desire and longing, but that you gradually come to in the solitary fires of experience and responsibility and error and decision and suffering. A responsible representative has a soul and retains it.

THE CHARACTER OF
REPRESENTATIVE RESPONSIBILITY:
BEYOND YOUR GOVERNMENT

I

R EPRESENTATIVE responsibility means, in the fifth place, that in a sense you are above the internal politics of your own country and even above your own government. Once outside of and speaking for your country, that which is eternal and essential in your own country and people, and not any transient phase in their development, looms foremost in your mind. Your sense of national responsibility abroad is altogether different from your sense of national responsibility at home. It is not that people cease to be critical of their country; it is that then they rise to what is above criticism—to that of which they are proud, to that which, despite every criticism, still enables them to claim it as their own. For there must be something *above criticism* if they continue to belong to it. Before "others" they suddenly realize that they do not belong to them, that therefore they belong "home," that no matter how critical they

13

may have been of their country and its policies they have not yet forsaken it, they still are citizens of it, and therefore there is something basic and enduring there which is beyond all criticism. We love home most away from home. Just as nihilism is essentially limited in its scope, so is one's criticism of one's own country: so long as it remains his own, there is a point at which he must stop in trying to tear it to pieces. Absolute not-being can never exist: being always breaks out upon you, even in the abysmal depths of not-being. A foreign minister may and often does come and go; a government may and often does come and go; a policy or a particular line of action is firm today and may become quite outmoded tomorrow; a whole regime may and sometimes does come and go; and yet with all these changes it should not be impossible for you, as a responsible representative, to outlive them all. Something then is permanent and endures amid all change, and you actually represent that enduring thing. Of the realities denoted by the terms instructions, policy, government, state, regime, people, and nation, what really endures is neither the set of instructions, nor the policy, nor the government, nor even the state or regime; what really endures is the people and the nation. That which is essential and in a sense eternal and of universal significance in your nation and people, *that* you really represent. To the extent then that you are able to rise above the flux of policy and government and state, without disobeying them while they hold sway, and even while obeying them; to the extent, therefore, that you fasten onto the distinctive being of your people, their permanent meaning and interests, such as their freedom, their security, their continued existence as a nation, their cultural significance in terms of human and spiritual values, what they have deposited in history, and what they have contributed to the world; to the extent that you firmly grasp these things and basically act in their name and feel first and foremost responsible to them, to that extent you are a good responsible representative. Nothing brings out more the essential and permanent in any people and nation—if there is anything essential and permanent there—than when it acts and makes itself felt on the international plane. The representative of the United States or France, for example, *is* his own nation on that plane. By the quality of his own action and thought a representative either justifies his nation—and sometimes overjustifies it, or justifies it more than is just, namely, more than it deserves—or invites ridicule upon its head and *a fortiori* upon his. And he who justifies his nation in truth, he who reflects honor on it, is the responsible representative.

II

It means, in the sixth place, that your responsibility transcends even your nation. The representative who is morbidly engrossed with his nation and its problems, who comes to the United Nations in effect only to orate and harangue and intrigue and maneuver, only to manipulate the World Organization for his and his nation's interests, who has no regard for the decent opinion of mankind, who bores the life out of you with his problems and his grievances and his points of view, who never tires of blaming people right and left for their perfidy and their wickedness, who never looks himself in the mirror, who never stops preaching, who sermonizes all the time about human rights to other people while his own people are plunged—and it would seem hopelessly plunged—in the darkest of dark ages, such a representative makes such a fool of himself that he soon becomes a byword and a buffoon. One only wishes he knew what people said of him! Would he amend then? That is the question. Now to be sure there is nobody who does not have some grievance against somebody, but life has the greatest grievance against us all, namely, that we are often so thoughtless and so ungrateful ourselves! There have been half a dozen such notorious characters at the United Nations, and everybody knows them. But the responsible representative is different, and fortunately the large majority is of this type. Surely he is loyal to his nation, surely he carries out his instructions, but this very loyalty makes him loyal also to that of which his nation is a member, namely, to the United Nations itself. He therefore enters into the corporate spirit of the Organization. He certainly insists on his rights under the Charter and under the Rules of Procedure, but he is keenly alive to the fact that he is in a sense a member of a fellowship, and others in that fellowship have their rights too. He therefore knows when to be silent, when to yield, when to give way, when to acknowledge the truth regardless of the lips from which it has fallen, when to give others, even his opponents, the praise if they deserve it. He acts, to a certain extent, as an organic member of a team. He plays the international game with due regard to its rules. He knows that if his nation wins but the United Nations goes to pieces, then his nation has not really won. The responsible representative soon acquires the sense of the whole and soon learns how not to offend that sense. There is fair play even in international relations: it "pays." He develops a genuine love for the United Nations; a love not mercenary, determined by some personal advantage, nor sentimental, arising from some silly pleasure or excitement. His attachment to the United Nations is ultimately grounded in the beauty of its idea and in the supreme significance for understanding and peace of its actuality. In his pronouncements and in his posture rings an unshakable faith in the United Nations. It is this evident faith that will stand him in excellent stead when he needs the United Nations most. The responsible representative could serve his country best if his colleagues had no doubt that side by side with his loyalty to his country he was loyal to them also, that is, to the corporate soul of the Organization. Many a good cause, needing just the two or three votes that would clinch the decision, has been lost because people were not convinced of the integrity of its defender, or had no doubt of the falsehood of his spirit. Many a borderline case swung the day because its defender was otherwise known for the integrity of his soul and the fairness of his spirit, and for his faith in the United Nations.

Even in international existence with its heartless clashes of power, it pays to lose oneself and to love; for you can never tell when you and your country will find yourselves in desperate need of just that marginal vote or two which, solely on the strength of the confidence that your love and your self-giving had won for you, will move either from the area of opposition to the realm of abstention or from this latter to the domain of approval. The spirit always and everywhere counts, and it counts most when it is needed most.

The unity of the world grows in the mind of the responsible representative despite all the world's inner conflicts and contradictions. In fact, he begins to suspect that these conflicts and contradictions might only be the growing pains of that unity. And if he is unhappy at times, it is not because he has not asserted himself or his nation has not asserted itself; it is because the unity of the world which he is just beginning to glimpse is still so rudimentary, so fragile, so imperfect, still in its earliest dawn.

III

It means, in the seventh place, that you soon acquire the habit of moving among "friends," or at least among intimate acquaintances, calling them by their first name, inviting them and accepting their invitations, having lots of fun with them at parties, in private visits, at the bar of the Delegates' Lounge, in the dining room of the United Nations, in the hundreds of lobbies and corners where you buttonhole them on some silly gossip or parley with them on some grave affair. How and when to invite; how to accept or gracefully decline an invitation; which to accept and which to decline when six of them come to you for the same afternoon or evening; how to make up with those whom you declined; how to bear the cross of the "white lies" you have to tell on such and on a thousand other occasions; what to say on formal occasions and what to say informally over a drink at a cocktail party; what not to say on either occasion; what to look for in what you see or hear; how not to presume too much on the "friendship" of your "friends," knowing that they too labor under their own necessities; how to understand a meaning without anyone ever having told it to you, without you ever pressing that it be bluntly told you, and knowing that you are expected to have understood it without exhibiting this childish curiosity; whom to salute and whom not to salute in public; whom to appear talking with in public and whom to be very careful not to appear huddled with or talking to or even looking at in public; whom to avoid seeing and at times even passing, and whom to seek purposely to see, and when; whom to ring up instead of seeing; whom to write instead of ringing up or seeing; when to ring up yourself and when to let your secretary do it; the thousand and one subtle ways in which you could intimate to a man that he was not quite saying the truth without crudely rubbing it in that he was what you would call a "damn liar"; how to bear your untenable existence when you bluff another and he bluffs you and both of you know perfectly well that you are bluffing each other, that is, how to look him then straight in the face without batting an eye; the shattering power of just neglecting people and not answering them, and leaving them alone; how and when to use this power; how to take a defeat with your head lifted up and without avenging it on your soul; how to recuperate after you have avenged your defeat on your soul; how to take a victory with grace and humility, knowing that a subsequent defeat is almost certainly around the corner; how, after you had gloated in your soul over your victory, to seek purposely a defeat in order to purge your soul of its impurity; the wonderful cleansing and liberation that then supervenes upon your soul; how to appreciate without being servile; how to criticize without appearing to damn; how to be courteous to everybody under even the most trying conditions; when to laugh or smile when you should, and when not to laugh or smile *precisely when you should*; when to intervene in a debate and when not to intervene, even though it would seem that you should; how to change your tack in the middle of a sentence if your assistant passes on a paper to you revealing a new fact upsetting all your argument; how to accept and treat every level of intercourse for what it is—the level of a mere passing glance, the level of a faint smile, the level of joking, the level of pulling your leg, the level of gossip, the level of the trial balloon, the level of probing, the level of finding out, the level of formal negotiation, the level of serious commitment; how not to interrupt your opponent when he is attacking you; how to wait for your turn in all patience and sometimes in all acute suffering; how not to take certain difficult situations too seriously, knowing that conditions, and therewith peoples and policies, change, and that relief may still come; how to hope and work for the coming of this relief in the face of all discouragement and contrariety, and how to take it if and when it comes, not as something the world owes you, but as a free gift; how to forgive and continue hoping and trusting and loving in the midst of your deepest trials, especially when dear friends forsake you; how to be exceedingly sensitive to the general moral sense of a Committee or a Council or the General Assembly, so as to know where to stop in pushing your cause lest a reaction should set in against you; how to be sensitive to the human needs of your immediate associates and co-workers and how to try to meet these needs; and the thousand and one civilities and proprieties and usages and customs and manners and points of etiquette and protocol: all these things soon become second nature to the responsible representative. International existence in action, namely, life at the United Nations, is a completely different beast from anything you are used to: it is a world by itself, with its own structures, norms, laws, expectations, temptations, seductions, pitfalls, slips, evils, beauties, and possibilities. There are other worlds in life, such as the world of the home or the world of the college or the world of the village, simpler, purer, more natural, more relaxed, and infinitely more beautiful; but the responsible representative must be hard on himself; he cannot hanker nostalgically after the protected and sheltered existence of these simpler worlds, nor can he look back yearningly to the peace and beauty which they vouchsafe; he must drink the cup of international existence in action to the last drop; he must accept the knocks and bruises he receives at its hands; he must thoroughly attune himself to all its weirdness and unnaturalness; he must bear its cross; he must pay its price; and withal he should beware lest, in winning for him the whole world, it should nevertheless cost him his soul.

4

THE LAST RESORT

I

FINALLY, representative responsibility means that, if you cannot stand it any longer, if it is too much for you, if you are fed up with it, then you can always resign. This is the limiting condition of all your work. I do not think representatives coming from behind the Iron Curtain enjoy the option of resigning as much as representatives hailing from this side of the veil. But representatives from free countries know that resignation always stands before them as a last resort, and this ought to lighten their burden. So long as you carry on with your job, you are wholly responsible for it. You can blame nobody but yourself if anything goes wrong. Nothing is more unseemly than for a representative to be naggingly dissatisfied and to keep on expressing his dissatisfaction with his government and its policies, or with the United Nations and the state of the world, and still to hang on to his job. This, of course, cannot go on indefinitely even if the representative in question is without a conscience, for governments soon realize what is happening and usually take steps to dismiss or transfer their man. But the possibility of resignation to a responsible representative serves as a liberating thought. No matter how many straws of compromise he may keep on piling on his stout back, there is always a last one that is going to break it. That last straw could be as much his own creation as the world's; he could be as much disgusted with himself as with anything the world had brought upon his head. For you could say, "I've had enough," as much *from yourself* as from the world. You begin by being pure and innocent and buoyant and boundless in your faith; gradually you are inducted into the horror of the world, into conditions and dealings too questionable to bear; and yet you bear them all the same. How do you rationalize it to yourself? It could be blind ambition; it could be the hollow glamour involved; it could be your rightly saying to yourself, "But nobody can do it better"; it could be your honest feeling that the moral sacrifice, whether of your own doing or of the world's, is nothing compared to the service of the larger cause. But a moment of revulsion can be reached when you brush aside everything, including "the service of the larger cause," because you have had enough. Thrown as we all are into this world of sin and suffering and imperfection, of which we are an organic and inseparable part, it is our responsibility to carry as much of the burden and dirt of the world as properly falls to our share, indeed as we willingly take on ourselves, even if in the process we should be tainted and soiled with that sin and suffering ourselves. But when the tainting exceeds a certain limit, when we can honestly no longer accept the moral sacrifice involved, when we have seen enough of darkness and craftiness and ruthlessness and falsehood and sheer injustice, then we had better leave the task to fresher hands to tackle, and to be soiled in their turn. All of us must share, not only in the glory of helping to create the world but also in its guilt, if for no other reason than to be humbled and, therefore, as much as possible cured of the unworthy pastime of self-righteously judging others. A responsible representative cannot stay at the United Nations one day beyond the moment when his conscience has had enough.

II

We may then say that representative responsibility and responsible representation consist in abstracting from your feelings and clinging to your instructions; in keeping many things —in fact the important things—to yourself; in entering deeply into the turbulent world of the United Nations and reporting it interpretively to your government; in taking care not to lose your soul in this process; in representing at all times that which is essential and eternal and of universal significance in your own people; in developing the deepest allegiance to the United Nations and to the barest rudiments of world order and unity that that Organization has been able to achieve; in quickly mastering the rules and usages and formalities of active international existence and profitably learning from its weird trials and experiences; and in standing ready at all times to quit if your conscience can no longer bear the moral burden of your responsibilities.

THE PHENOMENON

OF FRUSTRATION

I

IT MAY BE WORTHWHILE to pause for a moment at the personal phenomenon of frustration at the United Nations. This is one of the commonest of experiences. Nobody has served at the United Nations in any capacity, whether as a member of the Secretariat or as a member of some national delegation or as an elected officer, without this sense of frustration sooner or later overtaking him, if not also overwhelming him. This is an arresting fact. Here is a great world political organization, the greatest of its kind that the world has ever known; an organization with a truly great charter and a tremendous promise. Practically everybody belongs to its club. It debates and deals with real issues; its show is the greatest on earth; its platform commands the attention of the entire world. You meet and associate with great men in it, leaders in their own countries. There is plenty of fun and glamour and excitement about its work. And yet, despite all the glamour and reality and greatness, people's elation does not last long; sooner or later a sense of frustration and depression catches up with them. Why is frustration apparently inevitable? How does it creep upon you? What are its causes? What does it mean? Why this strange sense of unreality and hollowness?

II

It appears to me that people grow frustrated under the operation of one or more of six general causes.

There is first the sheer physical and nervous fatigue. Quickness to react; alertness to changes; making constantly sure that you are not in disharmony with the declared policy and ultimate will of your government with respect to a perpetually kaleidoscopic situation; keeping in touch with a hundred delegations, all of whom are also trying all the time to keep in touch with one another; keeping track of thousands of documents; listening hour after hour and day after day to endless speeches, some most important, some most boring and repetitive, some ridiculously unreal, considering who makes them and how they are made; attending parties and dinners every day; and doing your homework every evening in writing dispatches, preparing speeches, and organizing and following up the work of your delegation—all this varied and relentless and inhuman activity is taxing on the nerves. At the core of the whirl of the United Nations the undiscerning and superficial could perceive only madness. No wonder the nerves under such a maddening whirl need plenty of alcohol or other things to refresh and relax them! And when one is physically tired one usually slumps into a spiritual depression. The tired are frustrated by the least mishap.

III

A second cause of frustration is the fact that people in their self-expression find themselves circumscribed and hemmed in on every side. You must keep the fundamental policies of your government in your mind all the time; you cannot be too careful about your instructions; the sheer effort to keep so many things to yourself, when you know that everybody you meet with is doing the same, is most fatiguing; you must respect the rules; you must wait for your turn; you cannot answer every assault; you find things going on that you cannot condone and yet you cannot possibly help; if you have any self-respect you will swallow all sorts of awful situations and not make a scene in them or about them; you are only one of more than a hundred and therefore you can only occupy your modest place. In short, the challenge—the procedural and political and social and emotional and personal challenge—is crushingly varied and crushingly intense. There are people who go through all this without much feeling it, because their eyes have not been opened as to what is really going on. They live in blissful callousness and insensitivity. But it is impossible for the more sensitive and alive not to be frustrated when they clearly perceive that severe restrictions are placed upon their action and efficacy, and when they want to react practically at every turn but they cannot.

IV

A deeper cause of the sense of frustration is the fact that governments change their policies almost invariably without advance notice. This is an inalienable part of their sovereign freedom. You are sailing along beautifully in the happy conviction that those who support you or whom you support or with whom you are collaborating on a particular issue have such-and-such a clearly-defined policy; you make all your calculations and moves on that basis; and then you suddenly wake up one morning to find out that that policy has changed. The change may be administered to you in the nicest capsule of diplomatic decorum possible: you are to swallow it painlessly. But after you swallow it its painful practical effects immediately make themselves felt. The hell that you go through then nobody knows but God. Your sense of frustration is indescribable. You feel the world has been withdrawn from underneath your feet. And you literally tear your hair and cry, and sometimes you even take one or two drinks too many. It will take you some time to adjust to the shocks that sovereign freedom will repeatedly and apparently capriciously mete out to you, and even when you intellectually realize that this belongs to the nature of things, you are not thereby existentially relieved. Now it is true that sovereign freedom behaves in this way, that by its very nature it must always reserve a free hand unto itself, but is the theoretical realization of this truth any comfort to you when in actual fact the presupposition of your action and your expectation is suddenly obliterated? Frustration, then, is part of the price we all have to pay for living in a world of sovereign nation states. It is the price we pay for forgetting that what is hidden from us in national policy is far more important than what is revealed. It is the price we pay for our naïveté in supposing that what is told and promised us in any given situation is really all that there is. Freedom, as Dostoevski has shown, is a tremendous burden which only the strong can bear; and not until we all become spiritual members one of another will the freedom of one entail and enhance the freedom of all.

V

Much deeper than all this is the fourth cause of frustration. For who would not put up with any personal fatigue, with any restriction upon his freedom and any intensity of challenge, and with any shocking change of national policy, no matter how arbitrary, *provided* the United Nations itself were not limping, faltering, more or less trivial in the results it has yielded?[1] We get frustrated because we expect too much from the United Nations, way beyond anything it can reasonably deliver. We become frustrated because we idolize the United Nations and think that it is a panacea for the ills of the world. Those to whom the United Nations is the only outlet for their melancholia—and there are some of this description—will of course be continually frustrated by it. The United Nations in fact is much simpler, much more limited than people imagine. If we do not lose sight of its reality, if we take it just for what it purports itself to be, if we place no exaggerated expectations upon it, if we know how relatively impotent it is, then we will live much more happily with it. Frustration is often the measure of our feeling that the world is in desperate need and then of turning around and finding that the United Nations does not in fact meet that need. We are right in feeling that the world is in desperate need; we are right in desperately searching for something to meet that need; where we are wrong is in supposing and expecting the United Nations to meet it. Frustration is the measure of a misplaced and therefore mistaken expectation.

VI

But there is something still deeper than all this. At the United Nations, diverse cultures and civilizations meet and diverse national interests clash. Each cultural and political grouping is

[1] The positive possibilities and accomplishments of the United Nations are examined in Chapter 10. Here I am suggesting an existential analysis of the grounds of frustration, and at this point am saying that when the United Nations appears—as at times it most certainly does—limping and faltering in its progress and trivial and futile in its outcome, the United Nations representative or the United Nations officer feels a profound sense of frustration. He begins to doubt whether what he is engaged in is worthwhile. When after weeks and months of labor the mountain produces a mouse, and when even this mouse is stillborn, then you should see the faces of the poor representatives and officers!

summoned to be at its best. There is the keenest possible open contest between ideas and positions and policies and points of view. Now the historic moment is most serious and therefore the issue of this contest could not be more decisive; for what is ultimately at stake is nothing short of the cumulative positive values of the entire past. Therefore, if the idea and point of view to which you belong is not adequately represented and defended, you feel terribly frustrated. If the government that is supposed to be leading your point of view fails in its leadership, you feel terribly frustrated. If the opposite point of view keeps on registering one brilliant victory after another, not because it is more true or more just than your point of view, but because those who represent it are more integral and more single-minded in their dedication, then you feel terribly frustrated. If the representative who is supposed to stand for and defend your civilization proves unequal to the challenge, you feel terribly frustrated. And above all, if you yourself, due to some weakness in your own formation or character, or to some silly material or political impediments that have been placed in your way, should prove in your performance unworthy of the great trust that had been placed on you, and that you yourself had placed on yourself, then—if you should have any conscience still left in you—your frustration would know no bounds. Frustration measures the failure of leadership. Frustration measures the extent to which in trying to meet the incredibly exacting demands of the historic moment we have fallen short of our possible best and highest.

VII

The deepest frustration is spiritual: it arises when we do not know whom to worship and love, or when we know him but nevertheless worship something else. Your error is when, whatever your motive—and most such motives are not pure—you gave your whole soul to the thing. It is not worth it! From the corner of your being you knew all the time that it was not right; you knew it was not worth it. Even at its best, even when everything is perfect, without a single fault or blemish, even when the cause of "international peace and security"—a most noble cause—is absolutely served, still the thing does not satisfy. What you need above and beyond everything is love, friendship, trust, understanding, quiet, intimacy, laughter, the swing of the child, the rapturous freedom of the spirit. What you need is to "enter into the temple, walking, and leaping (and even dancing), and praising God." What you need is spiritual food—that moment of bliss and certainty and understanding in which you are caught up into eternity with a most wonderful hidden smile. What you need is Being. The soul that pants for this because *it knows and believes that it exists* will, if it gives itself completely to the United Nations, repeatedly feel frustrated there; it is not the function of the United Nations to provide or to foster this food, this ultimate bliss. It is most honorable to be and to serve at the United Nations, but it cannot take the place of Being. And of course the cynic will laugh because I have used "Being" with a capital "B." But if we do not know anything higher than the United Nations to which to give our lives even while and as we serve the United Nations, something which will absorb and efface and justify our frustrations, then of course we shall be continually frustrated. He who *worships* the United Nations will discover one day that he committed an error; for there is only one fit object of our worship, and certainly the United Nations is not it. Frustration measures our idolatry.

To survive frustration, to come out of repeated frustrations relatively unscathed, is a veritable grace. It is easy to speak of strong nerves and solid character, it is easy to use stoical language of that sort, but the thing is much deeper than that. How can strength and solidity and will power remain unsubverted before the absolute flux and fluency and corruption of things, before the impotence of even the best will in the world? You are inevitably thrown back upon a strength and solidity outside yourself. Blessed are you then if you know or had known such a strength and solidity. Blessed are you if despite yourself it makes its face to shine upon you. In its name and through its strength you survive. The deepest human experience is when experience itself points and demands and leads up to a wonderful, actual realm, quite independent of your experience, a realm, nevertheless, without which human experience is but a flickering shadow in the abysmal night.

6

THE BEING

OF THE PRESIDENT

I

WHAT HAPPENS when one presides over a United Nations body, whether over a minor subcommittee, or over a Main Committee of the General Assembly, or over a Commission, or over a Council, or over the General Assembly itself—I mean what happens *to him?* Into what strange mode of being is he then thrown? Must he be altogether colorless and "neutral" to be able to be impartial and preside? How much real power does a presiding officer have? How are people elected to such offices anyway? An existential analysis of what it means to be a presiding officer at the United Nations may not be out of place.

Presiding over the Security Council is a matter of automatic monthly rotation; your turn is simply your country's alphabetical turn. To the question, Who is presiding now? the answer is strictly, not the representative, but his country. Thus no person as such is elected to the presidency of the Security Council; the prior election of the country in question to the

Council carries with it the right to preside; and whoever happens to represent it at the time its monthly turn arrives presides. The five permanent members, therefore, enjoy a statutory right to this office. But in the case of the six non-permanent members, the situation is a bit more complex. When a non-permanent member is elected, the General Assembly certainly takes into account the requirement of what is called "equitable geographical distribution"; but people often also keep in mind who is likely to represent that country on the Council. The person who is likely to represent his country thus helps in determining the decision of the General Assembly. In this sense one may say that the Assembly's decision to elect his country was, informally, at once a decision based on the expectation that he would represent his country on the Council and therefore implicitly a decision to have him preside over the Council when his country's alphabetical turn comes. Thus a representative of a non-permanent member is more truly elected to preside over the Security Council than a representative of a permanent member.

In all other cases of elected officers (with very few exceptions with respect to some of the Councils and Commissions, but with no exceptions with respect to the presidency of the General Assembly and the chairmanship of its Committees), the permanent members of the Security Council have yielded the right to such offices to the other members of the United Nations; the presupposition being that, since these relatively smaller nations do not enjoy the power and prestige of the permanent members, it is only right to permit them to enjoy the honor of these offices.

Equitable geographical distribution plays a role in the election of officers. But the competition within the same region is very intense, and therefore the preceding campaigning is relentless. What is remarkable is that once governments give you their word, you can be sure they will vote for you in the secret balloting. (Once in a while there are one or two defections, and you suspect who perpetrated them, because the eyes of their representatives when they look at you tell you something, but you are not quite sure; but what is sure is that the number of votes counted for you is slightly less than the number of promises you had received.) You must keep on checking and re-checking and making sure—both from your home capital, at the offices of the various delegations in New York, and in the halls of the United Nations itself—until the very last minute. A Chekhov or a Tolstoi or a Dostoevski can write a delightful short story about the political, emotional, psychological, and personal phenomena which come into play in this little game. He can be supplied with fascinating concrete human data for such an account. There are the great political realities which impose themselves; but three elements are often no less decisive: (1) hard, continuous, vigilant, well-organized work; (2) certain remarkably dependable loyalties which stick by you through thick and thin; and (3) a certain strange element of chance. To say that this chance is not chance, but that there is a hidden providence behind it, is a matter of faith; all we can *see* from *this side* is sheer chance.

II

In the chair the officer *is* the mouthpiece *and nothing more* of the corporate will of the organ over which he presides. The organ *in session* is a living sovereign entity, with its own independent life and spirit, and the officer is only its first servant; he cannot direct it—it directs him. It is incredible how much the officer feels the living, independent, dominant reality of the body over which he presides. There is the subtlest and most real organic interaction between him and it, which reaches at times a point of utmost fineness and unity. His functions are strictly defined and delimited by the Rules of Procedure. He hardly has any freedom of action beyond the orderly conduct of business and the dutiful declaration of decisions. A matter is debated, briefly or at length (sometimes the deliberations of a single item last for weeks), and then the point of decision approaches; all sorts of maneuvers take place just before and during the voting. Situations at times arise which defy even the most impeccable interpretation of the Rules. The Chairman or President will then be helped out only by the original resources of his "common sense." He should never act blindly or rashly, partly because it is unbecoming of him to do so, partly because he need not at all act blindly or rashly if he fully and relaxedly falls back upon the light of his reason, partly because he can never tell who in the House is more wide-awake than he and therefore is likely publicly to make fun of him if he acted foolishly and is proven wrong. The creative rule of self-confidence in such situations is the simple moral maxim: *There is always a genuinely right way out.* If the right way does not at once reveal itself, one can quietly pray for it if he is a man of faith; and sometimes it is very expedient to take some time and think the matter over. With perspective gained, it is remarkable how many ingenious ways begin to suggest themselves. But the real crisis arises when the situation cannot wait and you must decide at once; it is then that your rational and spiritual resources alone can come to your succor. After the voting has taken place, the presiding officer declares the decision; the decision of that organ is *formally constituted by his act of declaring it.* If uncontested, that is the end of that item on the agenda; if contested, the House freshly sustains or overturns his declaration. But the formal decision is always some uncontested declaration by the Chairman or President.

In so far as it lies in him, everything in the smooth functioning of an international body depends on the degree to which the presiding officer succeeds in establishing a sense of trust and confidence between himself and his colleagues on that body. Because he has practically no material authority over them, he can never earn this trustful relationship artificially or by force. In the crucible of trial, experience, and suffering, he must prove himself worthy of it. His integrity, his dignity, his intellectual and moral strength, his unmistakable fairness, his absolute alertness to the intricacies and subtleties of situations as they arise, his unfailing sense of humor, his ability to put up with every personal annoyance and inconvenience in the overriding interest of the whole, his steadily maintained cordial relations with everybody at all times: these and these alone—in so far as he commands them—soon build up for him such a creative *rapport* with his colleagues that, if peace depended on such atmospheres alone, he is sure peace is simply and everlastingly assured.

III

But peace does not depend on the poor officer and his good intentions. Even if he and his colleagues were all saints and an atmosphere of heaven reigned in the international body, still peace might not be effected. Peace is a by-product of hard, independent, objective conditions. There are these sovereign and independent nations, each with its immense internal problems and pressures; there are these raging ideologies tearing the hearts and consciences of men; there are objectively irreconcilable national interests; there are small and ambitious and ruthless men everywhere; there are wobbly governments which are not sure of themselves, and which are either afraid to enter into the spirit of peace and trust lest that should bring about their downfall, or which intentionally create discord and turmoil at the United Nations in the hope that that would positively bolster them; and there is a demonic spirit of darkness and rebellion which sometimes seizes men and makes them wholly unreasonable. An international body is inalienably subject to all these outside determinations. And none of these determinations can be much influenced by the Chairman or President—the President even of the highest body; and were he even to have descended from heaven. Who knows why that ordinarily cooperative colleague has suddenly become abusive? He may have received new disturbing instructions from his government; one of a dozen vagaries may have assailed him; poor man, he may be under some terrific personal pressure— for some reason, his whole personal career may be at stake. Therefore, the presiding officer must be absolutely imperturbable. Nothing should ruffle him. Nothing that is said or hinted may he interpret personally. Even if he is personally attacked, he knows that the suffering attacker does not mean him personally. He should understand and forgive, and as he sits there in the chair he ought to have access to independent information about what is going on that would constitute and fortify his understanding. He should be wholly above his own person, *out there* in the independently existing, turbulent world, thankful withal that the world has not yet blown itself up to pieces. Personal self-transcendence under the most trying conditions into the independent, objective, tormented world of passion and conflict is the most important habit which a good Chairman or President soon acquires. So long as the House *is in session,* so long as it has not broken up, there is something transcending every ripple or turbulence within it; and he is the mouthpiece of that enduring thing; in a sense, he embodies it; in a sense, *he is it.* An international organization of the nature of the United Nations, by its mere existence and so long as it continues to exist, proves that the world, despite all its unbearable internal strains, has not yet completely fallen out with itself; and the President or executive officer, by receiving, feeling, and bearing these strains himself *without himself breaking down,* demonstrates the continued strained unity of the world.

IV

Presiding over an international body is wholly unlike any other mode of presiding. A chairman of a corporation or a university board or a church organization or a trade union or a parliament or a cabinet or a council of ministers is not dealing with *sovereign entities.* This fact is expressed by saying that he is vested with *real power,* a power defined in the bylaws or constitution and enforced by the persuasive and coercive machinery of that organization and ultimately by the courts and police of the country under which it functions. A presiding international officer, say, the President of the General Assembly, on the other hand, has no such power; he is for the most part —as the Rules of Procedure specify—to open and close the meetings, to conduct the business of the House according to the Rules of Procedure, and to announce the decisions. Rule 36 expressly stipulates: "The President, in the exercise of his functions, remains under the authority of the General Assembly." He is all the time literally dealing with sovereign governments—the governments of France, Ghana, Thailand, Chile, the Soviet Union, etc. These are not members of a committee in a university or a corporation, or ministers in a cabinet, or members of a national legislative assembly. Whether as a member or as a presiding officer, you cannot crack jokes or feel overly informal or lose your temper with these men as you do with your colleagues on these other bodies. A freshly appointed representative began once addressing a Committee of the United Nations in the familiar and joking manner he is used to in his home legislature: the entire performance fell ludicrously flat. Corporate decorum at the United Nations is entirely different from corporate decorum at any national parliament. The presiding officer, then, has no constituted authority over his colleagues. He sits there for the most part only as a convenient mechanism for affording these sovereign entities the opportunity of freely making their statements and freely putting forward their proposals. He cannot really interfere with their freedom. When a representative of a sovereign government uses violent and abusive language, the President cannot strictly call him to order, except perhaps by an indirect application of Rules 35 and 73. There is no explicit rule empowering the President to stand as censor of any language or mode of conduct the representative of a sovereign nation may choose to employ, including pounding the table with his shoes, or for that matter throwing them at the President himself. Even Rule 70, which authorizes the President to "call a speaker to order if his remarks are not relevant to the subject under discussion," if strictly and constantly applied by the President, will bring about a far more disorderly and spoiled and poisoned atmosphere than it will order and remedy. Who is to determine the bounds of "relevance"? The judgment of the President? Then that is a "ruling" of his which can be contested and appealed to the House. And this is more likely to compound the disorder. And even if the House sustains the President—which is what almost invariably happens in such cases—who is to prevent the representative of a sovereign government, bent on using violent language in urging its point of view, from asking for the floor again and continuing the interrupted tirade? Shall the President cause this performance to be repeated endlessly? If a government is determined to attack, the President cannot prevent it; he can only appeal to representatives to be reasonable and considerate; but even such appeals he should resort to most sparingly; the dignity of his office would certainly suffer if he protruded himself at every turn. The only real restraints are the intangible ones provided by the general moral atmosphere prevailing, an atmosphere constituted by whatever norms of conduct in international forensic matters have been established over the years, by certain elementary rules of protocol, by the special tone of that particular session, and by the political-moral situation of the world at the time. In international platforms thrust and counterthrust should be allowed to take place more or less freely: the free interplay of forces cannot be cramped. Whoever is attacked has every chance to defend himself—and to do so in any way he pleases. This freedom of attack and defense is the only possible order among sovereign entities. At the United Nations sovereign members bring their moods and their manners bodily with them, and there is no transcendent power limiting or constraining their freedom.

Behind the scenes the President can help a little: by quietly talking to people, by privately bringing them together, by suggesting alternatives, by helping to create through his good relations with all an atmosphere of moderation and reason, by giving private warnings of imminent storms, by intimating to friends possible counteracting moves in the interest of concord and peace, and by providing (through the Secretariat and to the extent the Secretariat agrees) innumerable little services to the representatives that ask for them. But the substantive efficacy of all this is exceedingly limited. The President cannot initiate national policies, nor can he conciliate much between such policies except if he is expressly asked to do so by the parties concerned. When the House is *in session* the President has no authority whatsoever over the representatives outside the extremely limited range of the Rules of Procedure; in substantive matters they exercise their sovereignty in full and complete freedom.

V

Can a presiding officer be absolutely impartial although he may hold decided views on all sorts of questions under consideration? Most certainly he can, if he believes in objective and independent truth.

First, it is quite clear that a solemn agreement subsists between the elected officer and the body that elected him, namely, that he be absolutely impartial. It was on this basis that it elected him, and he accepted this basis. If he had the slightest doubt that he might break this agreement, he should never have accepted to serve in the first place. And if he breaks it afterwards, the body over which he presides has every right to withdraw its trust in him. A solemn moral and legal contractual agreement, therefore, subsists between the two parties. When a man is elected he is supposed by that very act to lift himself above his point of view and become the exclusive servant of the international body.

Thus, if a cause in which he passionately believes is in danger of losing under his eyes, he will never attempt to manipulate the international machinery in the service of that cause, even if he could. He attributes the loss to ignorance or tendentiousness or passion on the part of those who voted against it, and to mediocrity of performance on the part of those who pleaded it. He will never take advantage of his position, even if he could; he respects the consensus of the House over which he presides without ceasing to believe in the lost cause and to hope that it will one day have better luck. He knows that all international decisions involve the inevitable risk of distortion and error through ignorance, tendentiousness, and passion. That is the stuff of which history is made, and *he is in history* and cannot get out of it except by faint-heartedly shirking all responsibility and closing his eyes ostrich-wise to it. But such a withdrawal does not stop history: history moves placidly on without him. Many tragic situations arise; he is profoundly sorry for them; he frankly does not understand many of them; often he comforts himself by saying, the world is full of error and injustice (which is perfectly true but which does not explain, much less justify, that *particular* error and injustice); sometimes he inclines to trusting a hidden wisdom which, however, may not exist.

But through thick and thin he sticks to the basic maxims: (1) There is a genuine truth for every situation; (2) he may be mistaken in seeing it, but that does not mean that it does not exist in itself; (3) he will hold on to what he sees as best he can until he knows better; (4) the consensus of the world community—no matter how accidentally or arbitrarily or imperfectly arrived at, and even if it should turn out to be against what he believes to be true—is more to be trusted in the long run than any pet idea of his, no matter how firmly he may hold it; (5) truth will certainly vindicate itself and it may turn out to be quite different from what he now holds; (6) man must be trusted to see the truth; (7) the truth of history, far from forming itself impersonally all by itself, is actually constituted by the decision, will, and effort of man; and (8) therefore, "the consensus of the world" moves and changes, and through his continued independent effort it may still, in ways altogether mysterious and unforeseen, make up for the error committed and redress the injustice caused.

The notion that a full-blooded man cannot serve as chairman or president or as an international civil servant, and that only a denatured, colorless, and characterless person can serve in these capacities, is ridiculous. It is obvious that the infinite challenges demand strength of character rather than weakness. You can be strong in faith and absolutely fair in service. You can be strong in conviction and being and still die for those who put their trust in you.

VI

What is at stake is the possibility of rising above oneself, of believing in and seeking a genuine world point of view. This is possible only if one believes in objective and independent truth, no matter how partial or dim our view of it might be, and no matter how much we might muddle it up in the process of seeking it. A man who believes that truth is identical with his own interests or the interests of his nation, and that he exists only to serve these interests, should never be elected to preside over an international organ or to serve as an international civil servant. A man who belongs to a militant movement which identifies all morality and all truth with "the cause" can never be trusted with presiding over an international body or serving the world community. It was not an accident therefore when Manuilsky in the chairmanship of the First Committee in 1946 and Jacob Malik in the presidency of the Security Council in August 1950 behaved as they did. Because international communism does not believe in objective and independent truth, it is not genuinely "international." It must conquer and dominate everything and whatever it does is calculated precisely to serve that end. Absolutely impartial international servants cannot be Communists—certainly not when crucial issues arise. Because they only serve *their* idea, they think everybody else, even when he is entrusted with international responsibility, has *an* idea to serve. That is why Khrushchev does not believe there can be a "neutral" international servant: he must serve either the Communist cause or the "capitalist" cause or—strange irony—the "neutralist" cause. But so long as spiritual cultures still exist on earth which believe in genuine, independent, objective truth, such cultures can produce men of absolute integrity and depth who will completely rise above their ideas and interests and *see the world as a whole.* Hammarskjold was absolutely right in affirming and sticking to this point. The whole issue today, in one of its deepest formulations, is precisely whether there is such a thing as "the world as a whole." Such men will always clash with a point of view that sees only itself; for such men see other points of view as well; and they also see that the objective relationship between different points of view need not always be one of absolute antagonism, in which one either destroys the other or is destroyed by it, but can also be one of mutual accommodation and tolerance. The deadlock could not be more complete than between the traditional concept of freedom and respect for objective truth and being and a revolutionary concept that makes short shrift of all that in order to posit only itself. There is here a radical spiritual rebellion which, by taking the initiative of the denial and the offense itself, has willfully placed itself outside the pale of any accommodation. It is not the fault of others if it is not accommodated: it itself does not want to be accommodated.

7

WHAT YOU SEE

I

PRESIDING dutifully day after day and month after month, what sort of panorama unfolds itself before you? The same panorama passing before your vision appears slightly differently from your presiding position than it does from your position as a member of the House. In the latter capacity you see things from the angle of the pull of your national interests. There is nothing shameful about this: a peace-loving man, representing a peace-loving country, peacefully defending and promoting its national interests, sincerely loyal to the United Nations, and honestly struggling in the service of peace, is a perfectly honorable creature. Even from such a perspective he could, although not without considerable moral effort, intellectually rise above his narrow national interests and see the world in itself and as a whole. But his constant preoccupation with his government and the interests of his country and the problems of his delegation could distort his vision so far as *seeing the world as a whole and in itself* is concerned. As representative, he cannot attend to everything; he must be selective. As President or Chairman, he must attend and listen to everything; he cannot select; he must see the whole; and from this non-selective, all-inclusive vantage point he soon acquires quite a different perspective. From the absolutely detached position of a President or a Chairman,[1] therefore, what do you see?

II

You see man in the struggle for peace concretely in all his tragedies and glories.

You see that in his actual, concrete struggle for peace, the mystery of man resolves itself into a finite number of basic states of mind (fear, envy, ambition, loneliness, spite, vanity, pride, domination, procrastination, competition, assertion, etc.), not more than thirty, although each such state of mind can articulate itself in a virtually infinite number of ingenious ways; and thus seeing man to be the same everywhere, you exclaim: *Is that man?*

You see the amazing fact that representatives of the whole world are at last actually meeting in one place under one roof, and this simple fact at times completely overpowers you.

You see the equally amazing fact that this meeting place is not in the Old World but in the New, and you deeply reflect on its significance.

You see the equally meaningful fact that for years this meeting has been presided over by representatives of small states— representatives and states in themselves altogether powerless, and yet somehow symbolizing the fragile unity of the world.

You see each nation wholly given to its own problems—

---

[1] The presiding officer of the General Assembly or any of the Councils is called "President"; the presiding officer of all subsidiary bodies of the General Assembly and the Councils, including the Main Committees of the General Assembly, is called "Chairman." In French, of course, only the term *"Président"* is used.

and you wonder who can possibly grudge it the happy solution of them.

You see the absolute reality of the issues preoccupying the nations, individually and in their relations to each other—and you wonder how abstract thinkers humming their own tunes to themselves can fail to see them.

You see the objectively clashing national interests—and you wonder how they may be reconciled.

As you sadly behold these objectively clashing national interests, you remember the words of Augustine and see in them the expression of an absolute truth:

There are two kinds of love; of these the one is holy, the other impure; the one is social, the other selfish; the one consults the common good for the sake of the supernal fellowship, the other reducing the affairs of the commonality to their own power for the sake of arrogant domination; the one subject to God, the other endeavouring to equal Him; the one tranquil, the other turbulent; the one working for peace, the other seditious; the one preferring truth to the praise of those who are in error, the other greedy for praise however got; the one friendly, the other envious; the one wishing for the neighbour what it would wish for itself, the other wishing to subject the very neighbour to itself; the one guiding the neighbour in the interest of the neighbour's good, the other in that of its own. . . . These two kinds of love distinguish the two cities established in the human race. . . in the so to speak commingling of which the ages are passed.[2]

You see the emergent nations eager to take their place under the sun, and you bless their good intentions.

You see the militant ideology of communism attacking and challenging the West, and you see a whole plenum of nations between them.

You clearly see the half dozen fundamental cultures of the

[2] Saint Augustine, *De Gen. ad litt.* XI, xv, 20. Included in Przywara, Erich: *An Augustine Synthesis* (London: Sheed and Ward, 1936), p. 266.

world, each delightfully expressing itself in its own inimitable way.

You see two more or less "equally good" causes moving towards a head-on collision, and you ask yourself: Are there *two goods,* and can the one world *contain* them?

You see two diametrically opposed points of view saying at times *exactly the same thing,* and you are completely lost —until you remember *what they did not say!*

You see two or more *worlds,* completely different, if not antagonistic, presenting themselves in succession, each complete with all its values, its laws, its expectations, its sense of humor, its outlook on man and the universe, and you wonder: Can the one world *contain two or more worlds?*

You see through the endless maneuverings and jockeyings that are going on, and you ask yourself: Do people never get tired; must they eternally play this boring game?

You see real men, great men, struggling like men—struggling with enormous problems—problems transcending their ability and at times even their comprehension.

You see the absolute necessity of secrecy, both because in international matters man is never quite sure of any position he takes, and because as a result he cannot act without the opportunity being guaranteed him that he can some day save face.

You see disgusting hypocrisy, self-righteousness, falsehood, shadiness, corruption, dirt, insincerity, untruth, rebellion, darkness—and yet the issues to which all these constitute a sort of delicately balanced background are most real and most true; and what disturbs you most is not what you see at the United Nations but the sure knowledge that the *world outside,* both inside each nation, and especially inside each government, and between the nations and governments, *is not better*; and so you resign yourself to the simple thought that "after all" the world of the United Nations only mirrors a world beyond itself, and you put to yourself the disturbing question: *Must there be a moral toll for every good?*

You see superb diplomatic presentation at its highest, and you see despicable diplomatic presentation at its lowest—and you wonder how spiritually uneven are the nations in the perfecting of this great art.

You see that, provided the basic will to some agreement is guaranteed all around, there is no situation for which expert drafters cannot find the acceptable language; and you marvel at the infinite ingenuity and resourcefulness of human reason.

You see real summits of vision and nobility and beauty, and you see real abysses of sordidness and ugliness and horror.

You see the absolute reality and goodness of human existence; but you also see the incredible vanity and pride of man.

You see how pitiful man is, and you say to yourself: Pity man, even the most unhappy and misguided of men; pity man that you may be pitied yourself.

You see everything straining and striving and travailing to *rise and be,* and inevitably you ask: Rise to *what,* be *what?*

You see the whole of humanity struggling and groping towards some end, perhaps blindly; and you instinctively ask: *What end?*

You see it also inexorably caught up into something, perhaps unawares; and you anxiously ask: *What thing?*

Seeing both of these things, you also ask: Is there anything that can open its eyes to what it is after; is there anything that can bring it out of the dark?

You see the strange phenomenon of fluency and change— every morning a new world, perhaps from morning to afternoon a different set of given facts altering the whole picture.

And yet behind this heartless kaleidoscope, you see eternal man desperately struggling for peace, for security, for salvation, and for being.

You see that history is never really decided *when it takes place,* but it is always the future that determines the present and the past, both because whatever "takes place" always takes place with an eye to the future, and especially whatever "takes place" can only be interpreted or confirmed or exalted or suppressed or established or permitted *to be* in and by the future; and thus you tremble before the tragic character of all historical decision, because each such decision delivers the world to the inscrutable mercies of the future.

You suddenly see that the ultimate principle of order is *fear of retribution,* and so you say: Fear is better than nothing; but fear is a purely negative principle. And so you ask: Is that enough?

You see how hopeless it is for these forces, left to themselves, to establish any semblance of permanent peace and order—and yet *where else* can you look?

You finally see a possible meaning to the whole show—but you would not dare express it!

III

In the contemplation of this rich and exciting panorama you are struck by its ten thousand concrete rhythms and beauties. The first virtue of the mind is to respect being such as it is. And so you are thankful for whatever order and firmness it presents. But *being as it is* is also most untidy, and this too has to be respected. Can you rest in its confusion, its disarray, its muddle, its disorder, its profound unrest? There is something obviously false and unreal about it. The unreality of the world of the United Nations, and of man in that world, is one of its deepest truths, and does not take long to reveal itself. Its very peace is not peace—it is so precarious that it could break down any minute; and the wonder is that it has not broken down. Its peace is a most uncertain *struggle* for peace, and one holds his heart all the time in his hands lest it suddenly slip away.

And so the question is absolutely inescapable: Is there *somewhere* an existing order of perfect and everlasting peace? Are we *condemned* to this world of unreality and confusion and falsehood and utter precariousness? Is there no *real* escape from it? The question must be asked, but we dare not lightly answer it.

It is always safe to exhaust the possibilities. There are only three possible answers to this question:

1. This is all that there is and we must do the best we can with it. But in the end this is a hopeless outlook; for there is no guarantee whatsoever that this "best" is even possible, and, if possible, that it is "good" at all. In other words, *if this is all that there is,* how can it possibly improve? How do I know that the future is going to be better? Why should it not rather be positively worse, or at least the same old, stale, drab, dull, and dreary confusion, recurring eternally—the "eternal recurrence" of Nietzsche? This answer shuts us up in utter darkness and despair. But it is a possible and honest answer.

2. There is "somewhere" an existing order of perfect and everlasting peace, but it is completely beyond this world and in no way impinges upon it. Whether or not we are translated after we die to that "other world," *it* makes no difference whatsoever to our struggles and tears while we are here. But now, since we are asking this question in and from and about *this* world, this second answer is as unprofitable as the first. We are equally before the bleakest of prospects. But again it is a possible and an honest answer.

3. There is "somewhere" an existing order of perfect and everlasting peace, and this "somewhere" is *both here and there.* It did not arise "here," but it *came* "here" *from* "there." A sure token of it wonderfully penetrates and leavens the world here, but it also infinitely transcends it. In this possibility we have complete hope, because when we do "the best" we can here,

we are grounding it in something solid and sure; and whatever is left unfinished "here"—and much indeed will be left un-finished—will be surely completed "there."

The interesting thing is that (1) and (2) cannot be proved, while (3) can; for you can never prove the non-existence of a thing except if it be self-contradictory. The holders of (1) do not really know that there is *nothing* but this world of con-fusion and struggle and recurrence. The holders of (2) cannot possibly know that there is a real world of truth and being and perfection wholly unrelated to our world. And purely formally, there is nothing self-contradictory in (3).

The most disturbing thing to the holders of both (1) and (2) is that there are perfectly rational human beings, by the millions, with their feet firmly on the ground, knowing as much mathematics and science and philosophy and economics as they, and having as much fun in life as they, who neverthe-less hold (3)—and can prove it!

And, what is more, the proof is not theoretical; it is not just in the order of ideas; it is not something "cosmological" or "teleological" or "ontological"; Kant was right in holding that these proofs do not satisfy; where he was wrong was in main-taining, or in thinking that he himself had "proved," that there was nothing in them. No, the proof of (3) is in the order of being and life. What can be pointed out to the holders of (1) and (2) is that there is an actual, existing order of perfect and everlasting peace here on earth, here in history. Surely it is not the order of the nations, nor of the United Nations, but *it ex-ists. And now that it exists,* the ultimate problem is *not whether it exists or can exist*: the ultimate problem is simply whether the pride and blindness and rebelliousness of men permit them to *recognize* it, once it is pointed out to them.

8

LIFE GOES ON

I

ONE OF THE DEEPEST JOYS of life at the United Nations, especially if one stays there any length of time, is the cultivation of life-long friendships. The camaraderie which one enjoys at the United Nations is very rare—I believe it is unique —in the history of international relations. Permanent friendships are struck, developed, and sustained throughout life. Most of the men who later on assume national responsibilities, especially in Asia and Africa, have had part of their political and international apprenticeship at the United Nations. You get to know these men well, some of them very intimately, and hardly a day passes without reading that one or another of them has had such an achievement to his credit or such a failure to his embarrassment or woe. In the one you take a special personal pride as though it were your own, and in the other you join in the embarrassment as though you helped in perpetrating it or you suffer the woe as though it smote you personally. When a dear friend of yours with whom you worked for years becomes Prime Minister or Foreign Minister or President in some far-off country, you rejoice and celebrate; and when he resigns, is dismissed, imprisoned, or assassinated, you accept that as in keeping with the turbulent and tragic times in which we live; and you always find yourself writing letters to him or his people suitable to the occasion. At the United Nations you make real friends, you enter into real fellowship, you really know people, and those who have known each other well constitute a sort of secret international fraternity, completely unorganized and informal but nevertheless real. Under the stress and challenge of events people either rise to their highest or sink to their lowest, or more often they do both. Nothing brings out more the best and the worst in man than the challenge of great crises, and you never really know yourself and others except in the testing crucible of such crises. Man is eternally unhappy and fallen without transcendent aid, and so you take the ugly revelations of human nature in your stride. The moments of pure friendship and fellowship and trust you enjoy at the United Nations you will never forget; they are among your dearest possessions; they will stay with you for life.

If personal relationships make a difference to the course of events, and I am certain they do, the theories of Karl Marx and his ilk notwithstanding, then the friendships established and sustained at the United Nations are among the important determinants of history. Can one measure the influence upon the tone and even substance of international relations which such friendships ultimately exert? Who knows under what crisis and at what point and in what guise these relationships will not assert themselves in rescuing this or that tough situation, in salvaging this or that lost cause, in averting this or that hopeless impasse, in resolving this or that fateful crisis? By personalizing diplomacy, the United Nations helps immeasurably in determining the course of history.

II

Thought and experience have different scales of time altogether. You may spend a lifetime wondering about what happened to you in the twinkling of an eye, and there are certain classical events in history which occurred within the space of a few years on which mankind has meditated for thousands of years without exhausting their meaning, and the likelihood is that it will continue to ponder them until the end of time. The comprehension of life, especially in moments of genuine ecstasy, is infinitely more spacious than the comprehension of thought. Whole worlds are actively present and in the midst of them you feel yourself at the very tip of time. The whole of history—past, present, *and* future—converges *there*; and when they pass on, they can never be captured again in their immediacy. They can only be "remembered," "reflected upon," "mediated." Before this sad phenomenon of inexorable passage, Whitehead had to invent what he called "the consequent nature of God" as that region where all historical immediacies remain eternally in their fullness, unabstracted from and undiminished. He felt that that alone can *make up* for the essential injustice of time. It is somehow not *right* that immediacies with all their richness and wonder should be doomed to perpetual perishing; therefore, postulates Whitehead, there must be a realm of being, outside the abstractive processes of time altogether, where all immediacies are absolutely deposited and conserved. This is a bold and noble speculation, out of keeping with the spirit of this timid age. What one goes through at the United Nations lives perfectly in that realm. But what Whitehead does not speculate upon—what within the bounds of his metaphysics he cannot speculate upon—is whether personal existence is such and the nature of being is such that "one" shall "one day" relive and see his whole temporal experience *in that realm*. For *one* is not particularly comforted that *his* "occasions of experience" are each absolutely eternally intact *there*: *one* craves for and *needs* wholeness, eternity, unity *himself*. But within time and history one must sooner or later "graduate" from the United Nations; and as he steps forth into the world of men and things, he breathes a fresh and most reinvigorating air—an air he is not used to, or at least an air he has now more or less forgotten; a demanding and challenging and strange air. His experience, then, is somewhat that of the man in Plato's allegory who emerges from the cave; for a while he is not sure which are the shadows, the objects he left behind or the realities he now sees. And the term of his "adjustment," both as to its length and its quality, depends on how far his roots extend beyond time. Two things now haunt him: to reflect—alas it is now only "reflection" and not "being"—upon his experience in detachment and perspective, and once again to contemplate the ultimate issues of life and death for which he had really found no place reserved at the conference table. Each of these matters raises its own poignant question: (1) Which yields the greater reality, the being of the United Nations experience or the detached reflection on it? (2) What bearing does that experience have upon—what enrichment does it offer to—the contemplation of the ultimate issues of life and death which never really departed from his mind for one minute?

III

Now life never leaves one alone. There are always fresh challenges, fresh burdens, fresh duties; and you can muster interest to dwell on the fundamental issues of thought and life only in the thick of the immediate concrete demands made upon you. You never step out of history, and you never succeed in freeing yourself from the clutch of the unknown—the *Um-*

greifende of Jaspers—that encloses and converges upon you within it. The formal fullness of life on earth, to repeat a Whiteheadian theme, consists in the active present forging ahead into the inexorable embrace of the future on the basis of the settled and peaceful past.

Service at the United Nations, if only one listens and sees and observes and feels and thinks, puts one in active personal touch with what is really happening in the world. There is nothing really like it. Before the concerned and thoughtful and thinking servant at the United Nations, whether he serves his own country or the Secretariat, or whether he is an elected officer, there are disclosed in all their shattering dimensions the great issues of the cold war in their most concrete manifestation; the historic crisis of the peoples of Asia and Africa; the tremendous and apparently irresistible onslaught of the international Communist movement; the militant assertion by man everywhere of his fundamental rights and freedoms; the contrasts and clashes in culture and civilization and spirit between the children of men; and, above all, the fact that Western civilization, with all that it holds dear and ultimate, is being put today to the test perhaps as never before, first by appearing as only one among many, and then by being actively and dangerously challenged to rise to its highest and deepest, namely, *to justify itself before man and history*. Gone forever are the days when anything can be taken for granted. Gone forever are the times when people can complacently say, "I need not justify myself; *I am,* that is enough, and let others all go to hell!" No one and nothing can be exempted any more from the necessity of justifying itself in the great crucible of being.

Thus, service at the United Nations enlarges the mind, tests the character, and humbles the soul, as practically nothing else does in this troubled age of crisis and conflict. And addressing myself at this point specifically to American youth, I say:

When the turn of any of you comes to serve, I hope you will prove worthy of being entrusted with real responsibilities at the United Nations. I hope also that at that moment some of you, both through the improved state of the world and through your fortunate personal development in the interim, will be in a position to sum up in the depth of your being, in the truth of your words, in the strength of your convictions, in the beauty of your vision, and in the simplicity of your life, the deepest that there is in your great heritage. I say this because you have no idea how much the world awaits the *Word* of America.

PART II

The United Nations:
A Political Interpretation

CHAPTER

9

THE LIMITATIONS

OF THE UNITED NATIONS

I

Part I sought to give an existential interpretation of the United Nations. By this phrase I only mean an interpretation in which actually existing man is at the center of our thought. Not only for the United Nations, but for everything else there is an existential interpretation, namely, the bearing of that thing upon and its meaning in and for man's existence; and whoever has had some intimate personal experience of that thing can, if he is interested in existential matters, work out his own existential interpretation of it. As a matter of fact, the foregoing account is but the barest introduction to what can be done in this field with respect to the United Nations. The possibility of a more complete account depends on how much day-by-day patiently recorded and existentially conceived material there is. Whether such a full existential elaboration will ever be attempted cannot now be known or promised. Existential interpretation can be done in one of two ways: the way of philosophy or the way of literature—the way of discursive phenomenological elaboration, or the way of dramatic, literary creation. Whatever modest powers I command fall entirely within the former domain. But I recognize that dramatic imagination on the Dostoevskian style, in which eight or ten created characters develop existentially between themselves the whole theme of the United Nations, is perhaps superior to the abstract method of philosophy. What is needed therefore is a Dostoevski who *knows the existential facts,* or to whom *these facts* can be made available; he alone can then creatively interweave this material into a superb living structure in which the eight characters, amidst the infinitely fluctuating moods and scenes at the United Nations, can each speak and act from his own unique personal point of view. What is needed is a sort of *War and Peace* written on the United Nations by a Dostoevski. He must further have the love and understanding and tenderness of Dostoevski; he may not treat man cynically; he must see reflected in every situation, no matter how sordid or meaningless, how hopeless or dark, a gleam of something wonderful and transcendent; he must have the magical power of *saving* everything he touches; he must be able to see, as Dostoevski saw, everything bathing in a light and a grace coming from "beyond." In the absence of the creative loving poet, the philosopher is at best a "second best."

But there is, of course, a sense in which the United Nations is a being in itself quite apart from the human actors in it. *It is this particular international organization.* In this sense, what happens to the persons who act in it, what they go through, who they are, what they see—all this is irrelevant. There is this Charter, there are these six principal organs, there is the record of these sixteen years, and there are these issues that have been debated and acted upon. What is at the center of thought here is not man, but "the polis"—humanity organized on the basis of ruler and ruled—these 110 governments, each ruling a separate nation, coming together through their representatives into this particular *international political organization*. The United Nations as such, then, is a fit subject of discourse; one can then set about elaborating its origins, its structure, its purposes, its functions, its successes, its failures. I am not detailing in this part all these features of the United Nations. In addition to the vast existing interpretive literature on this subject, the student should consult the records of the proceedings of this organization. I am here only attempting a political interpretation, that is to say, I am inquiring into the nature of the United Nations considered as a subject of discourse in itself, and, in the light of that nature, I shall appraise the present crisis through which it is passing. These two interpretations, the existential and the political, complete my study of the United Nations so far as man in it and through it is engaged in the struggle for peace.

II

There are two mistaken views of the United Nations. The first view expects the World Organization to solve virtually every problem, to be finally responsible for peace, to guarantee the observance of human rights everywhere, indeed to be a sort of super-government—all-powerful and all-effective. If things go wrong, blame the United Nations; if something should be done, ask and expect the United Nations to do it. This view expects too much from the United Nations; there is in it a sickly irrational exaggeration of its importance. And when the actual results do not square with the false expectations, people immediately flag into a state of despondency. The United Nations forthwith becomes of no use.

The second mistaken view holds that the United Nations is a mere debating society. It does not appear to make any difference to the question of peace or of human rights. Nations go on quarreling with each other and even hot wars break out between them as though the United Nations did not exist. Governments are not bound by its decisions and, as is well known, there are many resolutions by various organs of the United Nations which have not been implemented. One may even go further and show that in the implementation even of those resolutions that have been implemented there was always something defective, always a blemish. And what is the effect of the United Nations upon the greatest issue facing humanity today—the issue of disarmament and of the resolution of the cold war? Practically nil. Indeed, it is possible to show that the public and unlimited handling by the United Nations of certain cold war issues, far from having helped in easing them, has actually tended to aggravate them. The result of all this is to hold that the United Nations does little or nothing, that it is a mere debating society, and that, considering the harm it is doing, it should be scrapped. In this way, the second mistaken view underrates the reality of the World Organization. It is no less sickly and irrational than the first.

The one view expects too much, the other too little, from the United Nations. The one view exaggerates, the other underestimates, its importance. No one who knows anything about the United Nations holds either of these views: for you never exaggerate or underestimate *when you really know,* knowledge being the giving each thing exactly its just value. But there is a fundamental reason why these two views are widely held. This reason is the desperate world situation where, however one turns, one finds himself before so many problems, so many stresses and strains, so many dangers and conflicts. The problems are so exacting, so menacing, so unprecedented, so challenging, so complex, so impossible, that one view—in its utter perplexity before them but also in its ignorance of the nature of the United Nations—desperately expects the United Nations to solve them; but, of course, the United Nations, by virtue of being what it is, cannot do so. The other view, equally perplexed and overwhelmed by the problems, but knowing that they are really too much for the United Nations, turns its gaze away from the United Nations, looking upon it as completely ineffectual—indeed as nothing, which of course it is not; and in its despair, it seeks solace and comfort elsewhere. Before a great crisis—for instance, an apparently incurable disease—we either give up and say, What is the use? or we become so panicky that our mind suddenly takes on a magical or super-stitious bent, feeling, in its moment of softness, that if only we manipulated this or that object, everything would be solved and all would be well. Before the Chinese provocation or the Soviet provocation people desperately cry out: Where is the United Nations? As if the United Nations were a sort of Aladdin's lamp which will answer every wish and overcome every difficulty! It is often the case that the holders of these views suffer from a certain fundamental instability; for they often vacillate overnight from one extreme to the other—today ex-aggerating the importance of the United Nations and expecting everything from it, tomorrow, in the next swing of their mood, asserting that the United Nations is good for nothing.

Thus the ground for the two mistaken views of the United Nations is one and the same; it is none other than the desperate world situation which completely overwhelms the poor human mind. One is baffled where to look for succor, what to do. Both views are flights from reality; both are aberrations from the truth. What is needed, therefore, is a sense of realism with re-spect to the United Nations, a sense which views it exactly as it is, with all its limitations, but also with all its real possibili-ties.

III

I ask then: What are the limitations of the United Nations?

In the first place, the United Nations is the offspring of World War II, bearing in its concept and body the marks of that period with all its peculiarities and limitations. There was a grand alliance which beat Hitler, Mussolini, and Japanese militarism, and the United Nations reflected the will of the victorious powers as to how the peace after the war had ended and the peace treaties concluded would be maintained. Since they were the sponsors of the Organization, they saw to it that its provisions suited their interests. It should never be forgotten that the United Nations is not an idealistic construction, but an international organization that arose in a concrete historical context reflecting in its own constitution all the clashing and conflicting tendencies of its period; and any concrete product of history necessarily embodies the limitations of the epoch in which it arose. It took them two or three years to agree on the Charter, and the mutual suspicions between the great powers could hardly have produced a better instrument. It was in a sense the Yalta agreements, especially as to voting in the Security Council and the admission of the Ukraine and Byelorussia, that finally clenched the whole matter; the San Francisco Conference only ironed out the details. Considering the profound conflicts of interests and orientations in the world today, it was a miracle that the world finally agreed on the United Nations and the Charter. It was only the immediate background of three or four years of collaboration—strained and imperfect as it was—among the members of the anti-Fascist alliance that generated a sufficient political and spiritual impetus to make possible the United Nations such as it is. If the birth of the United Nations had been delayed six months or one year, it is likely that it would never have been born. History moves by one imperfect creation succeeding another; but history moves.

Second, the United Nations is strictly limited by its Charter. For instance, there is the veto in the Security Council without which neither the United States nor the Soviet Union would have ratified the Charter; and in the General Assembly every nation, large or small, has one vote, and the decisions of the

Assembly are mere recommendations with which the nations concerned may or may not comply. Every provision in the Charter is an agreement, but for that very reason it is also a strict limitation. Thus, it is inconceivable that the great powers would yield on the right of veto, or that the sovereign state—large or small, huge China or little Luxembourg—would agree to limit its sovereignty under the United Nations much more than is the case under the Charter. *The Charter is the extent to which the sovereign states in an age of nation-states and at a particular concrete moment in that age sovereignly agreed to limit their own sovereignty on a world scale.* The United Nations cannot rise above its own fountainhead which is its own Charter, and those who expect all sorts of fantastic miracles from the United Nations, as though it were a sort of *deus ex machina,* should first humbly sit down and read and ponder the Charter.

Third, this question of sovereignty bears a closer examination. No nation by becoming a member of the United Nations has thereby foregone its sovereignty. One of the Purposes of the United Nations according to the Charter is "to develop friendly relations among nations based on respect for the principle of equal rights and self-determination of peoples" (Article 1, Paragraph 2); and its first Principle is "the sovereign equality of all its Members" (Article 2, Paragraph 1). No nation by joining the United Nations has ceased to entertain normal diplomatic and international relations with the other nations as though, in a sense, the United Nations did not exist. The United Nations aids—it does not displace—normal international interaction; foreign policy is not determined by the delegations at the United Nations; foreign policy remains the exclusive province of the home governments. Thus the United Nations is not something apart from, much less something above, its sovereign members: it is nothing more than what its members will it to be. It is true that they have willed the

Charter, but they have not willed it as something above them or apart from them; for in the functioning of the Organization that they have willed and in the interpretation of its fundamental statute they do not always agree, and there is nobody above them to arbitrate their disagreements for them; and where they agree, their agreement is mostly on formal, thin, non-substantive, secondary matters. The United Nations then is a derivative reality of which the original is the sovereign nations which compose it. When one thinks of the United Nations, one should not confuse it with the United States just because both names use the same word "united": the United States is a substance and being apart from its component states; the United Nations is not such a being; when one thinks of the United Nations one should think more of its members than of it. The United Nations, then, reflects whatever world unity an order of sovereign and free nations permits at present.

It follows, fourth, that the United Nations in its activities mirrors the objective political realities of the world. It is virtually nothing apart from these objective realities. For instance, the so-called cold war—the tension between the Communist and non-Communist worlds—determines all activities at the United Nations. Nations form their stands and take their positions for the most part in terms of this tension: in important issues you are either with the West or with international communism, or of course you may join the neutralist bloc. But the very definition of neutralism is in relation to the cold war. The world drags itself into the United Nations, and the United Nations is for the most part nothing apart from this world that comes in and seizes it. Similarly, if the United Nations is considering some dispute, say, the dispute between Cuba and the United States, or the dispute between Yugoslavia and the Soviet Union, or the dispute between Israel and the Arabs, then that dispute determines the whole atmosphere and activity of the United Nations at the moment it is being debated. Thus the United Nations is delicately responsive to the concrete world situation which develops and unfolds itself for the most part, certainly in its decisive moments, independently of the United Nations. You are essentially limited if the original ground of your freedom lies outside you; for the United Nations, the original ground of freedom lies in the world and not in it.

Fifth, the United Nations has no army, no police force, no income from taxes, and a modest budget of the order of a few hundred million dollars, depending on how you compute it; this budget is contributed by its members according to a scale determined by the General Assembly, and for years now the Organization has been in profound financial difficulties, largely because some members do not pay their dues. The forces utilized by the United Nations, for instance in the Near East and in the Congo, are modest *ad hoc* contingents voted for specific and limited purposes, and supplied by member governments under the general oversight of the Secretary General; the governments can withdraw them any time they like, and in fact there have been cases of such withdrawals; they are not United Nations forces in the sense that they *belong* to the United Nations, and the world body can use them anywhere it pleases. And as for real estate, all that it owns is a somewhat imposing building on the East River in New York City, another palace in Geneva which it inherited from the League of Nations, and one or two other pieces of property elsewhere in the world. Compared to the smallest principality, Monaco, the physical assets of the United Nations are practically nothing. International politics is basically a matter of the sanction of power; and if these are the physical and power assets of the United Nations, how can it bring to bear upon events the decisive sanction of power except through the moral force of world public opinion *and through the power backing of its interested members*? The United Nations determines events, not independently, not originally, not in itself, but through those of its powerful members which lend it authority and sanction for the occasion in question.

IV

These, then, are the principal essential limitations of the United Nations. It follows that it is a very modest thing, being just that sort of thing which its Charter says it is and nothing more; and just that thing which the conflicting interests of its members permit it to be and nothing more. The United Nations will not achieve miracles; it will not solve all the problems of the world; it will not alone establish and secure peace; it will not even completely fulfill the purposes for which it was originally set up; for historical entities develop and grow; they have an independent life of their own; and in their independent growth they sometimes develop into forms completely different from the structure discernible in their original bud. Nor certainly does the United Nations have anything to do with our deep human and spiritual problems which education and religion alone can touch. Those, then, who, simply basing themselves on the first Purpose of the United Nations, namely, "to maintain international peace and security," expect the United Nations by itself to secure peace, betray their own ignorance of the nature of peace and the nature of the United Nations. Those who seek an outlet for their personal melancholia *at* the United Nations or *from* the United Nations are in a state of utter self-delusion. International existence, and *a fortiori* United Nations existence, is essentially limited.

Does it follow from all this that the United Nations is altogether useless? Not at all.

If you expect an apple to be an automobile—if you expect an apple to be anything except itself—of course you will be disappointed. While you cannot ride in an apple, you can nevertheless eat it. The apple can only be an apple—but that is something. And to him who loves apples it is a very interesting thing. Similarly, if the United Nations cannot by its very nature meet all the expectations of mankind, all the yearnings of the present moment of history, still it is not nothing. The United Nations is just itself—a very limited but a very real and useful international organization.

What, then, are some of its uses, some of its possibilities?

10

THE POSSIBILITIES
OF THE UNITED NATIONS

I

THERE IS IN THE FIRST place the importance of the great debates which unroll themselves at the United Nations. The opening general debate at the beginning of each session of the General Assembly is a marvelously reasoned distillation of all the issues (explicit and implicit) facing and agitating humanity today. For three or four weeks each year the nations forcefully put forward in orderly fashion through their authoritative representatives (mostly foreign ministers) their policies and fears, their complaints and problems, their proposals and points of view, before the whole world. There is no more authoritative annual compendium of world problems and issues anywhere in existence. This compilation should be made required reading of every student of world affairs, especially of every statesman; infinitely preferable would be to attend the fascinating show and follow it closely hour after hour and day after day. It is impossible to convey the overwhelming sense of these opening general debates by abstract, remote description.

There is nothing like them. Other great debates take place during every session of practically every organ of the United Nations on a variety of specific subjects: disarmament, some colonial question, some cold war issue, etc. In these debates the policies and points of view of member nations undergo a fundamental confrontation and a mutual elucidation, definition, and challenge. This elucidation and challenge, by argument, debate and rational elaboration, taking place at the United Nations, is one of the greatest educational forces in the world today. There is nothing more instructive, for governments, students, and thinkers, than to follow and ponder these debates. What is fascinating is not only the substantive issues discussed; that by itself is most important; but to see *how* people argue, *how* different minds and cultures marshal their evidence, the diversities of *humor,* the diversities of *spirit,* the utilitarian employment of *reason,* the *dialectical inventiveness* of the human mind, the varied and often opposed *scales of importance,* all this is a formal education by itself. Some of the speeches are truly great, the result of weeks of artistic and political creation by teams of experts. One may think that he knows quite a lot by reading the newspapers and magazines and listening to the radio on world affairs; or by reading books and secret briefs, or taking advanced courses of instruction, or sitting at the feet of great authorities; or by talking to experts and statesmen; but all this is second-hand and quite pallid and lifeless compared to the concrete, full-blooded, face-to-face, living confrontation and controversy about the great issues of the world that is all the time being enacted at the United Nations. People poke fun at the United Nations because they see it as a "mere debating society"; I myself see nothing reprehensible in a serious debating society even if it were further qualified by "mere"; and *if the United Nations were absolutely nothing but this particular debating society, where the official representatives of the governments of the world debated in public and in all seriousness and responsibility the issues weighing on their countries and governments, it would, despite its obvious weaknesses and its frequent frustrations, fully justify all the effort and all the money that is being invested in it.* Purely educationally, purely from the point of view of authoritatively elucidating the issues facing humanity today—disarmament, the great ideological conflict, nationalism, the rise of Asia and Africa, nuclear weapons and tests, the various forms of colonialism, anti-colonialism, human rights, self-determination of peoples, the question of freedom, the question of economic and social development, the specific spots of friction throughout the world—purely from the point of view of responsibly elucidating these issues, there is no platform, there is no learned treatise, there is no professor, there is no course of instruction, there is no university, comparable to the debates and encounters at the United Nations.

II

Second, the United Nations provides a place and an occasion for a permanent encounter and conference between the United States and the Soviet Union. In the actual world in which we live, practically everything in the international political order depends, as Mr. Khrushchev always rightly points out, on the understanding or lack of understanding between these two powers; it follows that the mere existence of a recognized permanent place where they can meet and argue and negotiate with each other is a great boon. What is especially valuable is the informality, the leisureliness, the casualness, the indirectness of diplomatic contacts at the United Nations. There have been and there will continue to be, whether or not the United Nations existed, the traditional diplomatic channels through embassies and ambassadors, and through secret emissaries. But United Nations contacts, while certainly not displacing traditional diplomacy, make four distinctive contributions to the conduct of diplomatic relations:

1. There are agreed rules of procedure within which the soundings and negotiations can take place; therefore, nobody need be embarrassed as to whether he or somebody else should initiate these contacts (often a very crucial question), or as to the mode of their development, or if they should break down and amount to nothing. The dispersal of interest and participation at the United Nations has this beneficent effect that nobody need feel that he is "put on the spot," not even those most directly concerned, and not even at the most critical moment. The world is around you, and you feel considerably relieved. The rules and amenities of the United Nations can bear and absorb an immense amount of jockeying and maneuvering and embarrassment, without anybody being worsted on that account alone.

2. The casualness of contact—in a committee, in the Delegates' Lounge, as one chances to be smoking or walking in the corridors and lobbies, at luncheons and parties, etc.—could be most useful. It was while casually chatting with each other at the bar of the Delegates' Lounge in 1949 that Jacob Malik managed to communicate to Philip Jessup the barest hint that the Soviet Union was at last prepared to call off the Berlin blockade; whereupon talks were started and that most dangerous situation was finally brought to an end. In traditional diplomatic communication you have first to seek a formal appointment, etc., and that always produces a stir and always raises the delicate question of who should approach whom first.

3. The sheer joint preoccupation, in committee and consideration, of the two great powers with problems of third parties—and many problems at the United Nations are of this character—relaxes them vis-à-vis each other. Such problems may be called "buffer problems," for the two great powers are

not then colliding head-on, and so they can breathe more freely. They try each other sportively and vicariously on third parties, and this could strangely bring them closer together; at least they are not then pitted in absolute dead earnest against each other.

4. Even in head-on collisions on issues vital to the United States and the Soviet Union, the presence of third parties who have under the Charter the right to a voice and who can make their voice heard is sometimes most useful. Such presence exerts an appreciable—sometimes a decisive—mitigating and mediating influence upon the giant contenders. If the United States and the Soviet Union originally do not want to agree, then the existence of the United Nations is not going to force them to agree. But if there is to start with a will to agreement, then the United Nations can facilitate the execution of that will in perfect dignity and honor. This has happened again and again.

These helpful opportunities of contact and negotiation are open not only to the Soviet Union and the United States, but also to all the membership of the Organization; and the quiet, daily diplomatic business that goes on at the United Nations between all governments that wish to transact such business is simply enormous. And third parties always play the twofold beneficent role of mediating and moderating disputes and of taking the minds of disputants off their own problems, as everybody is considering in an atmosphere of joint responsibility matters in which he is not directly concerned.

It follows from all this that *if the United Nations performed no other function than simply providing the United States and the Soviet Union, and indeed all its membership, with a stable opportunity of conferring with one another and constantly taking one another's pulse, with the restraining or mediating services of third parties always available in the background or foreground, it would, despite its obvious weaknesses and its many frustrations, fully justify all the effort and all the money that is being invested in it.*

III

Where the vital interests of the great powers clash, the Security Council is automatically paralyzed: the veto then immediately comes into play. Even when the Security Council acted under Chapter VII of the Charter (that is to say, when no veto was cast; as, for example, on June 25, 1950, with respect to Korea, by default of the Soviet Union), its decision, in the absence of any functioning Military Staff Committee as set up under the Charter, was not automatically enforceable; to the extent that these decisions were enforced, that was due to the fact that interested members *wanted* to enforce them. All other decisions by the Security Council, even where the Security Council "orders" and "asks," are essentially of the nature of recommendations, and many such decisions have not been heeded, or at least have been quietly allowed to lapse. The decisions of the other organs of the United Nations possess even more clearly the character of recommendations, and are even more readily subject to noncompliance; and, as was pointed out in the previous chapter, practically all United Nations decisions have been imperfectly implemented. All of this, and more, is true. But two things do not follow therefrom.

It does not follow that members never in any way heed the decisions of the Security Council or the General Assembly. In fact, virtually all such decisions are tailored to the readiness of the interested members to enforce them; preliminary, secret, informal consultations are conducted to find out how far these parties are prepared to accept certain texts; and when these texts are adopted, regardless of how the interested parties vote or speak at the time (sometimes they are violent in their opposition and actually vote against the draft resolutions), there is nevertheless *tacit prior agreement* with them on the measures taken. All this secret probing and consultation belongs to the warp and woof of international diplomacy. Thus, if one were to make a systematic study of every single decision taken by every organ of the United Nations with respect to the mode and degree of implementation it subsequently received (this appears to be a fit topic for intensive research), one could show, through the development of objective criteria, that the *extent of compliance* has been quite impressive. Think only in this connection of the Middle East and the Congo; think also of the many decisions taken with respect to the Trust territories, and of reports and studies on all kinds of subjects.

Nor does it follow, even if no degree of implementation took place (which is decidedly not the case), that the consideration of specific issues by the United Nations was altogether futile. The force of public opinion generated at the United Nations, and as a consequence throughout the world, has often exerted considerable pressure. When the spotlight is focused on an issue, and when this issue is freely and thoroughly debated at the United Nations, international tension is likely to abate. The mere exposure of a problem helps, sometimes decisively, towards its solution, and no nation will lightly take—even if it should afterwards spurn—any moral or political censure it may receive at the hands of the United Nations. People have often feared debate at the United Nations more than anything else, and just to forestall the display of their dirty linen before the world, they have offered or accepted all sorts of concessions and compromises. It is true that such debate sometimes exacerbates tensions, but this is the abuse and not the positive use of free international debate at the United Nations; and if people were to shrink back every time such hazards arise, they would never take one step forward. If the objective clash of interests and forces makes it impossible for a party to receive adequate satisfaction for its justified complaint, the notice which the international community has given its complaint and the mild or strong, but relatively ineffectual, resolution it has adopted on it could serve as a sufficient moral substitute. Many a good cause has been enhanced and strengthened, not because the United Nations did anything about it, but because it just took notice of it. However limited the United Nations may be, there are no limits whatsoever on the freedom with which the issues at the United Nations are considered, once they are placed on the agenda (and even, when they are not placed, in the preliminary discussion of whether they should be placed), and such consideration is exceedingly potent in influencing and directing world public opinion.

It follows from all this that *if the United Nations did nothing but (1) secure limited enforcement of its decisions, (2) serve as a moderate curb on the reckless by inducing him either to desist or to make concessions on penalty of exposure and sanctions, and (3) mobilize world public opinion so as to have it bear upon the determination of crucial issues, it would, despite its obvious weaknesses and its many frustrations, fully justify all the effort and all the money that is being invested in it.*

IV

The United Nations, under resolutions either of the Security Council or the General Assembly, has deployed diverse agencies in the Far East, in Southeast Asia, in the Middle East, and in Africa for keeping watch over certain tense situations. The late Secretary-General Hammarskjold used the term " the presence of the United Nations" in referring to these operations. They were entrusted to his oversight and administration assisted by a most able staff. Regardless of how one might judge this or that operation, or the way its terms were actually discharged—and I have my reservations on some of them—it is humanly certain that without this "presence" many a situation would have dangerously deteriorated. The United Nations Emergency Force in the Middle East has now for more than five years effectively stood between Egypt and Israel. In the rapidly evolving African situation, the United Nations is destined to play a creative role; nor have we seen as yet the end of its constructive action—which is much more than just a "presence"—in the Congo. When the Cuban crisis almost exploded into general war in the fall of 1962, the world no doubt was grateful that the United Nations was around; for in its own way this world body, through its diverse organs and facilities, played, at least at one stage in the development of the crisis, a modest but fairly decisive role. And even with respect to Berlin, there are a number of possible modalities, some suggested by the great powers themselves, under which it could be of help.

Thus, *if the United Nations were nothing but a standing agency to shoot its "presence" to a few critical foci of tension whenever there is agreement that its "presence," as the representative of humanity's collective interests in peace and concord, is desirable there, so as to try to relieve tension, prevent breaches of the peace or acts of aggression, promptly report on them when they occur, and quietly mediate disputes on the spot, then it would, despite its obvious weaknesses and its many frustrations, fully justify all the effort and all the money that is being invested in it.*

V

The United Nations has served as a benevolent matrix within which and through which there has taken place an orderly emergence of many young nations. Indonesia, Israel, Libya,

Morocco, Tunisia, Algeria, Cyprus, and other emergent nations in Africa have all benefited from United Nations consideration, decision, and agency. In fact, Asia and Africa have been the chief beneficiaries, in a variety of ways, of the United Nations so far. If now this process of the birth of new nations were historically inevitable, it was far better for it to have taken place in the relatively peaceful manner in which it has been taking place, before the eyes of the whole world and under the benign aegis of the United Nations. Think of the endless bloody conflicts, in addition to those that have actually taken place, that would in all probability have marred the birth and development of these new nations if the United Nations had not existed! For the whole world, as it were, to preside over and seal with its own blessing the birth of a new nation is most reassuring both to the newly born and to the rest of the world; to the newly born, because it realizes that it has come into existence with the blessings and good wishes of the whole world; and to the older nations, because they take pride in having, as it were, fathered the newly born, and since the emergent nation has appeared, not so much thanks to violence and bloodshed, but in the willing bosom of world solidarity, they are entitled to expect it to feel and be responsible to the whole world. When at the time of the admission of a Ghana or a Tunis to the United Nations, every nation takes the floor to join in the universal rejoicing that a new portion of humanity has attained full nationhood and is now an integral member of the family of nations, and to wish it progress and prosperity, and the fullest realization of its peaceful dreams, we are in the presence of much more than a mere formal ceremony: we are then witnessing an act of human solidarity of the utmost importance; we are before a most solemn affirmation by the whole world that a certain people or culture has the right, in the peaceful and equal company of other peoples and cultures, to be and develop, in freedom, in independence, and according to laws of its own creative choosing. Nothing can be more moving than such a scene.

If the United Nations were nothing but this modest means whereby new political communities are given the seal of their nationhood, in a relatively orderly and peaceful manner, and with the blessing of the whole world, then it would, despite its obvious weaknesses and its many frustrations, fully justify all the effort and all the money that is being invested in it.

VI

There is offered at the United Nations for the small and weak and young a warm fellowship, a real sense of being included, a rigorous training in international responsibility. It is remarkable how small nations grow in stature by this experience and participation. Certainly, they begin by being fresh, childish, boisterous, self-important, even at times brash and insolent; they want to show off and assert themselves at every turn. But let the strong and wise (the strong can afford to be wise), let the old and experienced, display some forbearance and understanding towards them, and they are bound soon to outgrow their childish ways. The path to growth is always through error and suffering, and one of the conditions of genuine community is that the wise *stand* the foolish. In community, nations soon find their place, and those who do not will keep knocking their heads until a place is *found* for them. Moreover, the United Nations has provided a certain measure of protection—in some cases, the only measure of protection—to the weak and exposed. Although this protection is not much, although the weak and lonely would do well not to rely on the United Nations alone, still in some cases it is the only security available —and the hungry person cannot be too dainty about his food. Many governments, in Asia, in the Middle East, in Africa, in

Latin America, have repeatedly included in fundamental statements of national policy the provision that they base their orientation upon the Charter of the United Nations. They look to that instrument for peace and protection, and they take pride (sometimes a necessity converted into a virtue) in the fact that they are involved in no "entanglement" and are parties to no "alliance" but that which the Charter imposes upon them, and which they had freely and willingly subscribed to; and since everybody has subscribed to the Charter, in subscribing to it themselves, they have shown no partiality to any special cause. It is excellent to have an opportunity in the company of the big and mighty to exercise responsibility—in consideration, in debate, in statesmanship, in decision—not only with respect to one's own problems, but in matters, big and small, affecting the destiny of the whole world.

If, then, the United Nations were nothing more than an organized means of training nations in international responsibility, of giving them a sense of belonging, of making them feel that they can depend on something, or at least that they are not altogether forlorn, it would, despite its obvious weaknesses and its repeated frustrations, fully justify itself and all the effort and all the money that is being invested in it.

VII

The United Nations appears to be peculiarly fitted to treat problems of intermediate areas, such as in the Middle East and Africa. In a sense such huge political systems as the United States or the Soviet Union or Europe do not *need* the United Nations; they are quite competent to look after their own affairs independently of the United Nations; but regions that are not integral to them or that are between them or that are contested by them, the United Nations can, when they raise international issues, quite properly deal with. These are sensitive spots; they lie astride conflicting spheres of influence; they are not strong enough to cope with the endless international complications which their peculiar situation generates; they are too hot to be handled by one side alone, because the other side would object; and yet they are too precious and central to be allowed to rot into breeding grounds of chaos. For these reasons wisdom has determined that they be turned over, in some aspects of their existence at least, to the care of the United Nations. This is what has happened in relation to several problems in the Middle East. When I say "wisdom has determined," I do not mean some strange, mysterious, extra-mundane power: I mean the concrete necessities of the international political situation, whereby—since a political vacuum is impossible in this world, since both sides immobilize each other when it comes to dealing with these areas, and since they are not vital enough for either side to cause that side to secure its exclusive influence in them at the risk of war—there is nothing left in the political plenum but the international agency to attend to some of their problems. Thus the intermediate areas, some of whose problems involve international complications, appear to present a special domain for the concern of the United Nations; and it is in serving them as an agency of the world community that the United Nations has been most successful. Just as under the League of Nations ambiguous areas existed with respect to which the League had to develop a special competence, so intermediate regions will always exist, although their location on the map will vary from epoch to epoch and even their needs will change, and therefore there will always be room in them for some creative contribution by the United Nations, or by whatever agency is representing the world community at the time.[1]

---

[1] In many of his works, Professor William Ernest Hocking treats the problem of the mutuality of obligation as between the world and what I

If the United Nations has done nothing more than serve (and if it does nothing but stand ready to serve) in certain intermediate sensitive spots, as the authorized representative of the international community, and with the minimum necessary blessing (that is to say, without the active obstruction) of the great powers, then it has, despite its obvious weaknesses and its many frustrations, fully justified both itself (and it will fully justify itself) and all the effort and all the money that is being invested in it.

have been calling here "intermediate regions." This is how he expresses this mutuality of obligation with respect to the Near East in his *The Spirit of World Politics* (New York, Macmillan, 1932):

"Thus, French trade and French ideas are not a legitimate ground for French control of Syria. But world trade and the general spread of ideas are on a different footing; they give a legitimate case—I do not say for world control of Syria—but for some kind of international foothold, since the destiny of Syria is to be, not abstractly self-determining, but a world-member. Leave out entirely the interests of any nation's military strength in the Near East, and ask merely whether the crossroads of the world should be made safe, like other highways, for the traffic of goods and of thoughts. It is necessary to have there not merely well-meaning governments, but governments responsible in the wider sense—able to assess the weight of the valuables entrusted to them. Of the Near East in general we may say that it is fated by its geography to live more than its own life, to become world-conscious, to add to its local genius a general sophistication. The proper price of its independence, then, is not the *non-obstat* of any particular western state. It is simply a sympathy with, and an understanding for, the interests which from all sides are penetrating its territory; and, as a pledge of this, a readiness to admit the presence of an authoritative rep-*World Politics* (New York: Macmillan, 1932):

My point in reproducing this interesting passage here is to stress, in the words of one of the very few American philosophers who have profoundly interested themselves in concrete, world-historical issues (another such philosopher is Professor Northrop of Yale), the peculiar problem which intermediate regions present to the world community; were I to comment on this passage in depth, I would show where I would depart from it, both as to its letter and its implications; nor am I sure that Professor Hocking himself would not today (the passage was written in 1931 in the days of the Mandates of the League of Nations) agree with my criticisms and refinements.

VIII

The United Nations can serve, and has often served, as a mechanism for disembarrassment and disentanglement. When some big powers have overextended themselves, or when they are too much entangled in some situation, then one way of disentangling themselves is to turn the situation to the United Nations and have the world body make a decision which will enable them to save face both before their people, before those to whom they are obligated, and before the world. This has happened time and again (many examples can be given, some most instructive). The overextended or embarrassed nation can then gracefully withdraw by appealing to the decision of the United Nations. Some of the small nations have also availed themselves of this possibility: before their otherwise uncontrollable public opinion, certain weak leaders have on many occasions resorted to the United Nations to get them "off the hook." Speeches designed for home consumption have sometimes served the same end; although there is always danger here of these speeches boomeranging in other respects, since they usually bore the soul out of those who are plagued with listening to them. The problems of these governments were too much for them; so before their masses they could say: "This is the decision of the United Nations, and we cannot fight the whole world!" Far from being reprehensible, all this, from the point of view of world peace, actually serves a very constructive purpose. The active bearing of the whole world upon a particular situation modulates that situation and puts it in its proper perspective. The masses then realize that they are not alone, that there are others with whom they must constitute the harmony of the world. Reason comes into play as soon as the unreasonable confronts the collective wisdom of the world.

If the United Nations were nothing more than this protec-

tive face-saving device whereby the embarrassed may disembarrass himself and the overextended may get "off the hook," it would, despite its obvious weaknesses and its many frustrations, fully justify itself and all the effort and all the money that is being invested in it.

IX

The United Nations offers an ultimate recourse for one's basic complaints. Of course, this is not automatic: a nation cannot any time it pleases bring anything it pleases to the attention of the United Nations; it must first enlist the support of the necessary majority before its complaint can be placed on the agenda, but this diplomatic hurdle is a fair test of the seriousness and justice of its cause; and even if the matter is not placed on the agenda (this happens very rarely) in the preliminary debate as to whether it should be so placed, much can be said. It is most important that nations feel and know that such an ultimate recourse exists. The Charter, in Article 33, stipulates that "the parties to any dispute, the continuance of which is likely to endanger the maintenance of international peace and security, shall, first of all, seek a solution by negotiation, enquiry, mediation, conciliation, arbitration, judicial settlement, resort to regional agencies or arrangements, or other peaceful means of their own choice." But what now if all such means fail? The first thought that comes to any nation when it is in the thick of a dispute or a situation leading to international friction is: *Shall I or shall I not submit this matter to the United Nations?* The mere presence of such a high court of appeal in the international political field provides a sense of ease and rest among the nations—*there is* a last resort, even if it should prove ineffectual. This very sense (1) helps to prevent issues from arising; (2) exerts a subtle pressure upon nations engaged in the means of settlement enumerated in

Article 33; and (3), should the dispute nevertheless persist, helps to prevent it from deteriorating.

If the United Nations were nothing more than this highest court of appeal which the nations keep in mind all the time as the last resort where persistent disputes can be aired and argued, it would, despite its obvious weaknesses and its many frustrations, fully justify itself and all the effort and all the money that is being invested in it.

X

In the economic, social, technical, and human rights fields, the United Nations has made great contributions; it can here make greater contributions still. From the very beginning the United Nations was conceived, not only as an international political organization, but also as one that deals with "the creation of conditions of stability and well-being which are necessary for peaceful and friendly relations among nations" (Article 55 of the Charter). This principle is firmly expressed both in the Preamble and in the Purposes of the Charter. Hence the Second and Third Committees of the General Assembly; hence the Economic and Social Council and all that proliferates from it; and hence the Commission on Human Rights. The programs for assistance, both under the Technical Assistance Board and under the Special Fund, are most impressive: since the start of these activities in 1950, hundreds of millions of dollars have been spent in scores of developing countries on most worthwhile projects—and all this in comparative immunity from the incursions of the cold war. The first proposal adopted by the General Assembly in this field in December 1946 had been sponsored and defended by Lebanon in the teeth of incredible cynical opposition. Very valuable studies have also been made by organs of the United Nations and by the Secretariat on a host of international economic and social problems. If only the exigencies of the cold war permitted, this whole economic and technical function of the United Nations could be almost indefinitely expanded.

The Universal Declaration of Human Rights, adopted by the General Assembly in Paris in 1948 without a single dissenting vote, is one of the fundamental documents of this age. It is true that, despite this Declaration, human rights are not now fully respected and observed everywhere in the world; but it is also true that in this whole realm a tremendous impetus has been generated by the Declaration during the last fourteen years. This document is a powerful, ringing, clear, unanimous proclamation by the United Nations—and not by an armchair philosopher or a well-meaning jurist—as to what belongs to every human being by virtue of being human. Never had organized humanity spoken with one voice so emphatically on the nature of man: there have been excellent statements by individual prophets, thinkers, poets, statesmen, but never by the whole world, in the only way in which the whole world can speak—through its official representatives. The message does not come from this or that positive legal system, this or that special religion, this or that special culture, this or that special outlook on life. The message comes from the combined and considered views of all systems, all religions, all cultures, and all outlooks. That a consensus in this field—and what a consensus!—has been achieved is absolutely remarkable. And the message assures man everywhere that there is something— a something spelled out in detail—that belongs by nature to his essence, to his dignity, to his inherent worth as a human person; and that this something is a fit topic of concern by the organized community of nations. One can show at length that the Universal Declaration of Human Rights has had a most distinguished career in influencing public opinion, determining legislation, guiding many a movement seeking greater support for human rights, finding its way to important texts adopted by the United Nations or by other international bodies, and in serving as a standard of achievement for peoples and nations throughout the world.

If the United Nations were nothing more than this humble servant of man, on a multilateral international basis, in the economic, technical, and human rights fields, it would, despite its obvious weaknesses and its manifold frustrations, fully justify itself and all the effort and all the money that is being invested in it.

XI

The Secretariat of the United Nations, headed since its foundation by three very able men, has rendered in a thousand and one ways invaluable quiet service to the cause of international understanding and peace. There has never been such a community of able men and women, assembled so to speak under one roof, recruited from every country on earth, working devotedly together under one chief, and dedicated to such high purposes as those enshrined in the Charter. No one can fail, on knowing this community well, to be deeply impressed both by its spirit and by the high intellectual caliber of some of its members. International communal living and co-working raises all sorts of problems—political, emotional, moral, spiritual, personal, existential; but this is the cross which the international civil servant must bear. His only reward—no one is thinking of a job whereby one just earns his living—is in the personal satisfaction of a task well done, in the occasional glimpses of strength and truth and beauty which the proceedings of the international body may now and then chance to throw across his way, and in the hope that, since humanity from now on must always have the opportunity of meeting and conferring, he belongs to a living historical organism which, despite all the ups and downs it may still undergo, has a real future. In addition to serving faithfully the delegations and the officers when the various organs of the United Nations are in session, the Secretariat has never failed to extend every courtesy and assistance to the member nations, through its advice when asked for, through its publications, through its studies, through the influence of its representatives abroad, through its ongoing formal operations in virtually every country in the world, through the quiet personal diplomacy of the Secretary-General, through the sheer prestige of the United Nations, and through the endless creative contacts and interactions, great and small, which are all the time transpiring between the United Nations and its members. The concrete political and psychological knowledge of world affairs, world cultures, and world personalities which the Secretariat—despite and through every suffering—has accumulated over the years is one of the priceless heritages of humanity today. It will be a great tragedy if this heritage is for any reason squandered, or just allowed to decay or lose heart; it has such an irreplaceable value that everything must be done to preserve and strengthen it, and to put it to the maximum use.

If the United Nations were nothing more than a training ground, at times through fiery trials, of a corps of international civil servants of the caliber and experience of which its present Secretariat can boast, it would, despite its obvious weaknesses and its manifold frustrations, fully justify itself and all the effort and all the money that is being invested in it.

XII

In Chapter 8, I commented in the first section on the friendships made at the United Nations. I attach the greatest importance to this fact so far as the possibilities of the United Nations are concerned.

It follows that *if the United Nations did nothing more than help in developing such friendships, so that the diplomats and statesmen of the world got to know one another well, and in the discharge of their state responsibilities later on they acted on a basis of personal knowledge of their opposite numbers and of the type of person with whom they were dealing, it would, despite its obvious weaknesses and its manifold frustrations, fully justify itself and all the effort and all the money that is being invested in it.*

XIII

The substantive issues debated and acted upon at the United Nations are of course the heart of the whole matter. They bring out the points of tension or conflict in the world. They have included so far, among other matters, the manifold problems of the Middle East, European postwar reconstruction, many aspects of the cold war, general disarmament, the banning of nuclear tests, the peaceful uses of atomic energy, the problems of space, diverse North African problems, the Trust territories, problems connected with Indonesia, problems connected with India and Pakistan, problems connected with the emerging African states, the complaint of Yugoslavia against the Soviet Union, Korea, Hungary, Cyprus, the Japanese peace treaty, the question of Chinese representation at the United Nations, the problem of membership, the appointment of the Secretary-General, such great debates as the debate in 1949 on the "Essentials of Peace" and in 1950 on "Uniting for Peace," economic development, technical assistance, human rights issues, etc.

The United Nations is nothing apart from these matters: *it is constituted by them*; it came into being precisely to treat such questions as they arise; the treatment of them, therefore, is its *raison d'être*. Its "success" is precisely how "successful" it has been in handling these matters; its "use" is precisely how "useful" it has been in dealing with them; its "possibilities" are precisely the opportunities for constructive international action with which this turbulent world has so abundantly and so unceasingly served it.

While the United Nations could in almost every case have done better, I believe that a fair detailed examination of the many substantive political issues with which it has been seized will reveal that it was an absolute world necessity, and that its cumulative humble achievements with respect to these matters, despite its obvious weaknesses and its repeated frustrations, fully justify all the effort and all the money that have been invested in it.

XIV

In this general account of the possibilities of the United Nations, I have not examined the relations between the United States and the United Nations: this is a matter to be treated separately in the next chapter. Nor have I touched upon the great humanitarian contributions of certain subsidiary bodies, such as the Children's Emergency Fund and the two refugee programs—the one for Arab refugees and the one under the High Commissioner for Refugees. As for the specialized agencies—the International Labor Organization, the Food and Agricultural Organization, the United Nations Educational, Scientific, and Cultural Organization, the World Health Organization, etc. (there are a dozen or more of these agencies) —although they are related to the United Nations and to one another through special agreements, they are almost completely independent intergovernmental organizations. Their contributions—which are distinguished and many—cannot be credited to the United Nations, although the United Nations does perform a modest coordinating function among them, and does refer to them now and then items for consideration and call upon them for assistance under a variety of resolutions. How much these technical intergovernmental bodies depend on the existence or non-existence of the United Nations cannot be assessed, each having an independent life and destiny of its own.

XV

This is, then, the simple, humble thing which is the United Nations. It cannot magically and suddenly transport us from this vale of suffering and struggle to utopia. It can do these other humble things—and no more; but these things which I have just enumerated are not inconsequential.

To be a free forum where the most important international debates take place; to be a natural concourse for permanent contact among the nations, and especially between the United States and the Soviet Union; to enable world public opinion to bear critically and sometimes decisively upon developing situations; to keep through its "presence" a vigilant watch over critical areas; to serve as a sort of midwife for the orderly emergence of new nations; to enable the small and weak and young to feel that they are included and that they belong, and to give them a training in international responsibility and participation; to have special opportunities in certain intermediate areas; to serve as a mechanism for the disembarrassment and the disentanglement of the embarrassed and the too-much entangled; to be a standing last recourse for whomever may feel his peace and security are threatened; to help a little in technical and economic assistance, and to have clarified and to continue clarifying what belongs to man as his essential, natural, human rights; to educate the United States (as we shall see in the next chapter) about the world and the world about the United States, and all of us about one another; to serve through the Secretariat as a source of helpfulness, including the unobtrusive reconciling diplomacy of the Secretary-General, in endless ways to those who seek its help; to be a place and an opportunity where the diplomatic and political leaders of the world cultivate and develop lasting friendships; and to receive, consider, and act upon the innumerable substantive questions that are constantly submitted to it under the Charter —to be all of this is not nothing.

Thus, the United Nations is an extremely limited international organization, but it is nonetheless an organization with immense, real possibilities. It is neither everything nor nothing; it is something—just its plain humble self.

And this plain, humble self is such that, despite its obvious limitations and weaknesses, and notwithstanding its repeated and manifold frustrations, the United Nations justifies more than a dozenfold all the effort and all the money that is being invested in it.

CHAPTER

11

THE UNITED NATIONS

AND THE UNITED STATES

I

THE DECLARATION by United Nations of January 1, 1942, which was largely inspired by President Roosevelt, marked the beginning of the concept of a United Nations. Secretary Hull gave a great deal of thought to a postwar world organization. A draft charter was drawn up at Dumbarton Oaks, and the present Charter was perfected at San Francisco. But with the first part of the First Session of the General Assembly, the United States has been from the beginning the home of the United Nations. The permanent headquarters is in New York. The Presidents and the secretaries of state of the United States have repeatedly affirmed that the United Nations is one of the fundamental bases of United States policy. One only among 110 members, the United States nevertheless contributes about one-third of the budget of the United Nations. The United States delegation plays a leading role in the deliberations of the world body.

This simple recital of well-known facts proves that in its

conception, in its origins, in its development, and in its functionings, the United Nations has a special and close relationship to the United States. Recent significant polls appear to show that four out of five Americans support the United Nations.[1]

For ringing statements of faith in and support of the United Nations by the United States, one can quote from every United States President, secretary of state, and representative at the United Nations at and since San Francisco. Moreover, in its important international actions outside the United Nations, the United States has always declared that it was carrying out a policy in conformity with the Charter of the United Nations. The necessity of making sure that its actions were not at variance with the principles of the Charter appears to have always haunted the mind of the United States.

I shall here cite only three passages from recent statements by President Kennedy. Speaking before the General Assembly on September 25, 1961, President Kennedy said:

Were we to let [the United Nations] die, to enfeeble its vigor, to cripple its powers, we would condemn our future. For in the development of this organization rests the only true alternative to war—and war appeals no longer as a rational alternative. . . . Already the United Nations has become both the measure and the vehicle of man's most generous impulse. . . . Until all the powerful are just, the weak will be secure only in the strength of the General Assembly.[2]

In his State of the Union Message to Congress on January 11, 1962, President Kennedy said:

But arms alone are not enough to keep the peace. It must be kept by men. Our instrument and our hope is the United Nations,

[1] For an endeavor to prove this claim, see an advertisement by the United States Committee for the United Nations and the American Association for the United Nations in *The Washington Post,* March 8, 1962, p. A19.

[2] *The New York Times,* September 26, 1961, p. 14.

and I see little merit in the impatience of those who would abandon this imperfect world instrument because they dislike our imperfect world. For the troubles of the world organization merely reflect the troubles of the world itself. And if the organization is weakened, these troubles can only increase. We may not always agree with every detailed action taken by every officer of the United Nations, or with every voting majority. But as an institution, it has in the future, as it has had in the past since its inception, no stronger or more faithful member than the United States of America.[3]

And in his message to Congress on January 30, 1962, asking legislative authority to purchase up to one hundred million dollars of a United Nations bond issue, he said:

The United Nations is faced with a financial crisis due largely to extraordinary expenditures which it incurred in fulfilling the pledges in its Charter to secure peace, progress and human rights. I regard it as vital to the interests of our country and to the maintenance of peace that the capacity of the United Nations to act for peace not be inhibited by a lack of financial resources. . . . Whatever its imperfections, the United Nations' effectiveness and existence are an essential part of the machinery to bring peace out of this world of danger and discord.[4]

These are strong statements of faith in the United Nations. Few other heads of state, if any, have expressed such firm support of the world body. It is part of American democracy— and this is one of its strengths—to discuss and debate freely practically everything in public; and therefore occasional widespread American criticism of the United Nations, no matter how violent or well-founded it might be, and no matter how important or influential those who make it might be, does not seem to alter the apparently unshakable faith of the United States, as a government and as a people, in the world organization.

[3] *The New York Times,* January 12, 1962, p. 12.
[4] *The New York Times,* January 31, 1962.

II

Although the United States defrays a considerable part both of the regular budget and the field expenses of the United Nations, this money is more than compensated for in four ways: (1) Thousands of Secretariat personnel are living in New York—this means millions of dollars spent back in the United States. (2) The proportion of United States citizens employed by the United Nations is quite high. (3) There are 109 foreign delegations accredited to the United Nations; the number of their personnel is considerably augmented each year at the time when the General Assembly is in session—a period of about three months; thus, thousands of non-Americans each year spend considerable sums of money from their home treasuries in the United States. (4) It is quite probable that if some of the peace operations of the United Nations— notably the operations in the Middle East and in the Congo— were not undertaken, the United States would have been forced to intervene directly, and this would have cost the United States, even apart from whether such intervention would or would not have provoked serious international complications, much more than its present share of expenditure on the United Nations.

It would appear, therefore, that the United Nations is not a financial burden on the United States. But beyond all these material considerations, there are the political matters which we took up in the preceding chapter. As every United States President and representative has affirmed, the United Nations —purely politically, purely from the point of view of fundamental United States policy, and regardless of any financial implications—is an immovable foundation on which United States policy is built.

This does not mean that it is healthy for the United Nations, every time it is in financial trouble, to turn exclusively to the

United States for its rescue. Ways and means should be found —and no doubt they will be found—to have every member, not only catch up with its arrears, but also carry in the future its fair share of the financial responsibility for every operation duly decided and embarked upon by the world body. As President Kennedy said in his message to Congress of January 30, 1962: "It is only fair that members that participate in the privileges of membership should participate also in its obligations."

<h1 style="text-align:center">III</h1>

In 1945 and 1946, when the question of the permanent headquarters of the United Nations was being debated, the slogan was, especially as people had in mind what happened at the time of the League of Nations: If you want to keep the United States in the United Nations, keep the United Nations in the United States. Today there is no danger that either will be kept out of the other. The United Nations, through its mere location in New York and therefore through the enormous press, radio, and television coverage it has received, has been a mighty force in educating the American people in the stubborn realities of the modern world. It has thus decisively helped to shake America out of any sense of isolationism. Without the multiform agency of the United Nations, the American people would not have awakened (to the extent to which they have been actually awakened) to what they know today of the irreducible facts that prevail in the Far East and China, throughout Asia, in the Middle East, throughout Africa, and in the Soviet Union. Also the thousands of foreign statesmen, politicians, officials, technicians, and government employees who have come to the United States in connection with duties at the United Nations have acquired a more concrete view of the United States than they could have acquired

in any other way. I am not implying that mere knowledge of
a country or culture promotes friendship or necessarily serves
the cause of understanding and peace; human nature being
what it is—I mean, human nature being essentially and mys-
teriously subject to envy, spite, pride, and inordinate ambition
—a certain degree of "distance" from a country or culture is
sometimes preferable to too intimate an acquaintance with it;
but on the whole, direct knowledge is preferable either to hear-
say or to the vagaries which ignorance breeds. Considering the
importance of the United States in this closely knit world, this
mutual educative function of the United Nations, as between
America and the rest of the world, alone justifies—as I pointed
out in the last chapter—the United Nations and all that is
being invested in it. Either one chooses to live in a fool's paradise to his eventual mortal peril, or one welcomes the knowledge of the truth, in the certain faith that one can adjust to and
live with it, no matter how painful and strange and exacting.
Revealing as it does an untidy world, a stubborn and recal-
citrant world, a somewhat shocking world, a world that does
not fit any preconceived categories, much less respond to the
naïve wishes of our childish dreams, the United Nations is a
hard training school in the objective truth of the world; and
after the first shock is absorbed, infinite possibilities of constructive action present themselves to the daring and self-
confident. It is impossible to assess how much history will owe
the discipline which the United States received at the hands of
the United Nations in New York.

Now the United Nations is a world body, and therefore the
location of its headquarters must somehow answer to the concrete balance of forces in the world. With Europe devastated
after World War II, and with Asia and Africa just beginning
to wake up from their slumber, it was inevitable perhaps that
the United States, and indeed New York, should be chosen
as the home of the United Nations. One can perhaps "logically

deduce" that decision. But at the next incarnation of the world organization—and there will always be a world organization from now on—the political-geographical center of the world may not be New York. It may be nowhere in the Western Hemisphere. It may not even be Geneva or anywhere in Europe. It is not clear yet that it will be Asia or Africa. I feel that a strong case can be made—on a number of grounds—that the most likely location of the United Nations if it is ever going to move from New York will be the Mediterranean region. The Mediterranean region is the center of the world historically, culturally, spiritually, geographically; in it, alone in the whole world, East and West and North and South meet; why should it not therefore be the meeting place, the political center, of mankind—now that the world has become physically one?

IV

The 110 members of the United Nations (they will number close to 130 before the present impulse of "freedom and independence" throughout the world has spent itself) are not so many independent and impervious atoms. Their relations to one another are not mechanical, external, monadic: there are internal groupings, linkages, understandings, among them. There is the Latin-American group, now cut across by a number of determinations, including above all the Communist infiltration, in its two forms, the Soviet and the Chinese. There are various shades of understanding among the Asian countries, with India playing a leading role; but always also with the India-Pakistan split in the background. The new African nations already display several structures. There are the Scandinavian countries, which usually have a mind of their own. There is the Arab bloc. There is Israel, with its influence and its vital interests. There is the monolithic Soviet realm. There is Western Europe, which does not always see eye to eye with the United States, although all form the Atlantic Community; thus the disagreements, for example, between the United States, the United Kingdom, and France on United Nations policy are quite revealing as to the inner spiritual unity or lack of unity of the Western world. United Nations action is always some resultant of these diverse and often conflicting forces. Thus, the United States in the United Nations always finds itself in the midst of a world teeming with clashing interests, each such interest just as tenacious, just as stubborn, just as ultimate and right in its own eyes, as its interests in the eyes of the United States. The art of helping to create some order out of this welter of confusion—from within the welter and as an element in the welter—is a tremendous and noble art. This is the art of world diplomacy practiced at the United Nations. In its most formal aspect, it is the art of patiently elaborating agreement among governments on specific texts. But prior to the final act of voting, whole universes of probing, negotiating, and maneuvering will have arisen, flourished, and dissolved. The Charter and the Rules of Procedure are the barest beginning of order; but these are only formal and regulative. There are natural communities of interest: material, political, geographical, cultural, and spiritual. These, too, aid in the creation of structure at the United Nations. But within every community there is always a germ of conflict, and between the half a dozen or so communities of interest into which the nations naturally fall there is always a residue of disorder. And so it comes about that no one nation, not even the United States or the Soviet Union, can dominate the United Nations; and the first virtue in international existence is to listen, to understand, to learn, and to accommodate oneself to the hard and stubborn facts.

And yet I do not think the United States has much to complain about at the United Nations. It is listened to with great respect. Its point of view usually prevails. An objective study of all the voting that has taken place since the foundation of the United Nations will reveal that the United States is rarely in the minority and that the overwhelming majority of United States proposals—at times, it is true, after some modifications —were finally adopted. While the United Nations cannot possibly be the handmaid of United States policy, I do not believe fundamental United States policies have suffered at the United Nations. One must qualify this statement by saying that some vigorous attacks against the United States have, regardless of the final voting, made a strong impression at the United Nations; that the number of countries which either vote against or abstain with respect to texts sponsored or supported by the United States has been on the increase in recent years; and that these countries are not confined to one political grouping or one geographical bloc, but are scattered all over the world. I consider this pattern to be more normal, more in conformity with objective interests and psychological facts, and therefore more healthy and challenging than what used to be the case ten or five years ago.

It is good to know who, when actually tested before the world, will stand up and be counted, who needs cajoling and appeasing, with whom there are honest differences of opinion, and who has reasons known—if at all—only to himself as to why he must spite and oppose and contradict, or at least keep happily sitting on the fence, watching and waiting. International existence has been for too long relatively easy for the United States. But now nothing can be taken for granted: the United States must argue and convince and work much harder than before. This is very good; for then the human and universal and genuinely true will come to the fore, and will have to justify itself. And "arguing" here means much more than the attempt at verbal persuasion; "arguing" includes the bringing of all one's resources—spiritual, moral, political, diplomatic, and material—to bear upon the determination of history; only this act of seriously "bringing to bear" makes possible "the attempt at verbal persuasion." It also means the re-examination of the whole United Nations machinery and presuppositions, and the reassessment of the place of the United States—and indeed of the whole of the Western world —in it, all in the light of what is radically at stake in the world today. The margin of one's life is not enough; it may have appeared enough in the past, but that was a great illusion; and if it "appeared" enough then, it is emphatically impossible for it even to "appear" enough today: it is his substance that must now come into play. And all this is wonderful.

V

The United Nations without the United States is ineffectual; the United Nations without the Soviet Union is dull; the United Nations with both of them is real. Nothing is more primordial today than that the United States and the Soviet Union keep on confronting, probing, arguing with each other, under every sign of the zodiac and whether the diplomatic weather be fair or foul.

There are radical ideological differences, not so much with respect to the economic process as with respect to the nature of man, freedom, society, history, government, and the ultimate things. But war is not the answer, although of course one cannot be weak or defenseless in this ruthless age. Moreover, war, even if possible, is—as I shall show in Part III, and as Presidents Eisenhower and Kennedy, and Chairman Khrushchev, have repeatedly declared—no longer a rational alternative.

The answer rather is untiring readiness to discuss in good faith, a genuine facing of facts, strengthening the United Nations on a realistic and non-sentimental basis, increased political, economic, and above all cultural contacts, the conduct of debate with superb and grounded vigor, putting one's house in order at all levels, an absolute firmness in the truth, and the perfecting of a wise, enlightened, daring, and vigorous leadership of the forces of freedom. I believe implicit in the expectations of this crucial moment of history are precisely these eight things.

There is full appreciation at the United Nations (despite criticism and opposition to the United States—for criticism and opposition are themselves often only indirect measures of respect, or of disappointment with the performance of one from whom much more was expected) of the importance of America in the modern world. Much indeed is expected from the economic, political, and spiritual resources of the United States. The inventiveness of the American mind; America's great industrial capabilities; the accent on hard work and just reward; a down-to-earth, practical wisdom; the principle that government, both as to its laws and to the people entrusted with its conduct, emerges from the free choice of the people whose common sense must, therefore, be trusted; partiality for the underdog; a certain humane, humanitarian, and idealistic outlook; love of freedom; hatred of tyranny; respect for the independent will; healthy pluralism; indomitable optimism; the exuberant spirit; and the free university and the free church —these things which constitute the soul of America are a great boon to the world. Immeasurably tragic for the whole of humanity shall be the day when these things—God forbid!—are weakened or neglected or undermined. Brought to bear— prudently, persistently, vigorously, and with the dynamism that once tamed a whole continent—upon situations as they arise at the United Nations and elsewhere, these total American assets will transform the world.

VI

Other nations do not like to speak of America as a "leader," and Americans shy the term, both in theory and in practice. But it is one thing to be self-respecting or to be shy, and it is entirely another to blink the facts. The facts are that the United States and the Soviet Union constitute two mighty poles of attraction in the world and that peace depends on some understanding between them. They both occupy "leading" positions and they both in fact have been "leading" from these positions. For to fail to recognize, and therefore be that which you already are, serves neither your interests nor the interests of peace. History's greatest testimony is when history proclaims of a man or a nation or a culture: "My expectations have been fulfilled, my prayers have not been in vain!"

Therefore, let whoever is called to lead, lead. Now the leader is sure of his stand and can argue it in full. He can therefore listen to counter-arguments with patience and without fear, and when the argument is compelling he will change his stand. But when the change comes, it must not be because the first stand was taken lightly or without due consideration; for nothing shakes confidence in the leader more than the knowledge that in the first place he was not really sure of himself, that his initial position was a veritable shot in the dark. Firmly grounded positions are of the essence of leadership.

A sense of humor is also necessary. This includes the realization that human beings, no matter how exalted their responsibilities, remain human to the core: they remain subject to the humors and follies to which human nature is heir. There is nothing more admirable and winsome about the leader than for him to feel and prove that, while in the respects in which his leadership is recognized he can and will lead with absolute vigor and resolution, in many simple human respects he is just like the rest—in desperate need of leadership himself. To lead, one need not be a philistine.

The leader is profoundly, really, demonstrably concerned for the interests of his colleagues. He understands their needs and their fears. He is solicitous about the least little one among them. He wins their complete confidence because he is prepared to lay down his life for them. He will never allow a situation to develop in which it will be necessary to sacrifice even the least little one for the rest. For every little one has a place —a real, tangible, secure place—and his non-existence must be felt.

A leader who cynically or regretfully sacrifices his old friends because of the seductive lure of the new will inevitably end by being trusted by neither. What is worse, he will sooner or later begin to distrust himself, because he will begin to suspect that there is no depth in him. Other things being equal, the near and close is more to be trusted than the distant and unknown; the old and tested than the new and untried. It is the unnecessary sacrifice that pains. The strange and different is always alluring, but the test of leadership is in remaining faithful to one's own. It is most strange—there appears to be a special seduction in sheer strangeness. One takes his friends for granted; one feels a special elation when he succeeds in appeasing his erstwhile foes; one says to himself, "Isn't it wonderful I have won him?" The question however always is: What price victory? It will be recalled that the faithful son was not disowned by the father when the father celebrated with his friends on the return of the faithless. Nor did the father go to the faithless who wasted his substance in riotous living, but the faithless returned to him. The golden rule is: Expand your circle of friends, but not at the expense of those who trusted you; welcome and win the new, but also preserve the old. And if the new lays it down as his condition for granting you the honor of his friendship that you first cast away the old, then you should be strong enough and honorable enough to tell him that you can do without that honor. If all this is dubbed sentimental, unpractical idealism, then it can be shown, both from theory and the facts of history, that it is far more pragmatic and hardheaded than all the unauthentic pragmatism that floats around.

In international politics three things count: questions of name, face, prestige, pride; questions of national security; and questions of economic welfare. The leader, therefore, must be sensitive on all three counts. He can lead in so far as he succeeds in helping to build up the name and authority of those whom he endeavors to lead, in so far as he can make a real contribution to their national security, and in so far as his association with them can advance their material well-being.

To lead, the leader must inspire. But only the inspired can inspire. And where does inspiration come from? It comes from vision and conviction. Without genuine faith and conviction, no one can lead. But no vision is more inspiring, and no conviction is more true and certain, than the vision and conviction which rest on the concrete knowledge of what the Mediterranean-Western tradition has deposited in terms of positive human, intellectual, moral, and spiritual values. Therefore, let America fully realize of what she is the integral heir, and there will be no limits to her inspired and inspiring leadership.

VII

In looking at the United States, the United Nations knows how much it owes the United States both in its genesis and in its development. It also knows how much it has helped in awakening the American people to the stubborn realities of the world. It is sure that America has now stepped forth into the world for good. It expects the United States to play her appointed role fully, fairly, vigorously, and with a due sense of human limitations. The United Nations insists on the positive alternatives to war and believes that the United States is by nature able to take full advantage of them. Grounded in her own material and moral resources, sustained by her faith that everything in the end is for the sake of man living under the rule of law, and resting both man and law ultimately on God, the United States can rise to unprecedented new heights of leadership. She can confidently negotiate with the Soviet Union in good faith; she can keep developing peacefully her own circle of friends and allies; and she can seek to meet in real self-giving the crying needs of the new Asia and the new Africa. For on these three things depends to a large extent whether freedom, justice, and peace shall continue to dwell on the face of the earth.

12

SOME FINAL THOUGHTS

I

OWING TO THE tragic death in 1961 of Dag Hammarskjold, the whole position of the Secretary-General has
come up for critical consideration. What are his powers? How
much can he develop into a sort of super-guardian of the
peace? What are the limits of the Secretariat's independence?
The Soviet Union proposed the troika system; has she really
suffered a setback—has the United States really won a victory
—by the election of U Thant?

Articles 97–101 of the Charter set forth the functions and
powers of the Secretary-General and his staff. The phrase in
Article 97 by which the Secretary-General is called "the chief
administrative officer" of the United Nations; the injunction
in Article 98 that he "shall perform such other functions as
are entrusted to him by" the organs of the United Nations;
the provision of Article 99 whereby "the Secretary-General
may bring to the attention of the Security Council any matter
which in his opinion may threaten the maintenance of international peace and security"; and the declaration in Article
100 of his complete independence from "any government or

from any other authority external to the Organization": all this language is wide enough and enabling enough to grant the Secretary-General much latitude in the discharge of his responsibilities. His powers, then, are not fixed once and for all: they are the organic growth of the exercise of his own initiative according as concrete circumstances permit. Put a man there, and his own personal character will then creatively mold the position of the Secretary-General according as the developing conditions of the world shall mold him.

It is true that Hammarskjold developed for himself a certain place and prestige. This is due in part to his own personality, which was very rich in subtlety, which has not been fully studied, and the mysteries of which I doubt will ever be fully known. But apart from his complex character, he was given the chance during the first five years of his incumbency gradually and securely to build up that position for himself. The two most critical issues which faced the United Nations during those five years were the Suez crisis of 1956 and the admission of new members, especially from Africa; and on these two issues the United States and the Soviet Union were in agreement. Had they disagreed as they did in the days of Trygve Lie with respect to Korea, and had they disagreed as they did later with respect to the Congo, Hammarskjold would not have been given the chance of establishing himself and consolidating his position. And when they did fall out with each other over the Congo, Hammarskjold's position was irreparably undermined. Like every other feature of the United Nations, the Secretary-General is a function of the objective world situation. It follows that U Thant, no matter how strong or weak his personality might be, will have a chance of succeeding in recapturing the position of Hammarskjold at the height of his prestige only to the extent the Soviet Union and the United States will not disagree on issues vital to them in which the United Nations is involved. Should they disagree again on such vital issues, U Thant or any other man in his place would be ruined, as his two predecessors were in 1950 and 1960.

It follows that the essence of the troika system was in actual operation even under Hammarskjold. Hammarskjold could not with impunity incur the wrath either of the Soviet Union or of the United States or of the world between, as was tragically proven in connection with the Congo. And U Thant today would not take a step—and survive—if any of these three worlds were radically opposed to his action. A troika—implicit, tacit, understood, but nevertheless in full operation—is today at the helm. In effect, then, there was no victory won and no setback sustained.

The last word about the tragedy of Hammarskjold is likely to be that he was a personal victim of the unwillingness of the great powers to confront each other directly and take the consequences. Someone had to be put between them—and crushed. Did he see or suspect that? Why did he accept it? Was he overly self-confident? These are questions that probably will never be answered. But his enormous penchant for the variable and vague and indefinite might throw some light on the last of these questions. Every text under which he operated—and, of course, he was consulted and he helped decisively in drafting every such text—was shot with some ambiguity; he felt perhaps that thus his hands would be free. If all that one requires is *some kind* of resolution by the Security Council or the General Assembly, regardless of the ambiguous terms in which it is couched, so as to have the authority of the world body thereby *formally* passed to him, then he must have extraordinary powers of self-confidence; for the Scylla and Charybdis of contemporary world conditions are infinitely more treacherous than the legendary ones of old. The agent insists on precise instructions, or else he asks his principals to act directly themselves. Excessive self-confidence could cost one his life; and depending on the cause you serve, nothing humanly speaking could be more heroic.

II

With the changes that have occurred since 1945, both in the balance of power in the world and in the membership of the United Nations, we may say that the San Francisco idea of the United Nations has now exhausted itself. An era has now come to an end. If in national existence governments and regimes come and go, I see no reason why world organizations should not be subject to fundamental change. The regime of San Francisco is now outmoded. This does not mean that the United Nations itself has now come to an end: there will always be from now on some world organization, whether this particular one or some other. So long as international war has not broken out on a large scale, the world which is already under one roof physically must somehow come together under one roof for purposes of perpetual contact and negotiation. And should world war—God forbid!—break out again, some world organization profiting from the experiences of the League of Nations and the United Nations is bound to emerge from it.

Profound thought therefore must be given by statesmen and thinkers to the present phase of transition in the life of the United Nations. Each nation must re-think its position, not sentimentally, not escapingly, but, first, in terms of its own interests, and, second, from the point of view of the ultimate human and spiritual issues at stake in history today. Mechanical adherence to the United Nations *as it is* may not be in the best interest even of peace; one can show how this is so at length. There is nothing unapproachably sacrosanct about the United Nations: what is absolutely sacrosanct is man, truth, freedom, justice, and peace; and that alone has a right to be and continue that serves these.

III

The two events which revolutionized the character of the United Nations since its foundation in San Francisco have been the "Uniting for Peace" resolution of 1950 which was sponsored by the United States and which empowered the General Assembly to act when the Security Council is paralyzed by the veto, and the doubling of the membership of the Organization for the most part by the newly emergent nations of Asia and Africa. Had the framers of the Charter foreseen these two developments, I am quite certain they would not have adopted the Charter as we have it today; and had the United States in 1950 foreseen the flooding of the General Assembly by new and inexperienced nations, virtually all suffering from a sense of grievance—be the grievance real or imaginary—against the West, she would either not have urged the "Uniting for Peace" resolution or she would have considerably modified its provisions.

Today the General Assembly, with its 110 members, is the center of gravity of the whole Organization. International communism has been even more potent in the General Assembly than in the Security Council. For the utmost mischief it can perpetrate in the Security Council is a negative one; it is just the use of the veto; its possibilities for intrigue and propaganda and formation of blocs are limited. But these possibilities are virtually unlimited in the General Assembly. There are four reasons for this greater potency in the General Assembly:

1. Anti-colonialism, an exceedingly complex phenomenon quite rife in the General Assembly, is both inflamed and exploited by international communism.

2. International communism has independently infiltrated Asia, Africa, and Latin America; and this infiltration clearly reflects itself in the conduct of many delegations from these continents.

3. The West is itself internally softened up and infiltrated, and is not quite sure of itself; and this too reflects itself in the General Assembly with its never-ending debates of every issue.

4. Even if there were no anti-colonialism and no Communist infiltration, when it comes to *open international conferences* and the spirit of the masses which, directly or indirectly, comes into play in them, international communism, through all sorts of secret and open tricks, is far more adept at injecting itself and manipulating these gatherings than the "civilized" West.

Communism, reflecting as it does proletarianism, is itself an expression in part of the dark spirit of the masses. It is precisely in such massive conclaves as obtain in the General Assembly, with its unlimited debates taking place before the eyes of the entire world, that communism is most virile and most at home. One may even lay down a general rule, that, if open international conferences were left only to the interplay of the conference table without other counteracting moves, there would always be a net gain for international communism from every such conference in which it takes part. It forces others to talk its own language and to appeal to its own ideals; and as soon as that happens, it wins a decisive point. Seldom do others succeed in forcing—seldom do they care to force—communism to talk the language, and to appeal to the ideals, of freedom. For all these reasons, the General Assembly appears to lend itself perfectly as a "front organization" in the strategy of communism. The West does not know the technique of "front organizations"; international communism has perfected that technique. The West never *needed* to "work with" others by guiding and boring and subverting them from within; international communism arose and flourished precisely in response to such need.

From all this nothing can be concluded against the necessity of maintaining constant contacts with the Soviets on every possible diplomatic level. Traditional diplomacy is more suited to Western mentality than flamboyant international conferences. Provided the negotiations are quiet and discreet, and regardless of whether they are formal or informal, the West should be able to exhibit the patience of Job and the subtlety of Solomon in sustaining them on any issue; if the Soviets can sit them out for five hundred futile meetings, the West should be able to sit them out for five thousand meetings; it should never break off negotiations because of apparent futility. The contest of will and wit and resourcefulness in the perpetual maintenance of contacts, discussions, negotiations, exchanges, should never be lost by the West.

IV

The Soviet Union will never withdraw from the United Nations; she will always try to use it as a front organization in the pursuit of her own ends. The United States, too, cannot withdraw from the United Nations, nor can she be the cause of its collapse. I tried to show in Chapter 10 that, despite the obvious defects of the United Nations, a world with it is better than a world without it. If the United Nations should collapse, let it then do so against the will of the United States. What is only debatable is the structure of the Organization and how much of United States policy should be channeled through, or should depend upon, or be influenced by, the United Nations. There is no general rule here: each case must be examined and judged on its own merits. Certain views have been expressed that the United Nations should serve, as it were, as the foreign arm of the United States, or that the United States should in every step she takes first make sure that it will pass the test of the United Nations. In so far as I understood these views, they appear to me to be decidedly sentimental, extravagant, and unauthentic.

Thus what is needed is to try from within the United Nations to transform that Organization into an effective world instrument that will help in maintaining the peace on the basis of law, justice, and mutual respect, and in preventing aggression, whether direct or indirect. Difficult and exacting—most difficult and most exacting—as this might be, it is the only open, practicable alternative.

Something radical must be done to counteract the unreasoning anti-Westernism that has lately developed at the United Nations. All you have to do now to be assured at once of sixty supporting votes is to denounce, whether fairly or unfairly, whether openly or subtly, Europe or America, or to put forward proposals whose direct or indirect effect is the weakening of the West. To be turned into an anti-Western instrument in the hands of the enemies of the West is obviously not the way of life for the United Nations. There are only three ways of combating this ridiculous phenomenon: (1) to develop a unified and far more vigorous Western diplomacy at the capitals of these sixty nations (the scandals of Western disunity are behind every setback the West has sustained); (2) to prove that anti-Westernism will not only be not unnoticed, nor only certainly unrewarded, but that it actually entails unpleasant consequences; and (3) to sustain a concerted and vigorous Western offensive in the halls and councils of the United Nations itself. So long as—either in the name of anti-colonialism, or in the name of neutralism, or in the name of "national liberation," but always in a profound and subtle spirit of anti-Westernism—the rest of the world succeeds in putting the West on the run, at least morally, at the United Nations, there is no hope for this Organization. This pernicious tendency should be reversed, and international communism and the rest of the world should themselves be put on the run, at least morally, except where the West is itself in the wrong. The British and the French are quite right in their anger; but the way out is not to sulk and withdraw, nor certainly to placate and appease, but to step forward and actually put in ten times as much effort in correcting this development as in externally lamenting it.

PART III

War and Revolution

13

THE QUESTION

I

THE ULTIMATE ISSUES of peace today transcend everything that the United Nations was, or is, or is likely to be, or that it can possibly stand for. Although there are people who appear to be prepared to settle for almost any kind of peace, provided only they got away with their skins, the problem is much deeper than people's "feelings" or "temperaments" or "predispositions" or even "good will." You may be honestly (rightly or wrongly) prepared to settle for almost any kind of peace, but what if peace is not granted you even then? You may be an absolute saint, and your whole country may be made up only of saints, but what if peace is denied even the saints? You cannot just subjectively *wish* peace: there are objective laws at work—economic, social, political, ideological, emotional, psychological, historical, human, and even superhuman. The fact that in history wars have always erupted and peace was the exception rather than the rule would seem to show that the phenomenon of war is something ultimate. There appear to be what I might call certain "cosmic dikes" that now and then break in the nature of man himself—including his society—beyond any one's ability to control or mend. A phenomenology of war, originally grounded in a fundamental ontological-existential interpretation of man, on the style of Heidegger, has not been worked out. How is war possible, considering how mad it is? Or is it as *mad* as it appears? How is it grounded in the nature of man? Is it enough to speak of "greed," "fear," "ambition," "security," "self-defense," and "love of money"? People have tended to take these matters for granted; they have looked upon the whole phenomenon as something "perfectly obvious"; and therefore they have inclined to the view that the "prevention" or "outlawry" of war, partly through measures of progressive disarmament, partly through treaties and declarations, supported by well-organized agitation, is something that good will coupled with strenuous effort would one day surely accomplish. What if the matter were infinitely more complex and profound? At least the persistence of war throughout history, despite all good will and all effort, would seem to indicate, *prima facie,* that war is something quite fundamental. When responsible representatives deliberated the United Nations Charter at San Francisco in 1945 nobody ever thought for one moment that the new world organization was going to abolish war for all time. That was the best mechanism for "maintaining international peace and security" the statesmen assembled there could devise for the moment, and people generally would have been quite happy if the new instrument only *helped* in the prevention or regulation of war or in the settlement of disputes for a decade or two. The possibility of war beyond anything the United Nations could do was clearly and wisely recognized in Article 51 of the Charter where "individual or collective self-defense" is described as an "inherent right" which "nothing in the present Charter shall impair." And Article 52 stipulates: "Nothing in the present Charter precludes the existence of regional arrangements or agencies for dealing with such matters relating to the maintenance of international peace and security as are appropriate for regional action . . ."; a language which realistically allows for the possibility of war, and which has been taken full advantage of in the formation of numerous defensive alliances, including the North Atlantic Treaty Organization and the Warsaw Pact. In fact, the whole Organization, and especially Chapter VII of the Charter on "Action with respect to threats to the peace, breaches of the peace, and acts of aggression," is predicated on the distinct possibility of war. Nor do the nations appear ready to trust their security entirely to the United Nations, for never in the history of mankind was the arms race as intense and as furious as it is today in this brave age of the United Nations. All this certainly does not mean that any particular war cannot be studied and analyzed as to its causes, or that its human perpetrators could not be identified, and moral, juridical, and political blame could not be truthfully placed upon them, or that it could not have been prevented. But the assigning of blame, be it noted, is itself an exceedingly complex and delicate matter, seeing that in general only victors write history; and as to the preventing, this judgment is in the nature of the case always arrived at by "hindsight," and by the same faculty it can be shown that in many—if not in most—instances the "preventing" would have been only a "postponing." War, then, belongs to the ultimates of human life; it is of a piece with life and death and destiny and truth and error. Man's struggle for peace is eternal, just because the possibility of war is itself eternal. And if in this struggle man should fail—and there is no absolute guarantee that he will succeed, just as there is no absolute guarantee that he will ever *by himself* overcome his folly or surmount his essential human limitations—or if he should not completely succeed, he should not on that account blaspheme God and conclude that all existence is evil. One does the very best he can (and this applies to governments, nations, and cultures as well) in this vale of sorrow and tears, trusting always a judgment and a righteousness altogether above himself. The sweetness and knowledge of tragedy is always a part of existence; and to be able to say with the author of Ecclesiastes: "To every thing there is a season, and a time to every purpose under the heaven: a time to be born, and a time to die; . . . a time of war, and a time of peace"; and to add to this: "Then I looked on all the works that my hands had wrought, and on the labour that I had laboured to do: and, behold, all was vanity and vexation of spirit, and there was no profit under the sun" (3:1,2, and 8; and 2:11); to be able to say all this and yet remain incurably cheerful and thankful and full of active hope is a tremendous gift that only the deep who are in touch with something above and beyond man and history and war and peace are entitled to enjoy.

Nor is peace just a matter of "mechanically" preventing the nations from falling out with each other. Internal conflicts within nations could be far more devastating than external wars between them; and "international peace" could not only conceal awful "international wars of ideas": it could also shield the most inhuman national injustice and therefore the most terrible "national wars." And the United Nations deals neither with "national wars" (i.e., internal revolutions) nor with "wars of ideas." Despite the activities of the United Nations in the economic, humanitarian, and human rights fields (and these are among its greatest achievements), its *primary* purpose is "to maintain international peace and security"; and since the Charter forbids the Organization from "intervening in matters which are essentially within the domestic jurisdiction of any state" (Article 2, Paragraph 7), the most important internal "material" conditions of peace, which are all in the sense of the Charter "essentially within the domestic jurisdiction" of states, fall outside the purview of the world body. Thus, the "maintenance of international peace and security" is understood only in the "international," "juridical" sense, and not in the internal, national, constitutive sense of the contents and character and social-human-spiritual conditions of peace. The peace of the United Nations, then, is fundamentally a "mechanical" peace. This is not to say that therefore it is unimportant: this is only to stress that as such it is essentially limited.

Even in the strictly international field it is not enough to "maintain international peace and security." The question is what *kind* of peace and what kind of *spirit* is going to pervade that peace. And since a mechanical peace maintained only juridically and by force is patently unauthentic, the question in a sense is the very *possibility* of peace. Questions of *kind* of peace and the *spirit* that pervades peace and the *possibility* of peace the United Nations has nothing to do with. Who then deals with these questions? Whose responsibility are they? Only the active social, political, intellectual, and spiritual forces in the world. These forces arise, develop, and mature *outside* the United Nations—outside any international organization—in the historical cultures and movements of existing peoples and nations. Any fundamental force for peace or for war at the United Nations or in any international organization is only a pale reflection of these original spiritual movements striking root in the soil of national cultures. One of the most important such forces today, flinging a radical challenge in the face of all men and movements and embodying at once a tremendous social, political, intellectual, and spiritual content and thrust, is international communism. The question of peace is whether international communism permits peace, or whether it is such a radical onslaught that it must either conquer or be conquered—*whether under conditions of peace or by war.* And at the United Nations itself virtually every issue affecting international peace and security revolves around the impact of international communism upon the world and the world's response to that impact. Man in the struggle for peace is neither man saving his soul—and his skin—alone, nor man saving the world through the United Nations, but man struggling politically and socially on the national level, and economically, intellectually, and spiritually both on the national level and within those universal movements which bear most profoundly on the question of peace—economic development, the university, and the Church; struggling, that is, in the fullest, deepest, most responsible, and most self-conscious response precisely to the challenge of international communism and of those ultimate human-spiritual causes which have brought it about. No man can talk about peace in the abstract today; no man can discuss peace just as an idea or as a general human *desideratum*. Whoever is really—and not just sophistically— interested in peace is under the absolute moral obligation to tell us what he thinks of international communism, what he thinks of the profound causes that engendered it, whether he has seriously grappled with it, whether and how he has come to terms with it, whether he thinks he can live at peace with it, and what he is concretely doing about its immense challenge. International communism is itself the question of peace or war today.

II

Because the astounding phenomenon of world communism *is itself* the basic issue of peace or war today, we must first establish the character of this phenomenon *in its totality*. There has been in recent years a veritable inundation of works on every aspect of communism. Any student can easily acquire on his shelf a hundred excellent titles in English and at least as many in German and French; all this in addition to the basic works of Marx, Engels, Lenin, Stalin, Mao Tse-tung, and Khrushchev, and the endless statements and declarations of

Communist leaders, conferences, and congresses.[1] There is thus nothing hidden either about fundamental Communist theory and intentions or about the actual Communist world-wide advance during the last forty-five years. People may, for various reasons, play the ostrich and "hide" their own eyes from seeing the perfectly obvious and "unhidden"; but *the thing itself* is there for all to see.

What is the character of the phenomenon of world communism in its totality? What are the topics which constitute this phenomenon? We can only give here the tersest possible summary. When we say that the following twelve topics constitute *the character of the phenomenon of world communism in its totality* we do not mean that this phenomenon is defined by these topics uniformly each in the same sense: we mean that each topic must be faced and gone into independently, and that only after one has thoroughly done this can he rightly say that he has grasped the full character of world communism both in its actual and in its problematic senses. The following, then, is our way of confronting the reader with the immense challenge of communism:

1. About a third of the world is directly and most tightly controlled by the Marxist-Leninist-International-Communist Party.

2. The remaining two-thirds are in varying degrees infil-

---

[1] The following works are among scores that discuss the whole question of communism; their importance consists also in the fact that they contain excellent bibliographies:

Communism—Menace to Freedom. Distributed by Reader's Digest, Inc. New York, 1962.

GOODMAN, ELLIOTT RAYMOND. *The Soviet Design for a World State*. New York: Columbia University Press, 1960.

KULSKI, WLADYSLAW W. *Peaceful Coexistence*. Chicago: Henry Regnery Company, 1959.

MAGER, N. H., and KATEL, JACQUES (eds.). *Conquest Without War*. New York: Pocket Books, Inc., 1961.

trated by it: this means (a) the active presence of Marxist-Leninist-International-Communist Parties; (b) the presence of many fellow travelers and sympathizers with these Parties; (c) the presence of people whose political tendencies would, whether wittingly or unwittingly, play into the hands of these Parties; and (d) the spread of the Marxist-materialist-atheist interpretation of life.

3. Never was communism freely adopted by any people; it was always imposed, through intrigue, conspiracy, revolution, and force, by a very small minority—not more than 1 or 2 per cent—constituting the Party. It follows (a) that no particular development of communism was at any point inevitable; (b) that nobody knows whether any people dominated by communism today really want to live under that system, since no people have ever been given the opportunity of expressing themselves freely on this question; and (c) that no question is more historically far-reaching than this: Where were the anti-Communist forces when communism succeeded by sheer conspiracy, subversion, intrigue, force, and considerable accident to seize one country after another?

4. A mighty state, the Soviet Union, with enormous nuclear capabilities and the means to deliver them, is behind this Party. This does not mean that the material might of this state will be automatically brought into play to support every Communist cell anywhere in the world; but it does mean that Marxist-Leninist-International-Communist purposes and policies are everywhere and wherever possible furthered and supported by the material and moral might of this state; and this fact engenders in these cells spread throughout the world enormous confidence and courage.

5. All these developments occurred in the last forty-five years.

6. The Marxist - Leninist - International - Communist Party uses every conceivable method and means for the propagation

of its ideas, the weakening of those who have not yet been overcome by it, and the seizure of power. These methods and means include the ordinary processes of diplomacy, infiltration (especially of the labor unions, the press, and the universities, and, wherever possible, of the government itself), intrigue, intimidation, character assassination, direct aggression, indirect aggression, subversion, front organizations, the manipulation of international organizations and conferences, the exploitation of grievances (real or imaginary), the exploitation of differences (national and international), the inflaming of the class struggle, economic and military assistance, etc., etc. Pope Pius XI, in his *Encyclical on Atheistic Communism* which was published in 1937, put it this way:

There is another explanation for the rapid diffusion of the Communistic ideas now seeping into every nation, great and small, advanced and backward, so that no corner of the earth is free from them. This explanation is to be found in a propaganda so truly diabolical that the world has perhaps never witnessed its like before. It is directed from one common center. It is shrewdly adapted to the varying conditions of diverse peoples. It has at its disposal great financial resources, gigantic organizations, international congresses and countless trained workers. It makes use of pamphlets and reviews, of cinema, theater and radio, of schools and even universities. Little by little it penetrates into all classes of the people and even reaches the better-minded groups of the community with the result that few are aware of the poison which increasingly pervades their minds and hearts.

The truth of these words, first uttered in 1937, is now confirmed tenfold.

7. The open aim of this world revolution is the overthrow, whether by peaceful or by violent means, of every existing non-Communist government, system, order, religion, and outlook on life, and the bringing of all men everywhere, in every aspect

of their life—political, economic, social, intellectual, spiritual —under the dictates of the Marxist-Leninist-International-Communist Party. It follows that this world-revolutionary aim involves the destruction, or at least the utter transmutation into the Marxist-Leninist-Communist image, of the basic political, social, intellectual, moral, spiritual, and personal values that have cumulatively come down to Mediterranean-Western existence from millenniums of human struggle, suffering, discovery, and attainment.

8. The question is often debated: Which is the instrument of the other, the State or the Party? That is to say, Is communism just an ideological weapon in the hands of the Soviet State, so that if this weapon should for some reason become obsolete the State would throw it away; or is the Soviet government itself only a tool in the hands of the Marxist-Leninist-International-Communist Party? This is a most fundamental question.

9. Significant tensions and rifts are appearing in the Communist realm itself—for instance, between Moscow and Peiping, and in the Soviet Union herself between diverse interests and schools of thought. On the other hand, the Yugoslav and Albanian breaches appear to be healing, or at least narrowing, and the outlook for some degree of freedom in Poland is far from clear. Thus we appear to be witnessing a significant phase of fluidity in inter-Communist relations.

10. So long as open international war has not broken out on a large scale—so long as there is no world war—the term "cold war" is used to describe the state of tension and conflict existing between international communism and the rest of the world, and especially between communism and the West. Here again a debate exists, some holding that the cold war is developing and will develop more in favor of one side, some more in favor of the other.

11. The problem of "peaceful coexistence" is also hotly de-

bated. How did this term originate? How is it used in Marxist-Leninist strategy? What do the Marxist-Leninists mean by it? How has the term crept into Western usage? What does the West mean by it when it uses it? Is "peaceful coexistence," in the non-dialectical, straightforward, honest sense of the term, possible? In the determination of the total character of world communism no questions are more important than these.

12. Will communism change, and what are the limits of its change? This is perhaps the deepest question of all.

These twelve topics appear to me to exhaust the theme of international communism. They present the character of this phenomenon in its totality. This total character can perhaps be presented in other ways, but this is one way of presenting it, and it can be shown that most other ways are either reducible to or derivable from this way. These twelve topics do not characterize the phenomenon of communism in a drably uniform manner; they are rather independent approaches, distinct themes, irreducible dimensions, different ways of reflecting on and asking fundamental questions about this great contemporary movement. Not one of them can be voided: they all cohere together. We shall refer to these twelve topics in their unmitigated entirety as *the total phenomenal fact of communism*. The first seven appear to be beyond debate; the remaining five appear to be debatable. Which is for the sake of which—the State or the Party? What is the extent and significance of the tensions and rifts in the Communist realm? Who is winning the cold war? Is "peaceful coexistence" really possible? Will communism significantly change? These are matters for which theses and antitheses can perhaps be put forward; but controversial as they might be, they should all be gone into as deeply as possible. Both the settled topics and the topics to be settled are of the utmost importance. The fact that the last five are perhaps debatable does not derogate from their belonging to the integral phenomenon of communism, for everything depends on the manner in which the controversy about each one of them is settled, if it can be settled at all. At any rate they are genuine questions to be asked about this tremendous thing. No one can get to the bottom of the deepest issues rocking the age in which we live, including above all the issues of war and peace, and of war and revolution, without responsibly ascertaining and unblinkingly facing the truth of the twelve topics which together constitute the total phenomenal fact of communism.

III

We cannot proceed in this essay without voicing a warning at this point. *It is most essential to keep in mind the total phenomenal fact of communism.* Of the many strange things happening in the world today nothing is more strange and more dangerous than the readiness with which some people forget one or another of these twelve themes (e.g., when they forget that communism negates the deepest convictions of their heritage, or that they are here dealing with the most superbly organized international political party the world has ever known); or fail to perceive them when they are pointed out (e.g., when they fail to see—and to draw the moral-political consequences therefrom—that in forty years the world is already either actually or potentially communized, at least in the sense that economic-social values appear now to overwhelm all other values everywhere); or lightly pass over them (e.g., when they talk about the whole thing as being "exaggerated," or the Communists as after all not being "ten feet tall," or people as being "pessimist" or "alarmist" or "panicky" or "extremist" or "rightist" or even "Fascist"); or too easily explain them away (e.g., when they speak of a worldwide revolution taking place independently of communism and the

Communists only riding on its crest, and therefore all they have to do is to "ride better" on its crest themselves); or fail to comprehend their incredible significance (e.g., when they tell you, as you point out these astounding things to them, "and what of it?"); or—and this is most dangerous of all— change the subject (e.g., when, in place of facing these things, they begin to talk about the wonderful movement whereby Asia and Africa are now becoming "free and independent," or about the great "affluent society" which is America, or about the wonders of science and technology, or about the peace of Laos and the Middle East)! It cannot therefore be too strongly emphasized that *everything—absolutely everything—depends on the honest, serious, unflagging, sustained, and courageous facing and taking in of the total phenomenal fact of communism.* A civilization that flags in facing and holding the truth can only survive by a miracle.

Assuming, then, that the gentle reader is holding the total phenomenal fact of communism immovably in his mind, I wish now to put a simple and direct question to him. What do you think of this fact? What do you make of it? How do you understand and interpret these twelve themes? I beg you to think, not just of a little recent improvement here and there (and when one fastens on such little things, it is always possible to cite other little things that would cancel them), but of the whole history of the past four decades, the sweep of a whole generation. Think of the phenomenal advance of communism, literally from zero forty-five years ago, to the commanding position it enjoys today—politically, militarily, and certainly ideologically—in Russia, in China, in Southeast Asia, in the Middle East, in Eastern Europe, in Western Europe, in Africa, and in Latin America. Above all, consider how the Marxist-materialist interpretation of things has invaded virtually all Western thought and valuation—everyone now talking and thinking (whether or not he recognizes it) as though he were a Marxist, economic and social categories overwhelming now all other considerations, such as free government, representative government, democratic government, free society, personal character, personal freedom, freedom of thought and conscience, and intellectual and spiritual values. My question therefore is (and I personify in the gentle reader the responsible statesmanship and thought of the West): Assuming that the radical impact of the total phenomenal fact of communism has now fully registered, *tell us what you think of this fact?*

14

THE FOUR ANSWERS

I

WE HAVE now before us a responsible mind which is seriously and unflinchingly thinking—and which is strong enough to refuse to "change the subject"—of the total phenomenal fact of communism. What does it think of this fact? How does it respond to it? What does it say about it? There are four possible answers:

The first is simply to say, communism deserves to win. It is the better system. It reconstructs society on a more just basis. Its spread has not been just accidental nor merely a matter of force; people responded to it and espoused it because it offered a superior alternative. Force may have been applied at the beginning; but that is only due, on the one hand, to the fact that the masses did not know what was best for them and had to be goaded into violent action by those who knew better—the magnificently organized vanguard of the working classes, the Marxist-Leninist Parties; and, on the other, to the resistance and active opposition of the capitalists, the bourgeoisie, the reactionaries, the exploiters, all the classes with vested interests. The working classes, according to this answer, were only claiming their rights; they were therefore only fighting a defensive battle; they used force only in defending and asserting their rights; those who were responsible for the force used were the established, decadent, exploiting classes; consequently, it was these exploiters who were the aggressors. As to the fact that it was always a tiny minority of not more than 1 to 2 per cent of the population that was the organizing and directing and farseeing mind behind the whole upheaval, this is no exception to any fundamental discovery or change in the history of mankind: it is always minorities that govern, always minorities that see the truth first, and the rest always follow the lead of the wise. In fact, every great thought began in *the mind of one man alone,* after whom mankind later followed like sheep. He was the prophet, the catalyst, the revolutionary, the seer, the reformer, the champion of ideas; he only gave conscious, forceful articulation to what was vaguely, dimly and dumbly, felt by the masses; and these followed him only because the historic moment was just ripe for the revolution: they were breathlessly *waiting* for his appearance. It was not *their* fault that Marx and Lenin appeared when they did; the objective, social-historical situation *demanded* their appearance, and *there they were*. This has always been the case and this will always be the case. This is the nature of things. Who started the American revolution?—*a very tiny minority!* What is important—regardless of whose fault it was (and, according to this answer, it was never the fault of the Communists that force was first used, because the exploiters refused to grant the laboring classes their rights) and regardless of the pointless question of minorities and majorities—is whether the outcome justified itself: the test is purely pragmatic. That communism fully justified itself can be amply proven (again according to this answer) by the uprooting of all exploitation, the establishing of justice, the peace and happiness and satisfaction of the populations ruled by it, the enormous rise (which all sorts of statistics appear brilliantly to prove) in their standard of living, and the myriad scientific, social, economic, and cultural achievements of Communist societies. That they have not yet quite caught up with the standard of living of America and Western Europe is due, first, to the initial low level from which they started and to the insufficient lapse of time since the onset of communism (How long did it take America to achieve its present standard of living?); and, second, to the fact that the capitalist countries do not leave the Communist countries in peace, but have forced them, in sheer self-defense, to divert much of their wealth and energy to the building up of a mighty military machine that will shield them against the wiles and stratagems of the greedy and fearful and envious. Give these Communists peace another twenty years, and let them concentrate all their energies upon economic and social development, and by 1980, or at most by the year 2000, they will far surpass anything the Western world will have achieved. Communism will continue to win until it engulfs and absorbs the whole world.

In the ruthless historical struggle for existence only the better and fitter survives. All power and honor and glory to communism, therefore, if it proves itself the best and fittest! Communism came exactly in the fullness of time: it came to pluck a perfectly ripe fruit. The rest of the world, according to this answer, is so corrupt, so rotten, so rigid and stiff and old-fashioned, so outmoded, so inertial, so inadequate to the exacting demands of the moment, so complacent, so soft and stupid, so reactionary, that no wonder it is falling piece by piece into the lap of communism. Look at Asia and Africa and Latin America; how can what these people dispose of by way of institutions and resources, human and technical, be adequate to their needs? How can the crumbs they picked up, like beggars, or even like dogs, from their foreign and native exploiters meet their requirements? They are perfect soil for the Communist culture. All that communism need do is just to announce itself in those areas and blow its trumpet, and then the people will voraciously gobble it up with astounding greed: it is a godsend to them.

And as for the West, it is so decadent and gullible that it believes almost anything the Communists choose to tell it. You kick it, and it thanks God you did not kick it more; you call communism socialism, and it thanks you it is not communism; you tell it to its face "peaceful coexistence" is precisely to bury you "in peace," and, enchanted by the melodious phrase "peaceful coexistence," it turns around and says, "let us then coexist peacefully"; you snatch away a portion from it here and a portion there, and it turns to you and thanks you for not snatching away more, in fact, it begins to search for and find all sorts of "reasons" why you should have done what you did and why it was not "in its interest" to stand in your way; you obliterate or replace its influence here and there, and it comforts itself with the thought that people have a right to their own ideas, as though there is an eternal law whereby people's ideas must necessarily be "non-Western"; you plant the poison of anti-Westernism in whole areas, and the West itself then races around to feed and replenish that poison with its own money and technique, without daring to say a word about you, in order to retain "a leverage of influence" in "peaceful competition" with your presence; and if you happen to believe in and practice Western values—and it becomes known of you that you are "Westernized" or that you are "pro-Western" or that you are "a friend of the West"—then God help you! for immediately the Communists and the anti-Westerners jump upon you and rend you to shreds and nobody lifts a finger to defend you, and the utmost that the West offers you is some place of refuge on its soil, as though the West is ashamed of its values being known and loved and practiced beyond its proper domain! Communism *uses* the West—especially the intellectuals of the West—all the time in the service of the proletarian revolution, and the West has not yet waked up to the fact. It makes them talk *only* of "progress" and "social justice" and "the independence of peoples"—always, however, independence only from the West. The West's powers of ingeniously rationalizing its defeats and retreats and cheerfully and palatably swallowing them are so infinite that you can literally do almost anything (subtly, of course) to it, and it will not feel it. No, the West is so hopelessly divided, so degenerate, so fat, so decadent, so pleasure-seeking, pleasure-surfeited, and pleasure-drunk, that it too is a ripe fruit for plucking. Give the Communists time, and the red flag will one day fly in all Western capitals, and it will be hoisted, not by Russians or Chinese, but by the Western peoples themselves. Communism is only rightfully inheriting a most rotten world—to remake it. *Communism cannot help winning.*

II

We have before us a fully responsible mind who has faced and taken in the phenomenal total fact of communism. To the question, What do you think of this astounding fact, what do you make of it, how do you react to it? he now answers as follows:

This second answer admits and regrets the fact. It fully recognizes that there are many peoples in Europe, Asia, Africa, and Latin America who have been overwhelmed by communism, and many people in the Western world itself who have been softened up by it; this is a sad fact and something must be done about it. It is also most regrettably the case that the Marxist-Leninist-International-Communist domain has expanded, as a result of World War II, westwards to the heart of

Europe, and, as a result of certain events immediately after that war, eastwards all over China and a goodly portion of Southeast Asia. World communism today is incomparably stronger, incomparably more extended and entrenched, than it was before World War II. *But give these people time*: *in time* they will absorb and assimilate the Communist shock and their nationalism will assert itself. By nationalism here is meant all the special cultural, moral, political, and material roots and interests of a particular people. The Chinese are Chinese first and Communists second; the Russians are Russian first and Communists second; the Cubans are Cuban first and Communists second. China, for example, has absorbed many a comparable onslaught in the past. What is Marxism-Leninism to the Chinese soul—700 million strong—with its millennia of history and cumulative culture? Time, therefore, is on our side; the people will wake up; their national interests will assert themselves; the best way to cure them of communism is to let them have a taste of it. Look at the many revulsions against communism by people outside the immediate Communist domain who have known it more or less firsthand. Even inside that domain, people are just burning to overthrow it, if only an opportunity presents itself. One should always remember the uprisings in East Germany and Hungary and the murmurings of the Poles. Wait a while, hold the line, contain the Communists, and you can be sure the nationalist reaction will set in. Nationalism is the strongest force, the strongest ally of the West, against communism. The West therefore should identify itself with nationalist movements everywhere; it should foment, inflame, and support nationalism all over the world. This second answer, then, reacts to the arresting facts of the past four decades by banking on *nationalism* as the savior of the world. *Nationalism will rid the world of communism.*

III

We are dealing with a responsible mind that does not "change the subject." It fully and unflinchingly looks the phenomenal total fact of communism in the face. It dwells upon it day and night. It admits and regrets it just as deeply as the second answer. It has nothing to do with the first answer; it most certainly does not want to see communism win; but it is not so much banking on nationalism to defeat it. This third reaction to the total phenomenal fact of communism formulates itself as follows:

What in the last analysis it is really banking on is *change in communism itself. Give the Communists time*; they will mellow and change; already they have changed considerably; this mellowing process will continue indefinitely; it belongs to the nature of things; in fact, we ourselves can help it along by wise policies and prudent measures, including the avoidance of any embarrassing rebuffs to Khrushchev who himself appears to be its most outstanding promoter and vehicle; Soviet society is already stratified and their ruling upper classes with their vested interests already think more or less as we do. Khrushchev appears to think and talk and act more like an ordinary Western politician than like a classical Communist pundit. In his case, the virus of ideology appears to have lost its sting. It is ordinary power, old-fashioned political responsibility, that now counts—not ideology. They are approaching us socially, politically, economically, and even ideologically, and we too are approaching them in these realms: we ourselves are becoming more and more socialistic and more and more materialistic, and when the two of us have sufficiently advanced in this process of mutual approachment, then such terms as "advance" and "retreat" and "won" and "lost" will no longer apply, for we will both then have more or less equally advanced and more or less equally retreated, and we will both have more or less equally won and lost, and peace and understanding then will prevail. The "ultimate adjustment" will have peacefully taken place without our even having noticed it. Firm, dependable agreements and accommodations will be reached one day, provided we do not in the meantime weary or lose our heads. "Time and chance happeneth to us all," as the author of Ecclesiastes would say (9:11), and one day all will be healed, all reconciled, all forgotten. Look at the social and economic changes in the Western world (social security, graduated income tax, governmental planning on a national scale, "mixed economies," etc.), and look at the economic, social, and even ideological changes in the Communist world (the new poets, the new criticism, the moral rebellion of youth, the quest—e.g., among some of the Communists in Poland—after the meaning of life, the penetration of jazz, the new air of freedom in the Khrushchev era as compared to that of Stalin, etc.); let this healthy, normal process of change on both sides continue sufficiently *in peace,* and in due course we will meet. *We will all one day become alike.* This third answer, thinking and talking in terms of "societies," faces the incredible fact of the Communist advance by banking on change so to soften and mellow and modulate Communist "societies," and so to soften and mellow and modulate American and Western "societies," and so indeed to "modernize" non-Communist and non-Western "societies" in the image of "socialist progress," as to enable all three "societies" *in time* to "coexist" ever afterwards in peace. *Change and time, then, are the saviors of the world.*

IV

A responsible mind has unflinchingly faced the facts. It does not like them at all, any more than the second or third answer did. But it banks neither on nationalism nor on change: it is much more red-blooded and vigorous. This is how this fourth answer goes:

We know what we are doing—only be patient. We are quietly and surely preparing ourselves for the showdown. We certainly are not depending on anybody's nationalism or on the painless processes of time, although of course we will not disdain to take full advantage of these things, wherever and whenever we can. If you like, we are depending in the final analysis on *our own nationalism alone,* and on such changes as *we* can evoke and master for our own purposes. Throughout we are holding the initiative absolutely in our hands. We still have some leeway; we can still afford to lose a little here and a little there; we can still afford to trade territory for time. We are counting on our diplomacy to be so fine and resourceful, so understanding and resilient and consummate, as to buy us the necessary time we need. Thus, there is much room still in Asia, in Africa, and even in Latin America for maneuver; many territories, many minds, may still be lost without our basic strategic position getting impaired or compromised. The line separating us from the Communists is still broad and flexible; we have not yet quite reached the point where we would say: "So far and no farther!" Surely we have yielded in Southeast Asia—but that is all peripheral. Even with respect to Berlin and Germany, we admit that Berlin is a different maiden today from what she was two years ago. The line is not yet absolutely rigidly drawn. We can still afford to yield in many minor matters *while we are preparing ourselves for the showdown.* There is still some time to buy and you can be sure we are not idly wasting it. Many, many things are being done and prepared in secret; we know the day of reckoning is coming; and when it comes *we shall lick these bastards*; we shall blast them out of existence altogether. By "licking" and "blasting" here is meant "destruction by war." War, then, is going to rid the world of communism. *War is the savior of the world!*

V

It appears that these are the four possible answers, the four fundamental attitudes, to the phenomenal total fact of communism: (1) Communism is the savior of the world; (2) nationalism is the savior of the world; (3) change is the savior of the world; (4) war is the savior of the world.

There are of course intermediate positions, but these are the four independent dimensions out of which every other position is composed. There are also "complex" and "impure" positions, in the sense of combining two or more of these basic attitudes. Thus the doctrine of "coexistence" in the Western non-dialectical sense is simply a mode of faith in change (the third position), and in the Communist dialectical sense it is a mode of the inevitable final triumph of communism (the first position). The Western (more strictly, the American) policy of independence and of what is called the choice between a world of free choice and a world of coercion is simply a version of reliance on nationalism (the second position). It is held that nationalism is such an original and powerful force that the diverse nations, jealous each of its "freedom and independence," asserting each its own spirit and genius, and each fanatically attached to its parochial deities, will sooner or later rise up against communism and reject it. Of a piece with this is the blithe reliance upon China and Russia, by falling out with each other "one day," to spare the Western world the greater effort needed in facing and dealing with world communism.

And so, to the fundamental question of the preceding chapter, What do you think of the phenomenal total fact of communism, what do you make of it, how do you (as a serious and responsible thinker or statesman who never "changes the subject") react to it? there are these four possible alternatives: You either expect it to destroy you (the first answer), or you plan to destroy it by force (the fourth answer), or you trust the diverse peoples themselves to reject it (the second answer), or you just trust the processes of natural change in you and it (the "time and chance" of Ecclesiastes) to bring about the necessary accommodation and adjustment (the third answer). There is no fifth position—or is there?

THE ANSWERS ANSWERED

I

THE FIRST ANSWER in the preceding chapter—that communism must conquer and inherit a rotten world—can only be held by Communists or Marxists of one type or another. Such people, whatever their reasons, believe in communism and wish it to succeed; indeed, if they are genuine Communists, you can count on their working day and night, each in his own quiet way in the immense international apparatus of the Party, to make it succeed. Even if they do *nothing else* except *hold the opinion* set forth in the preceding chapter; that is, even if they take no part whatever in any Communist Party activity, *the mere holding of that opinion is already something,* they are at least useless so far as any real opposition to communism is concerned; they are at least "neutralized." Actually, however, they are more than "useless"; they are positive dead weight for any attempt to stand up to communism; and because no one holds his views permanently to himself, they will be expressing these views in private or public on numerous occasions, and people will soon discover what they really think; and this helps to create an atmosphere of defeatism, helplessness, despair, and accommodationism, with respect to communism. Perhaps the point is reached today in history when more help is given the cause of communism by those who simply do not oppose it because they believe it is the inevitable wave of the future than by the active members of the Marxist-Leninist-International-Communist Parties. If this point is reached, then we are before the strange phenomenon of the entire world being converted into a veritable "front organization." It is then only a matter of time and modality when the *coup de grâce* is definitively dealt for the final take-over of the entire world; and those who still oppose communism and wish to see it defeated are only fighting a pitiable "holding operation." It can be shown that the whole attitude and presuppositions of many important Western leaders and thinkers strengthen this conclusion that the whole world is already converted into one vast "front organization," and that, while they wish to keep on fighting honorably and, if they should go down, to go down like men, in their heart of hearts they know that the only outlook left for them is to fight a "holding operation." The phenomenon of the world turned into a "front organization" and the mentality of the "holding operation" are two matters into which much deeper investigation is still called for.

One can quote thousands of statements by Communist masters, from Marx to Khrushchev, about the decadence of what they call the capitalist-bourgeois world and the absolute inevitability of the ultimate triumph of communism. A few passages from statements by Khrushchev will suffice:

The decadence and disintegration of the countries of capitalism represent an indisputable proof of the reactionary character of the capitalist order and of the fact that it is doomed; it is proof also of the futility of the reformist and revisionist attempts to improve and to embellish capitalism, to mask its flagrant ills and antagonistic differences.

It is now becoming increasingly clear that the rule of capitalism is coming to an end in other countries, too, and that capitalism is an outmoded system that is doomed to inexorable death. The future is ours. The future belongs to Marxism-Leninism. The future belongs to communism, comrades.

We live in a remarkable time when historical development leads inevitably to the final triumph of socialism and communism throughout the world. From a dream, socialism has turned in our day into a great and unconquerable world force that astonishes mankind with its magnificent victories.

I do not want to frighten the capitalists. We don't intend to interfere with their affairs, we don't think to wage war against them in order to set up our system in foreign countries. There is no need to do this. The workers, peasants, and working intelligentsia in the capitalist countries will do this themselves when they see that the people of our country, who were poorer than they, have begun to live a richer life. The working people will take our path, the path shown by Lenin.

More and more people are marching under the banner of Marxism-Leninism, and we can already see our ultimate goal appearing on the horizon—the victory of the working class throughout the whole world, the victory of the ideas of communism.

We live at a time when new millions upon millions of people are coming under the great banner of Marxism-Leninism. Marxism-Leninism is our main weapon. We will conquer the capitalist world by using this mighty ideological weapon and not a hydrogen bomb.

Prior to the Second World War, the Union of Socialist Soviet Republics was the only socialist country, with not more than seventeen per cent of the territory, three per cent of the population, and about ten per cent of the output of the world. At present the socialist countries cover about one-fourth of the territory of the globe, have one-third of its population, and their industrial output accounts for about one-third of the total world output.

The rotten [capitalist] world is collapsing. Friends, let's drink, let's laugh, let's rejoice.

Capitalism is at its ebb, heading for collapse. This does not mean that it is already lying down with its legs stretched out; much work has yet to be done to bring it to such a state.

We believe, for example, that there may come a time when the calendar will be based on the day of the October Revolution. But that is a thing of the future. When we speak of the triumph of communism all over the world, we have in mind, first and foremost, the inevitable victory of communist ideas and the triumph of the Marxist-Leninist philosophy.

Whether you like it or not, history is on our side. We will bury you!

The words "We will bury capitalism" should not be taken literally as indicating what is done by ordinary gravediggers who carry a spade and dig graves and bury the dead. What I had in mind was the outlook for the development of human society. Socialism will inevitably succeed capitalism.

Capitalism is a worn-out old mare while socialism is new, young, and full of teeming energy.

In the short time I still have to live, I would like to see the day when the communist flag flies over the whole world.

We have every reason to say confidently that under the present circumstances, war is not inevitable. Whoever does not understand this has no faith in the strength and creative possibilities of the working class, underestimates the power of the socialist camp, does not believe in the great power of attraction of socialism, which has, with full clarity, proved its advantages over capitalism.

Is the possibility excluded that the imperialists will start a war in the present circumstances? We have said more than once, and we repeat: No, it is not excluded. But the imperialist countries cannot fail to reckon with the might of the Soviet Union, the might of the entire socialist camp. It is understandable that the imperialists do not want to start a war in order to perish in it themselves. They would like to annihilate the socialist countries. Therefore, even the stupid, even the insane representatives of the imperialistic circles will think, and more than once, about our power before embarking on a military adventure.[1]

Today it is not imperialism, but socialism that is becoming the decisive factor in world development. The general tendency—the continuous decay of capitalism—has continued to operate ruthlessly. Capitalism cannot solve any of the urgent problems facing mankind. . . . We are confident that socialism will be victorious in the competition with capitalism. . . . The Soviet Union, in fulfillment of its internationalist duty, had been helping the people who struggled against imperialism and colonialism. There are those who do not approve of this position. But we cannot help that. Such are our convictions. From the bottom of our heart we wish success to those who are struggling for their liberty and happiness against imperialism. . . . We are convinced that in the end the Socialist system will triumph everywhere. . . . The people of a country who rise in struggle will not find themselves engaged in single combat with world imperialism. They will enjoy the support of powerful international forces possessing everything necessary for effective moral and material support.[2]

After his first personal encounter with Mr. Khrushchev in Vienna in early June of 1961, President Kennedy told the American people that he had "a very sober 2 days" with the Soviet leader, and he described that meeting as quite "somber." This is how he reported his impressions of the convictions of the leader of world communism:

[1] All the above sixteen quotations are taken from statements made by Nikita Khrushchev and reproduced in *Conquest Without War,* which is a useful compilation of statements by Khrushchev, compiled and edited by N. H. Mager and Jacques Katel (New York: Pocket Books, Inc., 1961), pp. 47–55.

[2] Speech by Mr. Khrushchev before the Twenty-Second Congress of the Communist Party of the Soviet Union, in Moscow, on October 17, 1961; from *The New York Times,* October 18, 1961, p. 16.

. . the facts of the matter are that the Soviets and ourselves give wholly different meanings to the same words—"war," "peace," "democracy," and "popular will." We have wholly different views of right and wrong, of what is an internal affair and what is aggression, and, above all, we have wholly different concepts of where the world is and where it is going. . . . We believe in a system of national freedom and independence. He believes in an expanding and dynamic concept of world communism, and the question was whether these two systems can ever hope to live in peace without permitting any loss of security or any denial of freedom of our friends. . . . Generally, Mr. Khrushchev did not talk in terms of war. He believes the world will move his way without resort to force. He spoke of his nation's achievements in space. He stressed his intention to outdo us in industrial production, to outtrade us, to prove to the world the superiority of his system over ours. Most of all, he predicted the triumph of communism in the new and less developed countries. He was certain that the tide there was moving his way, that the revolution of rising peoples would eventually be a Communist revolution, and that the so-called "wars of liberation," supported by the Kremlin, would replace the old methods of direct aggression and invasion. . . . But I believe just as strongly that time will prove [the Communist theory] wrong, that liberty and independence and self-determination, not communism, is the future of man, and that free men have the will and the resources to win the struggle for freedom. . . . We must be patient. We must be courageous. We must accept both risks and burdens, but with the will and the work freedom will prevail. . . .[3]

The importance of the President's report is that it was his firsthand personal impression, freshly and vividly conceived, of Mr. Khrushchev's mind. These are not the words of Khrushchev—these are the words of the President of the United States as to what he understood Khrushchev *to be*; and this is

[3] President Kennedy's Report to the People on his trip to Europe, May 30–June 6, 1961; Department of State Publication 7213, General Foreign Policy Series 171, released June 1961.

most important. It is one thing to gather the Communist frame of mind from reading about it in their classical statements, or in the interpretations of the experts, or in the briefs of your advisers and friends, or even from listening to their speeches: it is a wholly different thing to come to know it firsthand by direct personal confrontation, whether at the United Nations or in other international encounters, through vigorous debate and argument over concrete matters affecting the issue of war and peace. The "sober 2 days" of President Kennedy in Vienna could not have been more invaluable.

Communist speeches, statements, and declarations are never meant only theoretically. Their primary purpose is to guide and inspire the ongoing international proletarian revolution. Communists claim as their doctrine that the mind has integrally derived from matter and the economic struggle; despite this, they take the mind most seriously (in fact—and this is one of the great paradoxes of this age—they take it more seriously than the Western world; hence they are all the time stressing theory, philosophy, ideas); there is thus to them absolute attunement between the mind and action; "theory" to them *is* "instructions for action," and the action is the action of the worldwide, proletarian, Communist revolution. Mr. Khrushchev in all these statements is primarily speaking to his friends and agents all over the world, and secondarily to all the others in so far as they might weaken and soften and become one day his friends; that is, in so far as they are already *potentially* his friends and agents. The most elementary rule in understanding Communist language is to see through such revolutionary slogans as "imperialism," "colonialism," "capitalism," and "socialism." "Seeing through" them, and interpreting his semantics correctly, we at once perceive that what Mr. Khrushchev is here declaring is the certain doom of every non-Communist system and way of life and the certain eventual victory of the world-Communist movement in every country in the world, a victory for the consummation of which his Communist agents and friends can absolutely count on the material and moral resources of the Soviet Union and the other Communist countries.

We are not here arguing with Communists: nothing is more futile than that. The real argument is the issue of the great historic drama of this age. The "argument" in this case is the existential decision of history. In this respect Khrushchev is quite right: *history and history alone is going to be the arbiter.* Of course, believing Communists answer the fundamental question we raised in Chapter 13 as Mr. Khrushchev does, and the record of the last forty years appears to justify their confidence. *Their answer is itself the question we are putting to Western statesmen and thinkers: What do you think of Mr. Khrushchev's thesis, what do you make of it, how do you react to it, how do you answer it?* It is clear Mr. Khrushchev will endorse every word in our formulation of the first answer in the preceding chapter. Our argument is with the statesmen and thinkers of the West, and not with the Communists. We say to them: If you were Communists, you would answer the way Khrushchev did; but since you are not Communists, you are forced to fall back upon one of the other three answers. You must hold that what will arrest and beat back communism is either *nationalism* (the nationalism of the Chinese and the Indians, the Laotians and the Viet-Namese, the Indonesians and the Pakistanis, the Iranians and the Arabs, the Turks, the Cubans and the Brazilians; and indeed the nationalism of the Russians, the Poles, and Czechs, not to mention the nationalism of the French, the British, and other Europeans—and of course, the nationalism of the Americans) or *change* or *war.* We assume that you have no other alternative, and so we proceed to refute these three positions on which you appear to be pinning your hope.

II

THEOREM: *Nationalism is inadequate to resist and beat back communism.*

PROOF: 1. There is at least as much chance for nationalism to go Communist as anti-Communist. In a sense nationalism is neutral vis-à-vis communism. This is the deepest reason why the nationalism of Asia and Africa has in general adopted at least the neutralist stance. The hope that nationalism must go anti-Communist is a dogmatic hope; it could be sheer wishful thinking. In banking on nationalism to defeat communism or to prevent its entry, one possibly is expecting some strange dark law of national development to bail one out of his immediate responsibility. One really does not know that such a law exists. This expectation is all the more hazardous as one, by the very doctrine of national independence, has no control over the development of nations outside his own. How does he know the soul and spirit of the other nations? How can he fathom the depths of their development? Thus, an American or an Englishman or a Frenchman cannot control the development of nationalism in, let us say, Cuba or Brazil or China. By his own philosophy he must let them develop *in their own way,* and therefore how does he know they will opt for him? To make them opt for him, he must go *beyond nationalism.* Many nationalisms have turned Communist after communism got hold of them. It is doubtful whether the Chinese or the Cubans were ever as nationalistic as they are today. There is then absolutely no inherent incompatibility between nationalism and communism: communism need not be repugnant to nationalism; it all depends on how communism *treats* the particular nationalism. A rabid nationalism could become violently communistic. There is no essential natural law determining nationalism to be anti-Communist.

2. Nationalism today needs some international association,

some supra-nationalist fellowship. International communism appears to provide it with just that. In a world brought exceedingly closely together through the miracles of transportation and communication, nationalism cannot for long nurture radical exclusivism: even apart from all questions of security and economic interests, man craves that his narrow nationalism be complemented by some universalism. Nationalism could develop an unbearable form of claustrophobia that can only be relieved, in a world so closely-knit and of such constant danger, by some supra-nationalist association. One of the strengths of international communism—which the Western world appears to be incapable of matching—is precisely these "international conferences" or "congresses" at which Communist leaders from eighty or a hundred nations all over the world forgather for days and weeks in Moscow or Prague or some other Communist capital. At these "conferences" these men and women undergo a sort of "religious-spiritual experience" through the fun and *camaraderie* and fellowship and indoctrination they receive. They are made to feel that they belong to, and are supported and carried by, an all-conquering world movement, and this imbues them with tremendous zest and confirms in them the deepest confidence. They return home not the less nationalistic because they have become, through the "vision" they saw, fanatically Communist. Communism and nationalism fuse indissolubly in their souls; in giving their lives to the one cause, they are giving them to the other. Thus, the whole idea of nationalism is in a sense breaking down, and communism appears to have available to it universalist resources which precisely fit this moment of history. No matter how defiant and self-assertive at first, no matter how much they speak at first of their desire to be independent and to be left alone, the new nations really feel too lonely and exposed, not only economically, but also politically, intellectually, and from the point of view of security and defense. The pressure of the warmth, fellowship, protection, and assistance of the supra-nationalism of communism could easily iron out all intra-national frictions and conflicts in the Communist camp. And outside this camp, an Arab or Brazilian would turn to the Western prophets of nationalism and "freedom and independence" and say: "You want me to be nationalist? You want me to be 'free and independent'? I thank you for that, for this is exactly what I want to be. But I want to be much more. I want to be human, to enter into the universal company of man, to be taken once again onto the common active stage of history. I want 'freely' to come out of my 'independence and nationalism' into the reassuring warmth of some world fellowship. The Communists provide me with just that; you do not."

3. Those who rely on the nation and its spirit to resist the inroads of communism and to rise up against it when it strikes appear conveniently to forget that communism never consults the nation and its spirit. Communism spreads, not by election, but by coercion; not by "the nation" freely accepting and adopting it (whatever the term "nation" here may mean), but by a handful of people belonging to the Communist Party conspiring and intriguing and seizing the reins of government by force. After that happens, they introduce such a reign of terror and such a systematic domination of every aspect of life that no "nation" and no "national spirit" can by themselves oppose or rise up against them. Those who sit back and enjoy the comfortable feeling that the nationalism of this or that country—for example, Iran or Brazil—is going to protect it against communism should remember that communism knows all about these nationalisms and does not give a hoot for them, because it is boring and undermining them from within by the intrigue and conspiracy of a small handful of men.

4. Those who rely on nationalism as their salvation, either within their own country or vicariously abroad, appear to un-

derestimate the revolutionary fervor and the radical character of international communism. Communism inspires and satisfies; it gives a tremendous meaning to otherwise empty or insufficiently full lives; it fills the heart and makes one feel that he is playing a significant role in the decision of history; under its spell one is thrilled by the sense that he is the bearer of a message of salvation; it is universal and worldwide; it supplies its followers with a most reinvigorating fellowship; it feeds them with ideas; it affords them some protection; it is total, providing meaning and purpose and direction to one's life; it is full of content; it fires the imagination and steadies the will. Before this terrific spiritual onslaught, nationalism is puny and quite helpless. If all that guides and sustains the Iranian nationalist or the Brazilian nationalist is the power of the nationalist idea with which he is seized, it is quite certain that no sooner does he get initiated into the mysteries of communism than he forgets about the Iranian idea or the Brazilian idea. The Communist idea, with the tremendous support it receives from the Marxist-Leninist-International-Communist Party, is stronger than the nationalist idea. I have known nationalists who readily turned into Communists after the proper dose of frustration followed by the right measure of indoctrination.

5. No people have had deeper and longer and more intimate experience with "nations," "nationalisms," and "nationalities" than the Russians, and especially the Communists. The very term *international communism*," of which they are proud, indicates that they have come to take *nationalism* in their stride. Lenin pondered and wrote voluminously on these themes; Stalin was the Party expert on nationalism, and after the revolution of 1917 he was appointed "Commissar for Nationalities." Which Western leader wrote a standard work on nationalism? Stalin did, and as early as 1912–1913. Of course he wrote it from the Marxist point of view, but he wrestled

with the problem with the utmost seriousness. When Western leaders and thinkers sit back and hopefully talk about nationalism as the savior of the world from communism, they will do well to recognize that the Russians are their masters in these intricate realms: there is a whole body of Communist theory and practice on this entire question. The Russians know better than the Westerners what a multinational state entails, as witness how Western overseas empires (and even the continental Austro-Hungarian and German empires) have dissolved while the Tsarist empire was only taken over and expanded by the Communists. The United States concept of nationalities, since these peoples have uprooted themselves from their ancient homes and crossed the ocean, is slowly to assimilate them in the general American "melting pot"; the Russian concept of nationalities, since these peoples have remained rooted where they always were, is to grant them some cultural autonomy within a Soviet over-all rule. Certainly the nationalisms of the Eastern Europeans are important Western potential assets, but the decisive ingredient here is more the religious and cultural than the political; these peoples feel drawn to Western Europe far more intellectually, religiously, and spiritually than politically; and it is precisely in these nonpolitical, spiritual matters that the West apears to be particularly embarrassed, timid, and bashful. Think of the West appealing to the Eastern Europeans on other than political and economic grounds! There is no crudeness, no mechanicalness, no wishfulness in Communist thought on nationalism: there is realism, knowledge, experience, and finesse.

6. Nationalism is a real thing; the attachment to soil and countryside, the love of one's people and culture, of one's customs, history, and background, of one's peculiar outlook on life, of everything that is distinctively and uniquely one's own, is natural, human, and good. But just because it is human, natural, and real, nationalism is not just a vague idea enter-

tained by dreamers and poets: it seeks to embody itself in politico-historical institutions. The historico-political experience of the nationalisms of Asia and Africa is much nearer that of the Communist realm than that of the Western world. Asia and Africa are not used to freedom, in the Graeco-Roman-Mediterranean-European-Western sense; their conception of man and his destiny is different; the individual human soul is not ultimate to them; it is the collectivity, whether in the form of race or religion, the linguistic group or the cultural unit, the tribe or the state, that is ultimate. The rule of law, if it exists, is in general subordinate to the rule of force or of personality. Thus, Asia and Africa are in general quite "used" to totalitarianism and despotic rule. Moreover, all peoples lying beyond and just outside the Communist domain are culturally and humanly continuous with those lying within it; powerful affinities subsist across the dividing Communist line. The peoples of the Middle East, for example, find themselves much more at home in Russian literature than in Western European literature; they appreciate and understand Dostoevski and Tolstoi much more than they do Goethe, Shakespeare, Molière, or Emerson. Politically, socially, temperamentally, and culturally, most Asians and Eastern Europeans can think of the Communists (Chinese and Russian) as their "cousins"; and politically, economically, and socially, Africans too can claim them as their kin. How then can African and Asian nationalism as such, once awakened and kindled, and therefore once seriously attempting to articulate itself in real politico-historical institutions, possibly resist or oppose or beat back communism, when its whole historical existence, with all its native temperament, outlook, and experience, is so much nearer the historical existence of the peoples dominated by Marxism-Leninism than the historical existence of the peoples of Europe and America? The political, social, and economic patterns developed by the Communists would thus exert a much stronger appeal to the nationalism of Asia and Africa than would the corresponding patterns developed by the West. All this appears true in theory; and when we turn to what is actually happening, we find that it is eminently true in fact. The new nations, in their impassioned nationalism, are actually much more avidly imbibing Marxist-Leninist norms in the political, economic, and social fields, and even in their outlook on life in general and their understanding and interpretation of history and existence, than anything hailing upon them either from the experience of the British, or the experience of the Germans, or the French revolution, or the mind of Jefferson and his fellow revolutionaries. In Asia and Africa, nationalism is not even neutral towards communism; it does not just manifest a lack of an inherent, spontaneous hostility to communism; in Asia and Africa nationalism positively finds in communism a congenial friend and ally. It would thus appear that the more you inflame the nationalist sentiment and idea among these peoples, the more you drive them into the lap of communism.

It follows from these six considerations that nationalism is not the salvation of the world from communism. Those whose highest strategy is only to promote nationalism and what they call "independence" as their best insurance against communism are fighting a losing battle. Nationalism is inadequate to resist and beat back communism.

III

THEOREM: *The hope that communism will so change as to make it possible for the rest of the world to live in peace with it is an empty hope.*

PROOF: 1. This hope involves a reliance on some dark cosmological law of whose existence we cannot be sure. How do you know that communism will fundamentally change? May it not be all a desperate wishfulness on your part? Since communism has not yet changed to the extent of being able to live in peace with the rest of the world, how do you know that it will change to that extent in the future? One luxury statesmen cannot afford to indulge in today: a sentimental reliance upon the beneficent operation of the dark and unknown powers of the universe. It is too hazardous to base policy on the assumption that the Communists will change. This kind of hopeful (and helpless) fatalism is the last resort of the checkmated and cornered. To say, "Of course, communism will change when it becomes prosperous and rich and secure, when the standard of living has risen, when the new managerial class which came into being only in recent years has taken the reins of power into its own hands, etc." (this thesis has been put forward by many "experts"), is at best to express a pious hope based on a dogmatic stand, and at worst to be changed into the Communist image yourself. For in saying this, you are only expressing the Marxist philosophy which makes the spirit merely a function of economic and social conditions—change these conditions, and the spirit changes correspondingly. But what if Marxism-Leninism, despite its doctrine about the derivation of the spirit from matter, society, and economics, is first and foremost itself a *spirit* which does not change with changing conditions? At any rate, you cannot be sure that this is not its nature. To fight it (or to hope that you will be spared the necessity of fighting it) by adopting uncritically its own interpretation of existence is a most dangerous procedure. You may then have been already "buried" spiritually by it!

2. Point 4 of the preceding section, concerning the radical revolutionary character of communism, applies here. The Communist thrust is total and absolute, and such thrusts do not change. It is of the character of a great religion, and no matter what happens to great religions, no matter how many

successive "interpretations" they undergo, there is always in them an integral and unmistakable deposit of faith which never changes. The fluctuating interpretations are always controlled and restrained by the original, unchanging, spiritual deposit of faith. Thus, communism cannot so change as to cease *to be itself.*

3. Why should communism change when it is winning on every side without war? When it reviews its history during the last forty-five years and realizes that never once has it been dislodged by one inch from where it was fully entrenched, i.e., from where it was in full political control, why should it even dream of changing? It has every right, purely on the strength of the record, and especially now that it possesses nuclear weapons in abundance, and the means to deliver them, to feel that it is absolutely irresistible (over the long run) and, in any event, once it takes hold, absolutely irreversible. When you do not suffer one fundamental defeat, when you manage despite every difficulty always in the end to come out on top, you are entitled to unlimited self-confidence. This sense of absolute self-confidence must have filled the minds of Messrs. Shepilov and Khrushchev when they said:

Taking their wishful thinking for reality, they [the strategists of the bourgeois world] have begun to rely on some "evolution" of the Soviet regime and on our rejecting "some aspects" of the dictatorship of the proletariat, on our becoming if not "white" then at least "pinkish" . . . all those conjectures regarding an "evolution" of the Soviet regime towards a bourgeois regime are an empty figment of imagination.[4]

We have never abandoned and will never abandon our political line which Lenin formulated for us; we have never abandoned or

---

[4] Foreign Minister Shepilov, *Pravda,* February 13, 1957. Quoted in W. W. Kulski, *Peaceful Co-Existence* (Chicago: Henry Regnery, 1959), p. 135. Although Foreign Minister Shepilov later fell from grace, he made this statement, according to Kulski, "on behalf of all his colleagues, including Khrushchev."

will abandon our political programme. . . . This is why we tell those gentlemen who wait for a change in the political programme of the Soviet Union: "Wait till the crayfish whistles!"[5]

The same defiant ring of confidence breathes in every fundamental Communist utterance. Such absolute confidence is not to be found to the same extent in Western fundamental utterances. One always senses in these utterances a note of uncertainty, hesitation, and doubt. Their authors appear to be far more prepared to "change" and "mellow" than the Communists. And so they may only be "projecting" their own state of mind upon their adversaries when they expect them to "change." To be entitled to expect the Communists to change (1) you should be absolutely changeless yourself at some point in your being, and (2) you should have actually inflicted at least one fundamental defeat upon them.

4. Lenin said in 1918:

Marx and Engels said many times that our doctrine was not a dogma, but a guide in action. I believe that we must keep this in mind before and above everything else.[6]

Lenin himself took great liberties with Marxism. The successors to Stalin have also taken great liberties both with Stalinism and, it can be shown, with Leninism itself. Many Communists today, especially the "revisionists" among them, keep on saying that Marxism is not a fixed body of doctrine, that it can change and grow considerably. They also point out how it can be adapted to this or that "different" or "changed" situation. The inevitability of war between communism and what they call "capitalism" was a most sacred dogma up until the last years of Stalin, and it appears that the Chinese Communists still hold it; and yet today we hear Khrushchev say:

[5] This statement was made by Khrushchev in Bombay in 1955. Quoted in Kulski, *op. cit.,* pp. xviii–xix.

[6] Kulski, *op. cit.,* p. 544. See also *ibid.,* p. 65.

The thesis has been confirmed that in the present epoch, wars between states are not inevitable, that they can be prevented.[7]

He has repeated this "changed position" on many other occasions. Then there appears to be a whole new tone emanating from the Soviet Union in recent years, and those who have visited that country confirm that there have been genuine changes in the spirit and mentality of the Soviet people since the death of Stalin. This new spirit was quite evident in United Nations debates almost immediately since the death of Stalin in 1953, and certainly since 1955. The jovial, informal, relaxed, open style of Khrushchev appears to have been transmitted to his subordinates. You can see Gromyko now smile, and even laugh. It appears, then, that communism does change and is changing before our very eyes. Some conclude from all this that, regardless of what the Shepilovs and the Khrushchevs say, *with time* it is bound so to mellow and change as to be able to coexist peacefully with the rest of the world.

Of course, communism will change and the West will change, but the crucial question is: *How far* will they change? What are *the limits* of their change? *Can they so change as to become other than themselves?*

The following elements in the Marxist-Leninist-International-Communist doctrine and practice *cannot* change "till the crayfish whistles"; they constitute the irreducible core of communism; it is this irreducible core that those who are banking on change to save them and the rest of the world with them are always and beyond every superficial change up against:

1. *Radical militant atheism:* The absolute denial of any God, any Christ, any Holy Spirit, any afterlife; and the militant

[7] Khrushchev's speech before the Twenty-Second Congress of the Communist Party of the Soviet Union, October 17, 1961. *The New York Times,* October 18, 1961, p. 16.

attempt by the party and the state to uproot all religion and to propagate atheistic anti-religious doctrine in schools and among all levels of the population. That religion nevertheless has not disappeared in Russia is not due to the Communist Party, which is doing everything it can to extirpate it, but thanks to the simple fact that, despite all that the Communist Party has done and is doing, religion simply refuses to die. Give the Communists a perfect economic and social order *with God*: they will not accept it; they insist that God must not be there; the *sine qua non* of anything they are doing or are hoping to do is the absolute and final destruction of God and Christ.

2. *Radical moral relativism:* There are no absolute given standards of morality; the good is identically and only that which serves the proletarian revolution and its vanguard, the Marxist-Leninist-International-Communist Party. Whatever is regarded as "immoral" or "bad" or "wrong" in any other moral system becomes forthwith "moral," "good," and "right" in Communist "morality," provided it serves and enhances the interests and plans of the Marxist-Leninist-International-Communist Party. Nothing whatsoever is recognized *outside* the Party and its interests.

3. *Radical materialism:* Spirit, mind, reason, truth, culture, all these things are mere epiphenomena, mere froth, on the surface of the immense ocean of matter—an ocean, in the end, of sheer atoms in motion. Thus, everything comes from and returns to matter in motion, and the Party itself is the final phase, the most "progressive" form, of this eternally moving, brute matter.

4. *Radical economism:* Everything is a function of the economic process; therefore all means of production must be socialized, and private ownership of the means of production must be abolished; no independent economic activity can be

permitted, since the Party, of which the State is only the instrument, is the only reality that there is.

5. *Radical collectivism:* The individual human person has no ultimate worth of his own but is utterly subordinate to the collectivity; the state, society, the collectivity, is not for the sake of the human person, but the human person is for the sake of the state.

6. *Radical totalitarianism:* The Marxist-Leninist-International-Communist Party, the vanguard of the proletariat, has an absolute monopoly of all truth and all wisdom, and, therefore, all systems and orders must sooner or later yield to the dictatorship of the proletariat; there is no possibility of political opposition, of more than one political party.

7. *Proletarian internationalism:* Absolute proletarian solidarity of the Communist Parties throughout the world, all of them supporting each other in the unabating class struggle and in maintaining or seizing power, and all of them subordinating themselves to their elder sister and leader, the Communist Party of the Soviet Union. In this connection, while the apparent deviations of the Communist Parties of Yugoslavia, Albania, and especially Communist China (recent evidence appears however to indicate that these family quarrels, even with regard to Yugoslavia, are in process of being patched up) are, from the international-political point of view, quite significant, and while most important practical conclusions can be drawn from these deviations so far as Western high policy is concerned, there is no evidence whatsoever that in these countries the Party has ceased to feel profoundly responsible for the solidarity of what it calls the international working-class movement. Its final spiritual identification is with the proletariat and its outlook everywhere. There could be an internal struggle for leadership in the Communist world, but the basic spirit of international proletarianism is behind and above all such struggle.

8. *Unshaken and unshakable conviction as to the inevitability of the triumph of communism* (preferably by peaceful means, but where that is not possible, then "the possibility of non-peaceful transition to socialism must be borne in mind"[8]): the absolute determination that Marxism-Leninism should transform and dominate every outlook, system, culture and government.

9. *Radical dialecticism:* The essence of existence is conflict and contradiction; therefore essentially and fundamentally there is no peace and rest in life; there is nothing firm and solid and final to lean upon, save what sheer force vouchsafes; therefore real trust and confidence are impossible, and suspicion must regulate every relationship.

Let communism change as much as it may, these nine irreducible elements constitute the limits of its change. In these nine respects it will never "mellow," for it is these that constitute it essentially into *what it is.* The burden of proof is on those who trust the mystique of change to demonstrate to us that communism one day will believe in God and permit religion to flourish freely in its midst; that the Communist head of state one day will go to church and pray on his knees; that communism will one day allow real freedom of thought and inquiry in all fields; that it will give up the dictatorship of the proletariat, tolerating more than one political party; that it will believe and teach that economics is altogether secondary in human life, that dialectical materialism is silly and stupid, that there are absolute moral standards, that the state is for the sake of the person, that mind and spirit are original and are not derived from matter, that it would not foment revolution everywhere in the name of "international proletarian solidar-

[8] The language of the Declaration of October 1957, on the occasion of the celebrations in Moscow of the fortieth anniversary of the Communist Revolution of 1917, a language reiterated by every fundamental Communist Declaration since.

ity" and under the "victorious banner of Marxism-Leninism," and that it would believe, teach, and put into practice that it need not conquer and subjugate the whole world, and that fundamentally you need not contradict, but you can trust and believe. No, there is an absolute unity about the whole spirit of the thing: you smell it unmistakably from a distance.

In this connection the following words of Pope Pius XI in the *Encyclical on Atheistic Communism of 1937* appear to me of tremendous significance:

For the first time in history we are witnessing a struggle, cold-blooded in purpose and mapped out to the least detail, between man and "all that is called God" (II Thess. 2:4). Communism is by its nature anti-religious. It considers religion as "the opiate of the people" because the principles of religion which speak of a life beyond the grave dissuade the proletariat from the dream of a Soviet paradise which is of this world. . . . Communism is intrinsically wrong, and no one who would save Christian civilization may collaborate with it in any undertaking whatsoever. Those who permit themselves to be deceived into lending their aid towards the triumph of Communism in their own country, will be the first to fall victims of their error. And the greater the antiquity and grandeur of the Christian civilization in the regions where Communism successfully penetrates, so much more devastating will be the hatred displayed by the Godless.

The reason why some people are banking so trustingly on change as the savior of the world could be that they *do not mind* if communism did not change in any of these nine respects; that they themselves do not especially care about God or Christ, or absolute moral values, or spiritual truth, or the human person, etc. Economic and social and even cultural changes—these could be endless: and it is these that they are thinking of when they speak of change; but these other nine fundamental things—why, they do not care about and it never occurred to them to attach any importance to whether communism changed or did not change with respect to them. What has happened, then, is that *they have changed,* knowingly or unknowingly, into the image of communism itself, and, therefore, they do not now want it to change its image. This is the deepest fear that haunts whoever seriously contemplates the contemporary scene. The present crisis is precisely to ascertain *what has happened to the soul of the West.*

When we say that the essence of communism never changes, we certainly do not mean that this or that individual Communist will not change; any individual Communist may be converted to Christianity, or Islam, or liberal socialism, or what is vaguely called democracy, or any one of a number of other persuasions or non-persuasions. Nor do we mean that the Russian or Chinese or Cuban peoples are forever doomed to the Communist outlook; Khrushchev himself says that not more than 4–5 per cent of the population of the Soviet Union belong to the Communist Party; so the remaining 95 per cent, who now have no direct effective voice in their government, may one day "so change" as to rid themselves altogether of their Communist rulers. Nor, finally, do we mean that the Soviet government need forever remain in the iron grip of the Communist Party: not only the people, but the army itself may one day take matters into its own hands and set up a completely non-Communist government. One of the fascinating sagas of recent years has been the creative role one army after another (including, behind the scenes, armies of the Western powers themselves!) has played in the determination of history. There must be a profound reason why the military all over the world has been, precisely *politically,* even more important than the political. Therefore I do not exclude the possibility that the Soviet Army will one day overthrow the rule of the Party. We mean none of these things and we exclude none of these possibilities. What we mean is simply that there is in the world today a mighty international political party called the Marxist-Leninist-International-Communist Party; that this Party rules the Soviet Union, China, Cuba, and a number of other countries; that it has active agents working day and night in its service in every country in the world; that the core of conviction of this Party consists of the nine points we have enumerated; and that this core of conviction will never change. What will never change, then, is the essence, the spirit, of Marxism-Leninism.

It remains that the non-Communist world may change in the Communist image. To the extent that it will, communism will have won, and the first answer to our fundamental question has been vindicated. How much Asia, Africa, and Latin America will become and remain Communist is, of course, the great question today. There is the most intense competition between communism and the West over these continents. It is obvious that the outcome of this competition depends primarily on how much of the West itself has not changed in the image of communism. This then is the fundamental question: *What are the limits of change of the West itself?*

Such limits exist. I hope and pray and believe that the following constitute *the limits of Western change*:

1. God will always be worshiped and Christ will always be loved in the West. Incidentally, this too will always be the case in the Soviet Union, despite Marxism-Leninism, and it is this that is going ultimately to save both the Soviet Union and the West, in ways that we cannot now see.

2. Western governments will never sponsor anti-religious propaganda and will never persecute those who worship God and love Christ; and there will always be rulers in the West who unashamedly go to church and who pray on their knees.

3. The free university where the truth *in every field* is sought and discovered for its own sake will always remain one of the glories of the West, as it has been since the Academy of Plato.

4. There will always be freedom of association, freedom of expression, and freedom of thought and conscience.

5. The fundamental theory of government will always be that the people come first, in the sense that there will always be free elections with more than one political party competing for power.

6. In the legal system and in the traditions and customs of society the presupposition will always be that the human person has inherent natural rights, and that everything—state, society, tradition, and custom—is for his sake.

7. The doctrine that there is a realm of ascertainable law, above ruler and ruled, to which ruler and ruled alike must conform, will always hold.

8. It will always be held that there is an essential internal continuity of history; that the past is not relative nonsense; that there is never a radical break in the continuum of time; and so history did not begin in 1917, nor will ever come a time when, as Khrushchev hopes, the calendar will start with that year; former ages are not only preludes and preparations for Communist society; they have each an ultimate worth of its own, and each can be studied and appreciated in itself and for its own sake, and some of these ages, far from being "behind" our present brave and "progressive" age, are actually "ahead" of it, providing valid criteria for evaluating and judging our present life and our present ideals; and so there will always be scholars who will endeavor to work out "life and conditions" in Athens and in Rome, in Galilee and Antioch, in Paris and in Florence, not by arbitrarily cramping them into the strait jacket of some contemporary "ism," such as Marx-

ism or positivism or idealism, but by *letting these times and ages speak for themselves,* from the inner, concrete point of view of each one of them.

9. Trust, peace, and rest belong to the nature of things, and, therefore, we need not be all the time contradicting and fighting one another.

I trust that the West, despite its sickness and its troubles, will never outgrow these things. The Western world and the Communist world have both been trying to "change" each other, each in the image of itself. We shall see in the following chapter that the Communist world has more succeeded in inducing *Communist change* in the West than the Western world in inducing *Western change* in the realm of communism. If one responsibly meditates on the limits of change both of communism and the West, one cannot then lightheartedly bank on inducing change in the other fellow as the savior of the world. Such a hope is altogether empty.

IV

THEOREM: *To pin one's hope on war as a means of beating back communism may turn out to be a completely idle dream.*

PROOF: 1. There appears to be today nuclear parity between the Communist and the Western worlds. Each side appears able to destroy the other even if the other struck first; this is the meaning of the nuclear stalemate. Under such conditions neither side would start a nuclear war, or a war that might develop into a nuclear one. Should there be some fundamental breakthrough in the furiously secretly developing technological revolution (e.g., the discovery of a new kind of ray, or some other medium, that would cause missiles, airplanes, and bombs to disintegrate in space, or the developing of an absolutely watertight system of national defense, etc.), this rule would not hold. But this breakthrough under present conditions appears to be not more likely for one side than for the other;[9] therefore, relief arising from the possibility of a breakthrough is itself subject to the law of parity, and one cannot scientifically in this general account employ it as an element, one way or the other, in the proof. But it is quite true that this first part of the present proof is valid on two assumptions: that nuclear parity actually exists, and that it is not more likely to be upset by a breakthrough in favor of one side than of the other. Under these assumptions, it is idle for anyone to expect war to extirpate communism; because while he may extirpate it, he would just as certainly be extirpated himself. This is what both President Kennedy and Premier Khrushchev mean when they keep on repeating that large-scale war (i.e., world war) —in the words of President Kennedy—"does not appeal any longer as a rational alternative." President Eisenhower meant the same thing when he formulated several years ago the famous maxim: "There is no alternative to peace." Nuclear war is automatically abolished as a national policy: there is today mutual paralysis, mutual immobilization, when it comes to unlimited war, or at least when it comes to *starting* a world war.

2. But if the great powers under present conditions will not resort to nuclear war (much as the belligerents in World War II did not use gas), what about conventional war? Since the Communists cannot be beaten by nuclear war, are people then planning to beat them by conventional war, a war

[9] In this connection, the following disturbing observation is proper: while there are probably far greater scientific and technological skills and resources in the West than in the Communist world, if the Communist scientists and technicians are fired in their work by the fanatical zeal of "the cause" of Marxism-Leninism, namely, if they exhibit anywhere near the dedication and self-giving that the *political* Marxist-Leninists (e.g., at the United Nations) show, while some of the Western scientists and technicians appear not to be fired by a comparable "Western zeal" and "cause," then "the balance of probability" for a Western technological breakthrough is not certain. The West, *even in science and technology,* cannot beat communism without developing *among its scientists* at least as profound and soul-gripping a Western *faith* as *the faith* of Marxism-Leninism.

in which the Communists would not dare to retaliate by nuclear weapons due to the operation of the law of parity of the preceding point? But in conventional war the Communists always managed to win in the past, and for such a war they appear to be better prepared today—both through their inexhaustible manpower and the vast expanse of their territory. Again this proof is valid only on the assumption that there has been no breakthrough on the Western side which would annul the Communist advantage in manpower and territory. But the law of parity with respect to this breakthrough itself would seem to apply here also. If things in the conventional field are not much different from what they were five, ten, or fifteen years ago, the West cannot expect to win a conventional war against the Communists, even with Communist nuclear weapons completely immobilized by the law of parity.

3. To expect to win only in war is not to believe that you can win in peace; it is to admit that in peace you are licked, that under normal conditions the other fellow is cleverer, more resourceful. But this is a most damning admission: it betrays a terrible lack in your life, in your whole apparatus of conviction. If this is true, then the mere thought of it ought to keep you awake and sleepless for at least a month. And this for two reasons: (a) Since you are admitting that in peace you are licked, and since, by the preceding two points, you are denied the possibility of war, then *you are licked*; and (b) the true position is when you know your strengths so well (material, economic, moral, and spiritual), and are so self-confident and sure of yourself that there is no question in your mind but that you can confound and confuse and disconcert and overwhelm and beat the Communists *without war,* and that, should *they dare* to start war, you will come out of the thing victorious yourself; this is the true position, and not that you will "show them" in war. War, even when possible, is a desperate last resort; and so the question arises: Have you

tried everything *short of war?* The thought of war striking the mind quickly and nervously and impulsively could mean that one is underestimating his *peaceful resources.* When one had exhausted half of these resources, he might discover that he did not need the other half, nor did he need war at all.

4. Even if you can "win" in war, do you know what conditions will prevail after you have "won"? How do you know that a victory thus "won" is worth the ticket? Mankind has never known the kind of aftermath that is now likely to supervene upon a war fought *and "won"* under modern conditions. In his report to the American people on his trip to Europe in June 1961, from which we quoted on p. 153, President Kennedy said:

Neither of us [i.e., himself and Khrushchev] was there to dictate a settlement or convert the other to a cause or to concede our basic interests. But both of us were there, I think, because we realized that each nation has the power to inflict enormous damage upon the other, that such a war could and should be avoided if at all possible since it would settle no dispute and prove no doctrine, and that care should thus be taken to prevent our conflicting interests from so directly confronting each other that war necessarily ensued.

And Dr. Franz Josef Strauss, Minister of Defense of the Federal Republic of Germany, said in a speech at Georgetown University in Washington, on November 27, 1961:

Today it must be the supreme politico-military objective of the [Atlantic] Alliance to avoid the outbreak of a war, [rather than] to win a war after it has started.

The most responsible leaders never tire of reminding the world that in an all-out nuclear war there will be no victors, there will only be vanquished. *The concept of a lost peace as being possibly better than a won war is under modern conditions a perfectly entertainable concept.* I do not believe in it myself

at all, because I do not believe these are the only two alternatives. But such a concept is quite rational and quite entertainable today.

From all this, unilateral disarmament does not follow. In
fact, the entire proof is predicated on the existence of parity
in the balance of power, and this precludes any unilateral self-
abnegation, because then the balance will immediately tip in
the opposite direction, and the parity, on which we are basing
the proof, will be gone. We do not believe that communism
will not be tempted to strike in the presence of weakness, nor
that it is better to invite it in than to hold it at bay.

The confrontation with world communism cannot be re-
solved by war—not under existing conditions. Means of a
peaceful nature should be sought and devised, to be sure, from
a position of military and moral strength and not of weakness.
It follows that to pin one's hope on war as a means of beating
back communism may turn out to be a completely idle dream.

V

We have had before us a responsible mind which is profoundly
disturbed by the total phenomenal fact of communism. It will
not "change the subject"; it will not "drown" this tremendous
fact either in alcohol, or in some silly momentary excitement,
or in hectically seeking its own personal interests (as though
personal interests can any longer be sought and secured independently of this fact!), or in some clever rationalization
(and this is far worse than alcohol; in fact, it is the alcohol
of the mind!), or in sheer forgetfulness. On the contrary, it will
face it calmly, soberly, resolutely, unshrinkingly. To the question, What do you think of this fact, how do you react to it,
what do you make of it? this responsible mind has answered
either by blessing the Communists and saying all power to
them in taking over and remaking a rotten world; or by hold-

ing that nationalism will in time take good care of them, so it need not worry much beyond supporting nationalism wherever it finds it, and encouraging and inciting the national leaders to resist and fight them; or by trusting "time and chance" and the processes of change to soften and mellow them, so that it will be able in time to live in peace with them in one world; or by frankly planning to settle its accounts with them through war.

The first answer is in effect only a rephrasing of our own question. It puts forth the Communist position, which simply affirms: "We will bury you!" Presumably the responsible Western mind we are addressing will refuse to be buried. What will it then say to this challenge flung in its face? It will find itself compelled to fall back upon one or another of the three remaining answers: *Communism itself will be buried either through nationalism or through change or through war.* Being responsible, it must be thinking of something, whether or not it cares to communicate it to you; for if in the face of this terrific fact it is thinking of nothing, then it will justify communism's cynicism with respect to the decadence of the Western world. So you wonder, What can it be that it is thinking of? Try as hard as you can to guess: examine its actions, its life, its sayings in the minutest detail; try to infer back from these things *what it must be thinking of.* You finally come to the conclusion that it can be thinking of nothing save these three alternatives: it is banking on nationalism, on change, or on war! I have demonstrated in the preceding sections of this chapter that communism too refuses to be buried, through nationalism, through change, or through war. All three Western hopes are empty: the thing is much tougher and more resistant than people think.

Now tension may be defined as that state of affairs in which two forces engage each other with a view each to "burying" the other without quite succeeding. This is exactly the world in which we live. A world of such terrific tension, where nothing less than "burial" is the object, is obviously not a world at peace. We are, then, at some kind of war. The term "cold war" has been invented to denote this kind of war. The word "cold" is a bit misleading, for the issues in this "cold war" are as "hot" as the issues in the "hottest" of so-called "hot wars." According to the American science of behaviorism (which, it would appear, is not much different from the Pavlovian science of conditioning), you can fry a frog alive—simply by putting it in a comfortable, cool pan and steadily raising the temperature under the pan, but always at a rate at any temperature less than the threshold of the frog's sensitivity to temperature differential at that temperature. A moment will be reached when the frog will be fried, nice and sizzling, without ever having felt the heat. So the term "cold war" could be quite misleading: we may all be in a state where we are being fried alive, in the coolness of the pan! Stalin once said: "Who shall conquer whom?—that is the question." The issue of the cold war is nothing short of the fate of Mediterranean-Western civilization with its age-old values of mind and spirit and man and truth and freedom and God—its fate, indeed, not only at the hands of the Communists, *but at the hands of its own children*. It is important then to ask: *Who has succeeded in "burying" more of whom? Who is frying whom alive?* Communism relies on its revolution with its infinitely varied techniques; the West relies on nationalism, change, and war. Who, in this deadly contest, has "buried" more of whom? Who is really frying whom alive? This is precisely the question of the fortunes of the cold war to which we now turn.

CHAPTER

16

CRITERIA FOR THE COLD WAR

I

How is Mediterranean-Western civilization faring in the cold war? This civilization has been for decades under attack, from forces welling within it and forces infiltrating or swooping upon it from the outside. Its highest values are doubted and undermined by some of its deepest minds. Such aberrations as Hitlerism and Fascism are not simple phenomena: they are symptoms of a profound spiritual malady. To "explain" them by reference to the errors of Versailles, the shortsightedness of this or that statesman, the weaknesses of Baldwin and Chamberlain and Daladier, leaves completely unanswered two questions: Why these particular defects at this time, and why these particular aberrations—*and not others*—arising from them? Where was Western vision, Western sensitivity, and Western moral strength? It must be, therefore, that in a sense the West *willed* these things: the whole of Western civilization must, therefore, assume responsibility for them. To identify the Western malady that *willed* Hitlerism and Fascism, and that appears today to be *willing* communism, one can take up the innumerable inner strains afflicting the West—economic, social, political. One can depict—as Nietzsche power-fully did, though not necessarily from his standpoint—the weakness and decadence in many phases of the higher spiritual life of the West: in art, in philosophy, in morality, in religion, in the whole realm of vision, in the zest of life, in the goals and meaning of human existence. One can show that we are here before a phenomenon of total judgment, a sort of transcendental wrath. All of this is not our immediate task, although it would have a direct bearing on it. If it should become our task, and it might, we would attempt it only from the standpoint of positive vision and hope—hope in the living God, and hope that Western civilization, with God's help, is more than equal to the task of meeting the present crisis and rising to heights unprecedented and wonderful. But it will not rise to these heights by man lifting himself up, as Nietzsche taught, by his bootstraps. Man by himself cannot rise above himself. Nietzsche's commandment was: *O man, overcome thyself!*—and the Communists, without knowing it, obey this commandment strictly. Man's poignant answer, whether the Communists know or admit it or not, is: *I simply cannot!* Man's conquest of himself is a task, not just "beyond good and evil," but beyond man himself altogether. He needs outside help—from the source and mystery of all being. Of course this wounds his pride mortally—he must prove that he needs nothing and nobody, certainly no "source," no "mystery," and no "being"; and so he rebels. The deepest need of man is *not to rebel* in the face of the truth, especially of the truth of man himself. Mere destructive criticism of Western existence, of any existence, means therefore nothing to us—we consider it unworthy of a man. Moreover, in the unending dialectical process one negative criticism only leads to another negative criticism of itself, while life and being remain absolutely untouched. We are not interested in the mere game of dialectics, for we believe infinitely greater issues are at stake. It we have a positive vision we simply state it, and we see the world in its light. It must be genuinely beyond us and independent of us, or else we are not interested at all. Only a genuine, actual, existing, independent efficacy beyond man can save him. If we know it, then in *its* name, in *its* light, for *its* sake, we see what we see and we criticize what we criticize. Therefore, we always begin with a positive content which becomes itself then the instrument, the criterion, and the justification of our analysis. We stand or fall with *it*. *We believe and know something.* The breed of analysts of our day—infinitely clever, infinitely sharp, infinitely cutting, and therefore infinitely enjoying themselves—always leave you with the impression that they *believe nothing*; at least, their belief remains a *mysterium* (it is not an accident that many of them just before they die—and some, in anticipation, fairly early—begin talking a great deal about "mysticism"), because they have not yet told us what it is. Mere analysts are for the most part intellectual parasites: they live on the creativity of others. They sit at the edge of their chairs waiting for you to come out with a position—and then they jump on you like ravening wolves. Somebody must have labored for them and presented them with a synthesis before their wonderful analytical powers can come into play. They spend their time, as it were, "spying" on others, and they live (analytically, of course, never enjoyingly, never appreciatively, never lovingly, never thankfully) on the *crumbs of being* which they have been able to gather. What *positive vision* do they see, what *creative synthesis* have they worked out, what *original position* do they hold to, what *firm conviction* do they live by?—all this remains an impenetrable mystery. You can only infer it by reading back their fundamental presuppositions without which they could not have talked in the first place; but they never come out with it themselves. We hold that life is much too short for one day to be wasted on the analytical game of words; we hold that only spirit is worthy of spirit, only fundamental attitude of fundamental attitude, only mind of mind; we hold that nothing short of the highest concrete content of existence is worth our quest; and perhaps it is not the fault of the analysts that they do not know that such a "concrete highest content" exists. Again we ask: Where is the deepest in the West, what is it doing? Thus, our ideal is the poor man who knows he is dying, who sees a few things which he loves, who simply states them *while he has time,* perhaps in simple parables or stories, or in unsystematized aphorisms, and who lets the analysts then busy themselves until the end of time— if that gives them pleasure—with tearing them to pieces. Being is too voluptuously inviting for us to tinker with lesser things.

The critique of Western existence, then, even from the standpoint of positive vision and hope, is not our immediate task. What immediately concerns us is the question of the fortunes of the cold war. This is a fairly humble task, requiring only the establishment of certain complex facts. How has the West been faring in this struggle? It has almost become a mortal sin in certain quarters to speak of "winning" or "losing." The situation is "too complex," they tell you, for these "naïve" terms to be applicable. But surely there is a struggle and a kind of war going on, and surely the assessment of where one is in this struggle is not particularly sinful. We shall simpleheartedly use the terms "winning" and "losing"—indeed not sentimentally, not pathetically, not as though we were before a baseball game, but with the utmost and most sober realism. Politics, diplomacy, cleverness, embarrassment, calculation, personal interests, fear of offending others, making sure that nobody is hurt, all this we here completely and ruthlessly put aside: our aim is the truth, and the truth alone liberates and saves. And we believe there is a truth about whether Western civilization has been "winning" or "losing," a truth that can be "truthfully" and scientifically ascertained.

There has been an amazing recovery of Europe after the

war. The remarkable *rapprochement* that those great Europeans, De Gaulle and Adenauer, have fashioned between France and Germany does honor to them, to their great peoples, and to the whole West. One of the greatest events of 1962, perhaps in the perspective of history it will turn out to be one of the greatest events of this whole generation, was when De Gaulle and Adenauer knelt side by side, in July 1962, to pray at a High Mass at Rheims Cathedral. The potentialities of the Common Market, and of the whole movement for European and Atlantic unity, for the stability, strength, and triumph of the West are simply tremendous. There is much to be thankful for with respect to the Congo, to Africa in general, and to Berlin. The Communist camp itself appears to be plagued with serious problems and strains. The technological and military fields, in both Europe and America, are brightening up with accomplishment and confidence. There is youth, there is style, there is brilliance, there is vigor, there is stability, in some Western governments. There are also age and wisdom and a sense of historical depth in others. All this—and much besides—is wonderful, and it presages great things for the future.

But our unit of thought is not a day or a year or the life of a particular regime or government. Nor are we assessing praise or blame on this or that people or this or that statesman. We are thinking of Western civilization as a whole—the entire complex of values that Pericles and Plato and Aristotle and Cicero and Augustine and Aquinas and Dante and Pascal and Kant and Goethe and Pushkin and Dostoevski and Jefferson and Lincoln stood for, believed in, loved, and embodied in their own lives. We are thinking of freedom, truth, man, and God.

Concerned right after World War II for the fate of Europe, Karl Jaspers wrote a small essay entitled "The European Spirit." The Europe he was thinking of roughly coincides with what we have been calling here Mediterranean-Western civilization. In our present inquiry into the fortunes of the cold war, we would extend it to include the fate of America as well; for we believe the fate of Jaspers' Europe is inseparably bound up with that of America. And we would also have it cover those values and realizations which Pushkin, Dostoevski, and the great Russian saints would have loved and defended. This is how Jaspers defined the object of his concern:

If we want to define it by names, Europe is the Bible and the classical world. Europe is Homer, Aeschylus, Sophocles, Euripides, it is Phidias, it is Plato and Aristotle and Plotinus, Vergil and Horace, Dante, Shakespeare, and Goethe, Cervantes, Racine and Moliere, Leonardo, Raphael, Michelangelo, Rembrandt, Velasquez, Bach, Mozart, Beethoven, Augustine, Anselm, Aquinas, Nicolas of Cuso, Spinoza, Pascal, Kant, Hegel, Cicero, Erasmus, Voltaire. Europe is in cathedrals and palaces and ruins, it is Jerusalem, Athens, Rome, Paris, Oxford, Geneva, Weimar. Europe is the democracy of Athens, of republican Rome, of the Swiss and the Dutch and the English-speaking peoples. We could not make an end if we were to number all that is dear to our heart, an immeasurable wealth of the spirit, of morals, and of faith. Such names as these mean something for the man who has lived in what they represent, in the historically unique. The meaning of such a realisation would lead to representation and to the sources, to the towns and the countryside and what has been made, to the monuments and books, to the documents of great men. This is the best and fundamentally the only way of knowing what Europe is. It is in this way that our love is kindled and holds us.

Another way is to draw abstractions out of the experience of these sources. We want to know the principle which animates that richness and re-cast it in thoughts; we want to know what we are and what we can be. Every attempt of this kind is a game.

Three words may be taken to build the characteristic structure of Europe—freedom, history, science. (pp. 34–35)

But when for lack of firm ground we become dizzy—and the

extreme seems still to lie ahead of us—then it is true that when everything goes under, God remains. It is enough that there is transcendence.

Not even Europe is the last thing for us. We become Europeans on condition that we really become men—that is, men from the depths of the origin and the goal, both of which lie in God. (p. 64)[1]

Only the ignorant or the wicked can fail to be concerned about the fate of this incredible world of value and realization. The West has sinned towards Asia and Africa, and even towards itself; and the Asians and Africans, in their resentment, may not give a hoot for the fate of the West: they may even secretly wish it destruction and death. But this attitude is wrong: the positive values conceived, captured, and again and again confirmed by Western civilization belong to the patrimony of mankind; and if they should decline or disappear, not only the West, but the whole world would suffer as a result. In the calm consideration of the fortunes of the cold war it is unworthy to be oppressed by any resentful sentiment arising from jealousy or spite or nihilism or grievance or the sufferings of "imperialism" or the cheap pitting of East against West. One should rise above all such fatuity. Here is an exuberance of truth and value and meaning and achievement and being before which not even "Momus could find fault."[2] It is too much to wish to see the West expiate for its sins by the loss or even the weakening of this infinite wealth of positive and enduring achievement. In God's judgment, it may still *have* to do that; but secretly to *pray* that that be its fate is to take God's judgment into one's own hands; and he who does that may find himself stricken one day by the same hands he has usurped.

Our unit of thought in this inquiry is at least a generation. It

---

[1] Karl Jaspers, *The European Spirit* in the series "Viewpoints" (London: SCM Press, 1948).

[2] Plato, *The Republic*: 487A.

roughly spans the last forty-five years, since the seizure of power by the Marxist-Leninist-International-Communist Party in Russia. We are saying that during this entire period these fundamental values of the West have been mercilessly attacked by the international Communist movement, and Western civilization, which was carrying them, had to stand up in their defense. There is thus here a so-called "cold war." And we are asking: How has this civilization, that has been honored for so long by being the carrier of these momentous values, managed during this generation in this "cold war"? We are thus apologists for nothing and nobody: the issues at stake transcend all silly apologetics. What only interests us is whether Aristotle or Augustine or Kant or Dostoevski would be happy with the performance of Western civilization in its confrontation of communism so far in the "cold war." When people pass judgment on and philosophize about all sorts of things, we say within ourselves: Would that these good people knew that what is important is not their judgment and their philosophizing, but what Aristotle and Augustine and Kant and Dostoevski would say about them! What is therefore needed is the elaboration of *objective criteria* for the determination of the progress of "the cold war." And we will repeat here for the nth time: What is at stake is not this or that political interest, nor this or that government, nor even the security of the United States alone; what is at stake is the totality of Western civilization with its tested and wonderful values which have been cumulatively handed down for thousands of years. One can no longer think of himself or his interests or his country or his party or this or that superficial improvement or the span of a year or two when *this is the issue.*

II

I therefore suggest that the following criteria can objectively measure how Western civilization has been actually faring in the cold war. Every thinking man in the West must face up to these things and assume personal responsibility for them on behalf of his civilization. Doubtless there are other matters to be added, and doubtless some of these criteria themselves must be further refined. But it appears to me we can safely say: Here we have a means of objectively determining—beyond any possibility of superficial self-congratulation—who has been "burying" more of whom and who has been "frying" whom alive.

1. Have the Communists advanced in Asia, in the Middle East, in Africa, in Latin America, in Europe, into areas where they simply did not exist ten or twenty years ago?

2. Ten or fifteen years ago, Western policy in many areas of the world was: The Communists shall not have a foothold here. Is it not a fact that today, this policy is: Provided we are not altogether kicked out from here, we have no objection to the international Communists coming in?

3. Have there been instances of the overthrow of non-Communist governments by Communists?

4. Has there been one single instance of the overthrow of a Marxist-Leninist government by non-Communists?

5. Is it or is it not a fact that there are many countries which would not have dreamt of being "neutral" ten years ago, but which are now stridently "neutral" and some distinctly anti-Western?

6. Are there active Communist Parties outside the Iron Curtain countries?

7. Is there one single "free party" inside the Iron Curtain countries?

8. While the Marxist-Leninists never tire of inciting the world to revolution through the subversive activity of their agents, through daily propaganda (for example, revolution in Iran), and through the statements of their leaders and the declarations of their congresses, does the West dare incite the

Communist countries (for example, East Germany and Poland) to revolution?

9. Is the position of the West at the United Nations stronger or weaker than it was ten or fifteen years ago vis-à-vis international communism?

10. Is the Western Alliance more or less immune to divisive tactics (whether crude or subtle, whether direct or indirect) emanating from the Communist camp than this camp is to such tactics emanating from the West?

11. Is it not a fact that Communist dignitaries now travel far more freely all over the world than they did ten or fifteen years ago, whereas Western statesmen travel now far less freely than they did, say, before World War II?

12. In these travels, which side is more able to organize "popular demonstrations" against the traveling dignitaries of the other side—international communism against Western dignitaries, or the West against Communist dignitaries?

13. Who is capturing the minds of the students, the professors, the artists, the intellectuals in the so-called "neutral" world—Western thought or Marxist-Leninist thought?

14. Which literature has more inundated the bookstores and homes of Asia, Africa, and Latin America—Marxist literature or the literature of the West?

15. How much is the Marxist-materialistic-atheistic interpretation of life, society, man, destiny, and history penetrating Western thought, and how much is the Western-spiritual-Christian interpretation penetrating Communist thought?

16. Which interpretation of man is more and more finding its way into the educational systems, not only of Russia, China, and the Communist realm in general, but of the emerging nations of Asia and Africa, of the older nations of Latin America, and even of many countries in the Western world itself —I mean, into the actual textbooks of the fourth, fifth, sixth and seventh grades, and of the mind- and character-forming

courses of college and university education—the materialistic-naturalistic-atheistic interpretation, or the intellectual-moral-human-spiritual interpretation?

17. Regardless of direct Communist penetration, is it or is it not a fact that during the last two or three decades freedom of thought, freedom of conscience, and freedom of association and expression have virtually disappeared from (or have at least been considerably restricted in) many parts of the world, with no compensating expansion of personal freedom in other parts?

18. Khrushchev boasts that there are forty million dedicated Marxist-Leninists in the world. When he makes a speech or issues a statement, these forty million dedicated and disciplined agents and disciples take that document, read it backward and forward and upward and downward, memorize its contents, understand every word in it as a personal instruction to each one of them; then, they boil it and drink its syrup as a balsam to their heart, and they chew and swallow the dregs. Is there a comparable army of dedicated followers of President Kennedy or Prime Minister Macmillan or President De Gaulle or Chancellor Adenauer who chew and swallow and feed upon their words, and mold their thought and life in conformity with them?

19. Somewhat independently of their leadership, the Marxist-Leninists exhibit a tremendous degree of dedication, asceticism, and self-denial. Are there comparable dedicated ascetics on this side (outside certain religious orders), people who would deny themselves every pleasure and every interest in the service of their unselfish idea?

20. Who makes the greater appeal to the masses in the "neutral" world, who excites them, who talks their language, who succeeds in holding out to them (whether truly or falsely) greater hope and promise—Western leadership or Marxist-Leninist leadership?

21. Which side cares more for, knows more about, is more expert in, makes more full use of, wonderfully organizes, brilliantly splashes all over the world (and the press of the other side lends it a hand therein!), "world congresses" for all sorts of ends—for "peace," for "disarmament," for "banning the bomb," for "cooperation and fraternal association among the Asians and Africans," for some "anti-ism" or other—international communism or the Western world?

22. Who still enjoys an apparently wide lead in spectacular space feats—the United States or the Soviet Union?

23. Who can flout world public opinion with apparent complete impunity when it comes to the resumption of nuclear tests—Khrushchev or Kennedy?

24. From everything they say and do, who appear, on the basis of the record, to be more sure that they will *win without war*—Western leaders or Communist leaders?

25. Who is more and more debunking the whole notion of "winning"—the Communist realm or the Western realm? If one side both says and is absolutely convinced it will "win," and the other side neither says unequivocally nor appears to be really convinced that it will "win," which side then is more likely to "win"?

26. How much has the Marxist-Leninist advance depended on classified scientific and strategic data stolen and passed to the Marxist-Leninists by their agents, friends, and sympathizers in the West during the last twenty or thirty years? How much of this stealing and passing is still actually going on? And—most important—is any comparable stealing and passing going on in the opposite direction?

27. In an emergency, which side can count on more, and more effective, agents (saboteurs, obstructionists, spies, reporters, friends, etc.) helping its cause in the territory of the other side—the Communist realm in the territory of the West, or the West in the territory of the Communist realm?

28. Is it not a fact that the Marxist-Leninists did not have atomic and nuclear power fifteen years ago, while now they have such power to the point of apparently completely neutralizing the atomic and nuclear power of the West (at least so far as its employment as an instrument of policy for the defeat of communism is concerned)? And is it not the case that this fact has radically revolutionized the balance of power in the world to the disadvantage of the West? Has not the West here "lost"?

29. If it is certain that Communist ambassadors abroad constantly report back to their governments about conditions in the countries to which they are accredited from the point of view of the strict Marxist interpretation, do Western ambassadors abroad report back to their governments from the point of view of the strict Western interpretation of life, man, and destiny? What is *this strict Western interpretation today?* How much do these ambassadors know about and report on man and his freedom, the place of reason and free debate, the extent to which truth is revered and known, God and religion, the ultimate beliefs of that culture, the extent to which the government is representative, the extent to which it allows free political debate, the extent to which man in that culture is treated as an end in himself, and is not subordinated to some abstract idea or myth or system, or to the dark dictates of the police state under which he languishes? What is the proportion of this kind of reporting—if it exists—in relation to reporting on "independence" and "development" and "stability" and general "economic and social" matters and ordinary "political gossip" and whether the country is favoring the Soviet Union more? How then does Western reporting differ from strict Marxist-Communist reporting? And even if ambassadorial reporting is strictly and perfectly "Western" in the sense here defined, how much does it determine central Western foreign policy at home?

30. Some people in the West congratulate themselves on the fact that, whereas certain countries and regimes in Asia, Africa, and Latin America have friendly and even intimate relations with the Soviet Union, they have strictly maintained their independence from Moscow: they have even cast the Communists within their own borders in jail! This may be true and the self-congratulation may be quite legitimate; although in some instances it can be shown that it is false. But, with respect to the question as to how Western civilization is faring in the "cold war," there is first in this connection Point 2 above to be faced; and, what is far more important, there is the question: Where do these countries and men get their *master ideas* from—I mean, their actual ideas of political, social, and economic organization, and ideas of the interpretation of history and its sense and man and his destiny? Do they get these ideas from the spiritual heritages of Athens, Rome, Florence, Paris, London, and Boston, or do they get them from the writings of Marx, Lenin, and Mao Tse-tung, from the experience of Russia, China, and Yugoslavia, and from diverse other dark Oriental sources? Is it not cause for profound disturbance of the West—regardless of any question of alignment in the world power struggle—that its *master ideas,* in the political, social, economic, and human realms, do not appear to be loved by these countries and cultures, do not appear to be applicable in them? Should it not rather *not* congratulate itself seeing that the ideas of Marx, Lenin, Tito, and other dark sources appear almost everywhere to be displacing its own, or at least to be successfully competing with them?

31. Do the facts of the economic rate of growth of the Communist realm, when projected onto some point in the future—whether 1970, 1980, or 2010—point to a certain time when communism will have outdistanced the West in productivity and abundance?

32. What are the honest comparative figures as to the rate

of scientific and technological development in the Communist and the Western realms? Are the Communists by comparison producing more or less, better or worse, scientists, technicians, and engineers? At the present rate, is a point foreseeable in the future when they will become absolutely formidable scientifically and technologically? And what is the West planning against that day?

33. Does America really feel responsible for the whole of Western civilization?

III

These appear to me to be the real objective criteria by which the progress of the "cold war" can be gauged. There is nothing sentimental or wishful or subjective or politically tendentious about them. Fairly definite answers can be ascertained with respect to each of them. Responsible thinkers must face them and supply a truthful answer to each one of them on the deepest possible plane. These answers will reveal disturbing trends —even to those who are banking on nationalism and change, to those who are satisfied to leave, hopefully, the task of combating communism either to others or to the dark powers of the universe—trends that have been in progress for decades. It is not then difficult to perceive who is "burying" more of whom and who is really "frying" whom alive. Unless these trends are reversed, one cannot in conscience feel complacent about the "cold war"—whatever else he might find it expedient to say or not to say in public for political reasons or so as not to cause people to lose heart or panic. There is, therefore, something profoundly the matter with Western civilization as a whole to have allowed this situation to deteriorate to this extent, and its responsible children must wake up to this most disquieting fact. For the ultimate moral-spiritual-existential issues—as to the character of people, the character of Western civilization today, the degree of its loyalty to itself, the way it interprets the great historic moment, how much it is profoundly softened up, etc.—which these thirty-three criteria raise are of the deepest possible significance.

Put yourself in place of Mr. Khrushchev. You are entrenched in the Kremlin; there may be some internal intrigue against you, but let us suppose that for the time being you are firmly entrenched. At any rate, forget about this intrigue (it is possible to rise above and forget about your personal fortunes when it comes to great historic tides with which you, personally and existentially, absolutely identify yourself), and concentrate only on the larger issue of where the Marxist-Leninist-International-Communist movement, of which you are the leader and spokesman, is today. You contemplate profoundly each one of these thirty-three criteria. The pondering and complete taking in of each one of them may require months of thought and reflection; but let us suppose that through the dedicated labors of the thousands of your devoted assistants you can fully get to the heart and essence of all of them in a month, while you are vacationing on the Black Sea. Then you reflect that through your nuclear weapons[3] you have once and for all denied to the West any possible recourse to war as a way out of its dilemma. International communism triumphant everywhere; your adversaries amusing themselves with illusions, happy with momentary pleasures, satisfied with crumbs; no possible way of smashing international communism physically—are you not then entitled to the exultant toast: "The rotten capitalist world is collapsing. Friends, let's drink, let's laugh, let's rejoice!"

[3] Note in this connection the following statement made by Franz Josef Strauss in the speech he made at Georgetown University to which we had occasion to refer before (see page 177 above): "The means available to modern technology have caused the earth to shrink and become a very small unit; this makes the phenomenon of Communisim, possessing the most modern means of destruction, all the more tragic for mankind."

It appears, then, that Western civilization is being weighed in the scales of history and decision. We may indeed be before a judgment from something beyond history. Such is the lot of man that, wherever his judgment comes from, he can act only in time. And the question becomes crucial: Is there time still for Western civilization to act?

It is always possible to marshal evidence in such a way as to show that things could have been worse; one then sits back, relaxes, and feels thankful. What is important is to be able to show that things could not have been better. With respect to the "cold war," it is impossible to show this. It is certain that things could have been better, and that the present situation is not the outcome of inexorable fatal necessities. And, more important, in the future things should be better. There is no rest or stalemate in the cold war: if the West is not advancing, then it is certainly retreating. And if it cannot advance by war, and if nationalism and change are both hollow in this game, the question arises: What must it do?

CHAPTER

17

THE NEED FOR

A WESTERN REVOLUTION

I

WAR IS A great problem; but compared to peace, it is a fairly simple problem. The two constituent ingredients of the problem of war are to be strong enough to deter aggression and to be strong enough to win should war break out. Of course, to satisfy both ingredients calls for an immense amount of diplomatic, psychological, political, technical, technological, industrial, and military preparation and action. With the breathlessly-developing technological revolution, this problem becomes exceedingly exacting. For things are never static, disarmament—even were people to agree completely to its terms—could never affect the infinite inventiveness of the human mind, and a single breakthrough could suddenly upset all previous calculations. Moreover, the second element, that of "winning" a war, is, in the case of nuclear war, exceedingly problematic. But, difficult and demanding and problematic as the whole question of war might be, how not to "lose," and if possible how to "win," under peaceful conditions, is in-

comparably more difficult and demanding. The thesis I wish
to urge is that people who talk only about war miss the entire
point today; that the real problem today is not war but peace;
that the real problem is how to win, or at least how not to
lose, *under conditions of peace*; and that in this deadly game
of conducting war under conditions of peace it is entirely possible that the Communists, with their cumulative experience
since 1848, and especially since 1917, are more skilled than
any other people. It is absolutely necessary—and only natural
and realistic—to think and worry and take precautions about
the atomic holocaust, the destructiveness of the hydrogen
bomb, the fallout, and all the horror statistics that one reads
in the sensational accounts. We are indeed before a completely
unprecedented state of affairs, and these matters should be
treated with the utmost responsibility and seriousness. But
there is something even more serious; it is this: *What if international war on a large scale never broke out, and what if,
precisely under such conditions of no-war in the classical sense
of the term, communism nevertheless continued to advance
until it conquered the whole world?* One may thus formulate
a strange paradox, a paradox open to the most malicious of
misinterpretations: *In a sense, peace today is to be dreaded
more than war!*

George F. Kennan wrote a book, *Russia and the West under Lenin and Stalin,* which should be pondered by every
student of world affairs. We find ourselves in wholehearted
agreement with some—but certainly not with all—of the po-
litical-international-philosophical conclusions of this book.
The point we are here making, namely, that today the problem
is in reality *peace and not war,* is not unlike the thesis of the
following passage from Mr. Kennan:

How could outright warfare serve to protect against [the Com-
munist] danger? What could be the specific objective of regular
military operations undertaken to this end? To unseat the Soviet

government? But how? By occupying *all* of Russia? I think military authorities would agree that this is not technically feasible even if it were worth one's while to make the staggering effort. And what would you expect to put in the place of the Soviet government? Do you have a ready substitute? . . .

Besides, even if your military measures were directed, by intent, against the Soviet government, it would be the Russian people who would have to bear the brunt of them. Are you sure you wish to do this to them in the day of the horrors of the atom? The fact is that throughout all these years of anti-capitalist and anti-American propaganda in the Soviet Union, the Soviet peoples have remained touchingly well-inclined towards the United States, touchingly unwilling to accept the endless efforts of their government to persuade them that Americans meant them harm. You come here to the profound ambivalence in the relation between people and regime in such a country as Soviet Russia: to the fact that the interests and aspirations of these two entities in some ways differ but are in other ways identical, and that it is impossible to distinguish between the two when it comes to the hardships and injuries of war. Outright war is itself too unambivalent, too undiscriminating a device to be an appropriate means for effecting a mere change of regime in another country. You can not logically inflict on another people the horrors of nuclear destruction in the name of what you believe to be its salvation, and expect it to share your enthusiasm for the exercise. Even if you were sure that the overwhelming majority of another people wished in theory to be freed by external intervention from a given situation of political subservience (and in the case of Russia I am not at all satisfied that this would be the case today), it would still be senseless to attempt to free it from the limited internal embarrassment of an unpopular regime (which still permits it, after all, the privilege of life in the physical sense) by subjecting it to the far more fearful destruction and hardships of modern war.

All these things, I may add, would have been true even had the atomic and other weapons of mass destruction never been invented. The existence of these weapons merely adds another dimension of absurdity to the idea that the devices of outright war would be a suitable means of protecting the Western community from the kind of challenge with which Russian Communism has confronted it: . . . modern warfare in the grand manner, pursued by all available means and aimed at the total destruction of the enemy's capacity to resist, is, unless it proceeds very rapidly and successfully, of such general destructiveness that it ceases to be useful as an instrument for the achievement of any coherent political purpose. Such warfare (and this was true even in 1917) involves evils which far outweigh any forward political purpose it might serve—any purpose at all, in fact, short of sheer self-preservation, and perhaps not even short of that. Even if warfare had been the answer to Communism in a different stage of weaponry (and, mind you, I do not think it would), it would certainly not be the answer in the day of the atom.[1]

It follows that, while "the deterring ingredient" of the problem of war can never be relaxed for one moment, "the winning ingredient" under present conditions cannot be rationally entertained. This does not mean that one should not do his very best—and should not be prepared at all times to do his very best—under the absolute determination "to win" (no matter how absurd this might seem today), *should war be forced upon him* (and war, despite the fact that under the stalemate it cannot be rationally entertained, could be brought about through any one of a dozen causes: miscalculation, error, insanity, accident, the temptation which some technological breakthrough might exert, and everybody is feverishly working towards some breakthrough today, desperation, escalation, etc.). It does mean that no one can under the conditions of the stalemate coldbloodedly start a war (in the manner in which wars were almost always started in the past); that the *starting* of a nuclear war cannot be part of a deliberate national policy. Therefore, the fundamental problem today is

[1] George F. Kennan: *Russia and the West under Lenin and Stalin* (Boston, Mass: Little, Brown and Company, 1961), pp. 390–391.

peace and not war; how to beat the Communists, or at least how to prevent them from beating you, in peace and not in war; what to make of the peace, and not how to win a war.

II

Unless our argument in the preceding chapter is refuted point by point, or unless other criteria for the cold war are put forward that will materially alter the sense of the argument, it is apparent that *the Communists have been winning the cold war*. This is a conclusion that no depth of dialectics can alter, no amount of sophistry can modify, and no degree of apologetics can soften. There is a perfectly objective, non-controversial, universally valid sense in which Western civilization— whatever else it might be thankful for—has been retreating and communism and other non-Western and anti-Western forces have been advancing. This has happened partly through war (the results of World War II in Eastern Europe), partly through revolution (Cuba, and the clean sweep which the Communist Revolution made in mainland China), partly through quiet infiltration and subversion throughout the length and breadth of Asia, Africa, and Latin America under conditions of peace. The Marxist-materialist-atheist outlook, quite apart from the shrinkage of Western territorial, political, and economic influence, is, moreover, enjoying a field day all over the Western world.

The upshot of Chapter 15 is the demonstration that neither nationalism nor change nor war is the savior of the world from the scourge of communism. On the one hand, the Marxist-Leninists are handsomely winning in peace (cold war), and no matter how much this peace is prolonged *under the present rules*, it is hopeless to expect the forces of nationalism and change to beat or mellow them; on the other hand, they cannot be beaten if the peace (cold war) is transformed into war (hot war). *In peace they are winning, in war they are un-beatable*—this is the tremendous dilemma of the present moment of history.

And yet, there must be a way out. So long as there is time, there is hope; and since the world is not yet completely over-run, and since the creative possibilities of free and faithful men have not been exhausted, there is time and there is therefore hope—*provided the time that there is is fully made use of.* If the Communists are unbeatable in war, due to the continued existence of the nuclear stalemate, and if they have been winning under the present rules of peace, the only way out is *to change the rules of peace.* This means to seek such new rules as will enable you to turn the tide under peaceful conditions—*especially as the Communists themselves cannot win in war either!*

This change of the *rules of peace* is precisely the fundamental revolution in Western thought and living that I believe the present moment of history calls for. For what is it that is neither war nor peace, and yet that enables you to achieve the ends of a war that no longer "appeals as a rational alternative," namely, the defeat of the enemy? This can only be a revolution in your own existence; otherwise, you are only proposing to go on existing as usual, relying on the old methods and rules and expectations—but these only land you in the state of the cold war which you are losing. It is exactly existing-as-usual that is no longer possible. *That which is neither a losing peace nor an unwinning war can only be a fundamental human revolution which, in peace, can fully achieve the ends of war.*

Now the Communists seem to have perfected the art of revolution and subversion far more than the rest of the world —perhaps far more than any other movement in history. There is the real challenge: *To outrevolutionize their revolution and to outsubvert their subversion under conditions of peace, in peaceful competition!* To be able to do this—and remember, you have not yet done it—to be able to do it, not by words, not by idle dreams, not by falling back upon the empty hopes of nationalism, change, and war, but actually and historically, requires precisely the sort of revolutionary change in your existence and outlook that I believe the present moment of history absolutely cries for.

It appears that the Communists are prepared both for war and peace: for war through their armies, bombs, and rockets; and for peace through their Marxist-Communist revolution. On the other hand, it appears that the West is prepared for war and not for peace: for war through its armies, bombs, and rockets; and not for peace because it does not appear to carry the banner of some revolution.

This is the deepest observation that I can make, and that I believe any man can make, about the present world situation.

Because they appear to be prepared for war, the Communists are not afraid of war—rather, they are not more afraid of it than others. But because they are also prepared for peace through their revolution, they preach peace; they want peace; they develop peace movements; peace becomes one of the instruments of their revolution; in fact this is precisely their interpretation of their slogan "peaceful coexistence"—that it is but a special form of the class struggle, that it can never mean ideological peace, and that it is a special means, under existing world conditions (the nuclear stalemate, the enormously increased strength of world communism, etc.), of achieving their worldwide proletarian revolution without war;[2] they make the West appear to want war; they make the West appear to be the war party, while they are the peace party. The success of

---

[2] In his *Peaceful Coexistence* (*op. cit.*), Kulski discusses coexistence at length. In 1955, I gave two lectures at Northwestern University which the University then published in a pamphlet entitled "The Problem of Coexistence." See also all existing compilations of statements by Mr. Khrushchev. I believe the first, and perhaps only, theoretical discussion of "coexistence" at the United Nations occurred between me and Mr. Vychinsky in 1950; see the proceedings of the General Assembly for that year.

Communist propaganda on this point is measured by the simple fact that, whereas the West has lately, at the United Nations and in all its policy pronouncements, been stressing the theme of peace almost as much as the Communist world, the overwhelming majority of people (I know that from the United Nations) still believe that the Communists are more sincere in their desire for peace. By denying, through the nuclear stalemate, war to the West as an instrument, the Communists have forced the West to fight only peacefully; and by not developing an effective Western revolution, the West has so far doomed itself to be defeated in peace.

Nothing is more illuminating on this point than Walter Lippmann's interpretation of what Khrushchev means by "the status quo." Mr. Lippmann visited the Soviet Union in 1958 and had an interview with Khrushchev. Upon his return, he published in his newspaper column a series of articles on his impressions, which were subsequently put together in a book. Mr. Lippmann distinguishes three elements in Khrushchev's conception of "the status quo": (1) "that there should be no change of frontiers by military force"; (2) that there is a certain "military stalemate" between the Soviet Union and the United States, so that "neither country can defeat the other in a direct conflict"; and (3)—and this appears to be "the more important part of his conception of the status quo"—

In his mind, the social and economic revolution now in progress in Russia, China, and elsewhere in Asia and Africa *is* the status quo, and he wants us to recognize it as such. In his mind, opposition to this revolution is an attempt to change the status quo. Whereas we think of the status quo as the situation as it exists at the moment, he thinks of it as the process of revolutionary change which is in progress. He wants us to recognize the revolution not only as it is but as it is going to be.[3]

This is exactly the point: There is something important going

[3] Walter Lippmann, *The Communist World and Ours* (Boston, Mass.: Little, Brown and Company, 1959), pp. 12–13.

on all over the world which the West does not seem to recognize—at least not sufficiently—and adjust to, and when it recognizes this, it appears only to be "trailing along" behind the Communists. The awakening of the masses is as much provoked by the impact of the West during the last two centuries as by any Communist activity, and the West therefore must know how to take credit for it. The Communists have their revolution; what then is the revolution of the West? And it is not enough to *take credit* for what is happening: you must lead and guide it. You must also *distinguish* yourself from the Communists in this leading and guiding. You cannot go to these people and only tell them, "The Communists promise you something, I'll promise you more of the same thing!" You must provide a *distinctive Western promise*. This is the Western revolution called for, beside which what the Communists are talking about pales into stupidity and reaction. It must be distinctive and original, for an imitation revolution is a contradiction in terms.

It is most important therefore that the West be as prepared for peace as the Communists. But as it lives and thinks and acts and expects at present, it is not prepared for peace. This is the tragedy of the moment.

III

Revolution, then, is the fifth answer to the fundamental question we posed in Chapter 13—not a Communist revolution, but a genuine Western revolution which, seeing through the inadequacies of nationalism and change, and not depending on the mirage of war, manages nevertheless to beat the Communists in peace. Revolution is the only alternative whereby you can avoid being "buried" and being "fried alive."

But the mere word "revolution" frightens the West. What, do you mean—they ask—to subvert our laws, change our es-

tablished customs, upset our settled ways of thought, overthrow our institutions? One of course means nothing of the
sort: it is the Marxist-Leninist-International Communists who
are endangering all these; unless you acquiesce in being fried
alive, you must bestir yourself in the comfortably cool pan
while you are still alive—and do something. It is precisely for
the sake of preserving and deepening and extending your freedoms and values that the revolution appears the only way out.
What one profoundly fears is that in your heart of hearts you
are really hoping that somehow this cloud will pass and you
will be spared the effort of fundamentally bestirring yourself
—spared the effort, either through the operation of old-fashioned change, or through the laws of nationalism, or, finally,
through the holocaust of war. This hope is false, and therefore
you must arouse yourself despite the comfortable coolness of
the pan.

We are not thinking of mere people surviving: people will
always somehow manage to survive; they have survived in
Soviet Russia and China, and there will always be people in
Europe and America. The question is: What *kind* of people?
What do they live for? What do they hope for? What do they
believe? What do they love? What are their fundamental
values? We are thinking of the survival of Western civilization,
not of peoples inhabiting places where Western civilization
once existed; that is, we are thinking of peoples and cultures
believing in and practicing and loving Western civilization's
fundamental values: freedom, man, truth, God. We are not
thinking of "the survival of the human race," because we have
no fear whatsoever that "the human race" will not survive.

The test of the West's ability to survive in this sense is precisely whether it will cure itself of this emotional horror of the
very word "revolution." This horror is itself an indication of
the false sense that everything is normal and ordinary, that
existing-as-usual is all that the moment calls for, because

everything "will be all right." Centuries ago fundamental revolutions occurred in the West—in England, in France, in Italy,
in Germany, in America—and even the Russian revolution is
some kind of Western revolution, if Russia is part of the West,
which she is. Has the West lost its *capacity for revolution?*
This is the question. The truth I am trying to establish is that
nothing short of a fundamental revolution is adequate today.
He is the great and expected leader and savior of the West today who, completely rising above himself, and putting aside
all shallow optimism, can thoroughly and firmly din this fact
into its mind. In a great revolutionary age, for the West *not*
to be revolutionary is the tragedy of the day! If it were God,
the West could afford to be "the unmoved mover"; but being
a part of time and history, or, better, being itself essentially
temporal and historical, it must move and act—on the deepest
possible plane.

IV

Now what is meant by a revolution? You do not sit down,
work yourself up about "the world situation," take up the pen
at two o'clock in the morning, write down a series of twenty-
four revolutionary principles, proclaim them in a pamphlet or
in a letter to the editor of the *Times,* and then, *there* you have
the revolution! Especially as after you have done all this you
go back to sleep, get up in leisurely fashion at noon, drink
your morning (or noon) coffee, call in your valet to massage
you, and in the evening enjoy your magnificent Scotch and
smoke your pipe—as though nothing had happened.

Whatever else a revolution means, it means two things: (1)
It means *revolutionaries*—a revolutionary party, organized,
disciplined, dedicated, working day and night for its objectives;
and (2) it means principles and methods rooted in the political, social, psychological, and spiritual soil of the West, so as
to strike a deep chord of response in Western existence itself.

The only serious revolutionary party (in the socio-political sense) in the West is the Communist Party itself. There is no Western revolutionary party—not even in the West.

It follows that you cannot talk much about a revolution: a revolution just comes and proclaims itself. The revolution posits itself and then people must take a stand with respect to it. Nothing is more pathetic than when people begin vaguely to sense that there is something wrong, that some revolution is going on throughout the world, that, therefore, they must proclaim *their own revolution,* or ride on the wave of the one occurring. And what do they do when they do not want to appear only "riding"? They point to some revolution in the past, and they say, "There is our revolution which we proclaim to the world!" Besides the two relevant points (1) that this is a leisurely afterthought on their part, a reaction to what is happening in the world, and not an original, generous impulse, and (2) that the revolution they point to was created by their forefathers and not by themselves, there is this additional matter: *a revolution means revolutionaries,* and these worthy men, when you look at them and carefully study them, appear in their life and thought and expectations *anything but revolutionaries. Produce your revolutionaries first!* This is the maxim that governs every revolution.

Although only the revolution, when the revolutionaries themselves appear, can creatively determine its *kind* and set forth its own articles of faith and its rules of action, there is nothing to prevent us, in bringing this work to an end, and in supplying a sort of summary of many of the basic, positive positions we expressed before, from making a few general observations in the form of *notes about the revolution.*

V

1. Knowing the thinness and hollowness of the Marxist doctrine, and knowing the depth and truth and infinite richness

of the Western positive tradition of thought and existence, one should be absolutely persuaded that from the womb of this tradition a most authentic revolution of life and spirit can be evolved that will force the Communists to take to their heels everywhere and on every front; and as a result one should be living in the tension of the eschatological expectancy that such a revolution is assuredly forthcoming. This simple persuasion and that elementary knowledge are quite revolutionary these days, when the mind of the West appears to be confusedly and distractedly looking outside itself, outside its heritage, outside its depths, for guidance and for light, and when the only expectancy by which people appear to live is to look forward to more and more of the same old existence-as-usual.

2. The infinite possibilities, *short of war*, of causing the Communist realm to disintegrate from within, through political, diplomatic, economic, intellectual, moral, spiritual, and other measures, have not been sufficiently compassed, much less effectively mobilized and brought to bear. The children of light are unworthy of the light they enjoy if they do not believe that they can be, *precisely under conditions of peace*, infinitely more resourceful than the children of darkness; and if they do not translate this belief into actual fact. A believing determination to bring about the actual disintegration of the Communist realm *without war* is quite revolutionary these days, when people either do not want to see it disintegrate but prefer to coexist with it, or can only see it dissolve by war.

3. Just as the Communists find it possible, under the protective shield of the nuclear stalemate, to nibble with relative impunity at the periphery of the non-Communist world—for example, in Laos and Cuba—so the free world, under determined leadership, ought to find it possible, under the same protective shield, to nibble with relative impunity at the periphery of the Communist realm—for example, in Albania, or Poland, or East Germany, or North Viet Nam. To think

that the West is entitled at least to reciprocity in this respect is quite revolutionary these days, when as soon as you mention the word "liberation," people stare at you and say: "You are then advocating a nuclear war!"

4. There has been an enhanced recent interest in guerrillas. Here, too, at least reciprocity should be established. The extensive training of guerrillas, for a dozen different areas in the world, on a scale ten times the presently contemplated one, appears indicated. To think of the use of trained guerrillas as an answer to Communist infiltration and seizure is quite revolutionary these days, when the general assumption is that the sheer nationalism of these countries will somehow magically enable them to withstand and get rid of the Communist assault.

5. The clearest distinction must be maintained between the Communist Party and the captive peoples under its domination, and the most solemn assurance must be given that America and the West are friends of these peoples but cannot do business with the Marxist-Leninists. The torch of liberation from the yoke of communism must be unmistakably and fearlessly held up. There are three distinct things: Party, government, and people; with the people, "peaceful coexistence," in the honest sense of the term, is not only possible, but absolutely necessary; with the government, peace depends on its spirit and policy, and is quite impossible where the Marxist-Leninists are in power, but is quite possible if some other spirit replaces them; and with the Marxist-Leninists, peace, in any sense, is impossible. To maintain this distinction between these three entities and to formulate and execute policy on its basis is quite revolutionary these days, when practically everybody in the West is doing his utmost to confuse them with each other, not only beyond the actual facts, but beyond anything the peoples concerned—and even some elements in the governments—desire or wish or hope for or expect from the West.

6. The Marxist-Leninists openly and proudly declare that

their ultimate aim is the communization of the whole world. I see therefore no reason why, in sheer self-defense, if not also from motives of fundamental conviction, the West should not have as its ultimate policy—whether or not it openly and humbly declares it—the elimination of the Marxist-Leninist-International-Communist Party as a ruling Party anywhere in the world. The immediate aim should be to produce concrete examples which will invalidate Marxist analysis and prediction and thereby strikingly prove that communism, not only economically, but above all socially, politically, intellectually, and spiritually, is not the inevitable wave of the future. It is most important that a few such concrete examples be produced, especially in rolling back the Communist glacier from at least one country where it has firmly taken root. To think seriously of rolling back the glacier is quite revolutionary these days, when the very notion of roll-back is anathema, and when people seem to be perfectly satisfied if they are left alone defending their home and hearth, or at most containing the tide in Indonesia, India, the Middle East, Africa, and Latin America.

7. One understands how international communism lumps Latin America indiscriminately with Asia and Africa: they are all "underdeveloped," in the strictly Marxist-economic sense. But the lumping now is taken over by the West, so that all three are usually mentioned in the same breath. This one cannot understand, for the community of background, history, religion, art, language, and law, and culture and civilization in general, between Latin America, on the one hand, and the United States and Europe, on the other, does not exist between either of these and Asia and Africa. Here is one instance of how the West sheepishly falls for Communist slogans (one can make a list of twenty or thirty loaded Communist expressions which have crept into uncritical Western usage since 1917), a "falling for" which only expresses a deeper existential "falling into" or "conversion to" the Communist

ontological interpretation of man and things. One wonders if there has been anywhere near a corresponding Communist "falling," not only nominally, but in meaning and intention, "for" the Western language of freedom. We seem to have here a fruitful field of research as to who has held and retained "the terminological initiative"—the Communists or the West? To stress what unites Latin America with the West rather than what divides it is quite revolutionary these days, when all that people seem to care for is material values and "stages of development."

8. Because of the peculiar genius of the West, where variety, individuality, and freedom are ultimate, such an authentic revolution cannot come, cannot be imposed, from the outside. Mr. Lippmann is quite right when he concludes that:

barring a great catastrophe resulting from a war, the Communist system has no serious attraction for the highly developed Western countries, and that as an experience and an example, it is, in fact, irrelevant to them. . . . We have to live on the same globe with the Communist powers. But we do not live and we cannot live in the same intellectual and political world. Not now. Not in the foreseeable future.[4]

Thus, the true Western revolution can never be Marxist: it can only develop through and on the basis of existing institutions. The most important existing institutions which can amply do the job if properly mobilized and led—*of course, each within its own freedom and each in accordance with its own genius and competence*—are: *government, the press, industry, labor, the university, and the Church.* To think of these independent institutions of freedom galvanized and geared to the revolution is quite revolutionary these days, when governments are largely concerned with order, form, security, and politics, and if they turn to substance, only the economic seems

[4] Walter Lippmann, *op. cit.,* pp. 53–54 and p. 56.

to appeal to them; when the press, besides being quite weak on the fundamental issues involved, is so much given to sensuality, sensationalism, and violence; when there is so much wasteful uncoordination in industry, and when the rights of labor are sometimes selfishly denied; when labor, not always mindful of the larger, common good, often finds itself torn by strife both with industry and within its own ranks; when the universities are so much infected by materialism, atheism, indifferentism, and the cynical and self-sufficient spirit; and when the Church is scandalously disunited.

9. It is a shame that the West has been on the defensive all these years. The time has come to pass to the offensive on every front. The initiative should be seized in a dozen fields, especially the political, moral, personal, intellectual, and spiritual. To think of vigorously and relentlessly challenging the Communists on their theory of man, government, and history, on whether the mind is really free in their realm, on why they broke away from the wonderful spiritual heritage of their peoples, and on why they persecute those who believe in God and Christ, is quite revolutionary these days, when the utmost that people seem to be capable of thinking of is "systems," "societies," "gross national products," and who is going to reach the moon first.

10. It is necessary to think of economic and technical assistance, mutual security, meeting "the revolution of rising expectations," and raising the standard of living of the masses. But to think *only* of these things is to imitate the Communists and to play into the hands of their revolution. It is to confirm people in their thinking (they are already prone to this by nature) that these are the only things that matter, and this is precisely what the Communists love to have you mean and convey to them. In so-called "peaceful competition," one cannot be too wary lest one become so mesmerized by one's competitor as to turn into an exact copy of him. Hunger, poverty,

and disease are depicted as the worst enemies of mankind; actually, there are far worse enemies. When will the West move onto the plane of the fundamental spiritual values of freedom? When will it think and talk and act in terms of freedom of thought and conscience, free inquiry and free criticism, the dignity of man, the supremacy of reason, the ultimacy of the human person, personal depth and personal freedom, freedom of choice in the selection of the government, the rule of law, the conception of law as something not arbitrary, not determined by that fiat of the will, but as something natural, universal, inherent, objectively just, and independent of partisan interests? All this is quite revolutionary.

11. It is quite true that America and the West in general cannot be secure if they remain an oasis of abundance amidst a world desert of privation. A thousand people, both from the East and the West, have on a thousand occasions and in a thousand and one different ways given expression to this persuasion. But if this truth should cause America and the West to develop a guilt complex with respect to their wealth (and this is exactly what the Communists love to see take hold of Western conscience), then, weighed down by this sense of guilt, the West will not be free to think and talk in intellectual, moral, personal, and human terms. Allowing for all the possible "exploitation" (even in the exaggerated Marxist sense) that may have occurred, both internally and between the West and the rest of the world, it is certainly true that Western abundance is the independent creation of Western science, industry, and foresight. The West owes its affluence, with all its attendant ills, to nobody but itself. Those who suffer from privation today, especially if they have freely chosen to break away from the West politically, economically, and socially, have no strict moral claims on the fruits of Western industry. The mechanical equalization of merit, purely on the basis of counting heads, and without any regard for personal-moral-

intellectual-cultural worth, is one of the great fallacies of this age. To help the needy materially, not because you owe them anything, nor because you wish to bribe them, but in freedom and joy and liberality and out of sheer human solidarity, is quite revolutionary these days, when foreign economic assistance is so guilt-ridden and so politically determined.

12. Consider the following statement: "We are pledged, realistically, to defend freedom where there is a will to have it. There was no such will in Laos. There is some of it in Thailand."[5] You hear and read these days a thousand different variations on this same theme. This is completely unrevolutionary. A genuine revolution does not wait for people to will it: it creates in them the will to its major theme itself. "Existence-as-usual"—this is the great enemy today. You "have" "freedom"; others do not "have" it, and do not seem to "have" the "will to have it." This is the existing state of affairs, and so let us leave it at that! You do not want to be bothered; you do not want to be disturbed; essentially, you want to be left alone; essentially, if the "unfree" were not falling one by one to an enemy who at this rate would one day isolate, engulf, and destroy you, you would not give a hoot for them; therefore, you will not so deeply bestir yourself as to make others, whether or not they were falling piecemeal to your enemy, see and love and seek your deepest values. You do not then have an independent, original, distinctive, universal message yourself: your message depends on your enemy's being and action; it is a function of his will. And then you wonder why communism moves in and takes over! "Existence-as-usual" is the exact antithesis of any revolutionary spirit. Existing-as-usual, you dread to return radically to yourself. But only in this radical return can you "meet" your ground from whence all help, all hope, and all movement start. The will to freedom should be aroused, trumpeted, called forth. If it does not exist,

[5] Ralph McGill, *Washington Evening Star,* May 6, 1961, p. A9.

it is not the fault of those who do not "have it"; it is the fault of those who are free. For it is right that man everywhere should be free, and if you do not believe this, then you do not know freedom yourself, and communism has already won in your soul. How can any revolution start anywhere if it *begins* with lack of faith in its highest values? And the highest values of the West are man, freedom, truth, and God.

13. If you really believe in the values of freedom, you must remain faithful to freedom's lovers everywhere. Wherever there is the least trace of freedom, you must rejoice and do what you can to strengthen it. This is quite revolutionary these days, when the West treats almost equally the free and the slave, those who are attached to its values and those who hate them, nay, when it often delivers those who believe and love its values to the tender mercies of the dark and despotic.

14. One reason for the appeal of communism, where it does appeal, is that it makes its maker—the dread spirit of violence and revolution—available to others; one reason for the lack of appeal of the West, where it does not appeal, is that it keeps its maker—the creative spirit which ultimately fashioned it, the outlook on man and mind and matter, and on what is even above these, which it inherited from thousands of years of thought and struggle and toil and tears, the spirit which seeks and rejoices in the sight of being—hidden under a bushel. To even think of making this creative Western spirit available to others is quite revolutionary these days, partly because of fear and timidity, partly because the West itself is not sure of it.

15. Some Western authors refer to communism as a secular religion. This is what communism certainly is; and this is why it has developed such a radical hatred of real religion. But these authors fail to draw the only valid conclusion from their observation, namely, that secular religion can only be met by some kind of religion, not by the no-religion at all in which

they believe. Secular religion is of course a contradiction in terms; it is therefore false religion; and false religion can be met either by another false religion, or by the religion that is real and true. Communism is a spirit; and only the spirit can meet the spirit. The West, which knows the true spirit, the spirit of truth, and life, and love, has no excuse for not meeting communism on its own grounds—the grounds of the spirit —and overcoming it in the name of what it knows. One of the weaknesses of Western governments is that they completely dissociate themselves (in the name of pluralism) from the realm of the spirit, relying only on money, techniques, diplomacy, force, and politics; and if they approach the spirit at all, it is always the spirit of nationalism that they cuddle. The Soviet government deals both with spirit and with techniques; Western governments busy themselves all day long only with techniques. It is obvious that nothing short of a revolution can "spiritualize" Western governments.

16. There is much that is good and true and of enduring value in non-Western cultures. The West can only approach them with love and the utmost respect. All men share a common human nature and a reason that, under conditions of confidence and love, can by its natural light distinguish between right and wrong, true and false. And no matter how limited or colored, prejudiced, distorted, or warped his reason might be, no man is ever in principle hopeless so far as the possibility of seeing the right, the good, and the true is concerned. How to love the non-Western cultures without pampering them, how to learn from them without becoming their slave, how to challenge them without causing them to lose confidence in their genuine values, how to help them without sentimentally confirming them in their outworn customs and habits of mind, how to establish relations of equality, dignity, and mutual respect with them without either weakening yourself in your hold on the deepest you know or making them feel that

everything is as good as everything else—all this requires a hard, revolutionary bent of mind that knows what it believes, what it wants, and how to get it.

17. There are people in the West who take special pleasure in the fact that there is crop failure and famine in China and that Soviet agriculture encounters many difficulties. They sit back praying and waiting for the Chinese regime to collapse from these natural calamities, and for the Soviet system to totter. This can happen, but if it did, it would not be thanks to them, but to the inscrutable operations of Mother Nature; and Nature could one day as much chastise them as it had the Chinese and Russians. Besides, the sheer will of man has overcome many a natural handicap before. Those who are counting on Nature to relieve them of the necessity of facing up themselves to the challenge of China and Russia must remember that the important thing is, not what Nature may or may not do, but what they themselves believe in, and stand for, and are. The contest today is between man and man and spirit and spirit, and not between man and Nature. To see all this today in the comfortable and affluent West is quite revolutionary.

18. Dostoevski said somewhere that, if Christ came to earth again, he would appear in the form of a Russian peasant. I almost believe this. Who can read the great classical Russian literature without being moved from his deepest depths—without loving the Russians as though he were one of them. Consider this outburst by Belinsky as recounted by Berdyaev:

> The theme of the clash between personality and world harmony is very Russian. Russian thought experienced it with peculiar trenchancy and depth. In this connection the first place belongs to the revolt of Belinsky. . . . Belinsky says of himself that he is a terrible person when some mystical absurdity gets into his head. There are a great many Russians who might say that of themselves. After he went through his crisis Belinsky expressed his new thoughts in

the form of a reaction against Hegel, a revolt against him in the name of personality, on behalf of the living man. . . . The power of the universal idea, of the universal spirit—that is the great foe. "To the devil with all your higher strivings and purposes," writes Belinsky. "I have particularly serious grounds for being angry with Hegel, because I feel that it was my belief in him which led me to come to terms with Russian reality. *The fate of the subject, of the individual, of the person, is more important than the fate of the whole world.* They say to me, develop all the treasures of your spirit with a view to untrammelled self-satisfaction through the spirit. Weep so that you may be consoled; grieve so that you may rejoice anew; strive after perfection; climb to the highest rung of the ladder of development, but flounder and fall, and the devil take you. . . . I humbly express my gratitude to Egor Fedorovitch (Hegel); I reverence your philosopher's gown, but with all due respect to your philosophical philistinism I have the honour to inform you that if it were given to me to climb to the highest rung of the ladder of development, even there I would ask to be rendered an account for all the victims of chance, of superstition, of the Inquisition of Philip II, and so on and so on. Otherwise I would fling myself down headlong from that highest rung. I do not want happiness, even as a gift, unless I have peace of mind about every one of my brothers by blood. . . . This it seems to me is my final view of things and with it I shall die." "For me to think, to feel, to understand and to suffer are one and the same thing." "The fate of the subject, of the individual, of the person is more important than the fate of the whole world and the well-being of the Chinese Emperor, (that is to say, the Hegelian *Allgemeinheit*)."

Or consider this outburst by Dostoevski's *man underground:*

The man underground will not agree with the world harmony, with the crystal palace towards the achievement of which he himself would be nothing but a means. "His own, his free and voluntary desire," says the man underground, "that which is his own, even if it be the slightest caprice, his own fancy, even though it be at times carried to the extent of madness, in that you have something which is the greatest of all gains, a thing which enters into no classification and for the sake of which all systems and theories will gradually be consigned to the devil." The man underground does not accept the results of progress, of compulsory world harmony, of the contented ant hill, when millions will be happy in refusing personality and freedom. . . . The man underground exclaims: "Well now, I, for example, should not be in the least surprised if suddenly for no reason whatever, in the future state of general well-being, some gentleman emerges with an ignoble or rather a degenerate face, standing provocatively with arms akimbo, and says to us all: 'Well, gentlemen, wouldn't it be a good thing if we knocked all this rational well-being to bits with just one kick, reduced it to dust, with the one single aim that all these logarithms may take themselves off to the devil, and let us live once more according to our own stupid will?' "

Or, consider Ivan Karamazov's expression of his love for Europe:

I want to go to Europe. Maybe I know that I shall go only to a cemetery, but it will be to the dearest of cemeteries. So there you are. Dear ones departed lie there. Every stone upon them speaks of such ardent life in the past and such a devoted belief in its own achievement, in its own truth, in its own struggle and its own science. But I know beforehand that I shall fall upon the earth and I shall kiss those stones and weep over them, at the same time convinced with all my heart that all this has already been a cemetery for a very long time and is nothing else whatever.[6]

Finally, consider the following passages by the Elder Zosima in *The Brothers Karamazov*:

And another thing, mother, every one of us is guilty towards all men, of all sins, and I more than any. . . . Every one is really responsible to all men for all and everything. . . . Months and years! Why reckon the days? One day is enough for a man to

---

[6] The above three passages are taken from Nicolas Berdyaev's *The Russian Idea* (London: Geoffrey Bles, 1947), pp. 75–76, 77–78, and 70.

know all happiness. My dear ones, why do we quarrel, try to out-shine each other and bear grudges against each other? Let's go straight into the garden, walk and play there, love, appreciate, and kiss each other, and bless our life. . . . Yes, there was God's glory all about me; birds, trees, meadows, sky, I alone lived in shame and dishonoured it all and did not notice the beauty and glory. . . . Though I can't explain it to you, I myself like to feel guilty towards them [i.e., the birds, trees, meadows, sky], for I don't know how to love them enough. If I have sinned against every one, yet all forgive me, too, and that's heaven. Am I not in heaven now? . . . Indeed, precious memories may remain even of a bad home, if only the heart knows how to find what is pre-cious. . . . Good heavens, what a book it is, and what lessons there are in it! What a book the Bible is, what a miracle, what strength is given with it to man. It is like a mould cast of the world and man and human nature, everything is named there, and indicated for all time. And what mysteries are solved and revealed; God raises Job again, gives him wealth again. Many years pass by, and he has other children and loves them. But how could he love those new ones when those first children are no more, when he has lost them? Remembering them, how could he be fully happy with those new ones, however dear to him the new ones might be? But he could, he could. It's the great mystery of human life that old grief passes gradually into quiet tender joy. The mild serenity of age takes the place of the riotous blood of youth. I bless the rising sun each day, and, as before, my heart sings to it, but now I love even more its setting, its long slanting rays and the soft tender gentle memories that come with them, the dear images from the whole of my long blessed life—and over all the Divine Truth, softening, reconciling, forgiving! My life is ending, I know that well, but every day that is left me I feel how my earthly life touches a new, infinite, unknown, but imminent life, the presentiment of which sets my soul quivering with rapture, my mind glowing and my heart weeping with joy. . . . All creation and all creatures, every leaf is striving towards the Word, singing glory to God, crying to Christ, unwittingly accomplishing this by the mystery of their sinless life. . . . Gentlemen, look around you at the gifts of God, the clear sky, the pure air, the tender grass, the birds; nature is beautiful and sinless, and we, only we, are godless and foolish, and we don't understand that life is paradise, for we have only to understand that and it will at once be fulfilled in all its beauty, we shall embrace each other and weep.[7]

Pathos, suffering, loneliness, duality, inner contradictions, faith, spiritual freedom, wholeheartedness, self-abandon, intellectual asceticism, religious fervor, tension towards the end, self-identification with suffering humanity—nowhere else are these motifs as powerfully portrayed as in classical Russian literature. There is about them a liberating, universal, human appeal. The Russian soul may one day make the Russians forget all about Marx and Lenin; and who knows, they might forget about them sooner and cleaner than many people in the West! Nothing is more important therefore than to be absolutely clear on this: that the Russians are a great people, that they are a people of genius, that they are human to the core, that they are friends, that the enemy is not they but Marxism-Leninism, that their industrialization is a great achievement and the West has no intention of derogating from it, and that there is nothing to prevent a lasting peace with the Soviet government provided the Marxist-Leninists no longer control it. To love the Russians, to keep in mind that beneath the Marxist crust there is Pushkin and Gogol, Dostoevski and Tolstoi, and the great Russian saints, to feel humble before all these, to allow them in your mind to intercede for the present Communist aberration, to remember that the wonder that is *Doctor Zhivago* was possible even under communism, and that it was conceived in the suburbs of Moscow, whereas it is almost impossible for the suburbs of New York or Boston or London to produce a comparable creation, to be thankful because millions upon millions of Orthodox Christians in Russia

[7] Feodor Dostoevski, *The Brothers Karamazov* (New York: The Heritage Press, 1949), pp. 219–228.

are still immovably faithful despite all atheism, all persecution, and all materialism, to believe that the Church in Russia will never die and to praise God therefor, to identify oneself with all this intellectual-spiritual-human heritage and to keep on reminding the Russians of it all the time, to tell them boldly that you love them for *it*—all this is quite revolutionary these days, when all that people read about Russia is what Khrushchev and Malinovsky say, and what Tass publishes.

19. Policy is ultimately rooted in the way governments fundamentally interpret the historic moment. If Western civilization fails to see that communism is radically and unalterably sworn to destroy all its basic values; if fun is perpetually poured on the notion of "total victory"; if "neutralism" continues to be encouraged and anti-Westernism rewarded, not as a matter of tactics, but as a matter of policy; if the spirit of fear, accommodation, and coexistence continues to prevail; if the West fails to pass to the offensive so as to cause the tide really to turn; if the worst thing that can happen to a man outside the Western world—and I am afraid now even to some extent in the Western world itself—is to have it known of him and said of him that he believes in and practices the fundamental values of the West; in short, if the West's fundamental interpretation of the historic moment makes possible such understandings, policies, and atmospheres, then we have here a radical misreading of the crisis in its ultimate dimensions, and, as a result, we may be in for much tragedy and suffering still. A revolutionary awakening is needed. This awakening must embrace every aspect of human existence, not only the material and political, but, above all, the educational, the intellectual, and the spiritual. The character and possibility of this revolution are the greatest issues of the future.

20. Everything depends on the strength, vigors, and unity of the West. If despite every obstacle, external and internal, Europe succeeds in forging the unity now foretokened by the Com-

mon Market, the Western Hemisphere succeeds in integrating itself—economically, politically, culturally—with this unity, and this whole Western world succeeds in maintaining within its orbit Japan and as much of Asia and Africa as possible, *then the delinquencies and sins of the West will be forgiven. The West will have vindicated itself.* For then it becomes only a question of modality and of time as to how and when international communism will be forced to disintegrate *in peace* and the Marxist-Leninist nightmare lifted from the hearts of men. It takes a revolution in thought and life and law for the American to feel that he is organically no longer independent from Europe, and for the Europeans to feel that they now constitute an inseparable organism, both between themselves and with America. The consummation of this revolution is the greatest challenge of Western statesmanship.

21. The West prefers to deal (and perhaps is only able to deal) with "charismatic leaders" rather than with peoples. A great mystery resides here. This "dealing" is always in danger of turning into "double-dealing," especially on the part of the "leaders." Is the phenomenon of "hypocrisy," of "duplicity," whereby the "charismatic leader" tells the West one thing in secret and then turns around and tells his people the exact opposite in public, an inevitable phenomenon today? Is that the only basis on which "business" can be transacted? Has international communism so scared and intimidated everybody, has it so convinced everybody of its usefulness and inevitability, that no one would dare take a firm and open stand against it? The analysis of this phenomenon of "hypocrisy" as practiced today in the grand style, especially as regards its revelation of the *weakness* of the West, is fascinating. "Charismatic leaders" must thus develop two tongues and two faces, not only as between East and West, but as between either of these and their own peoples; they can never quite commit themselves; in this "tightrope balancing" they must always

provide themselves with a "way of escape," a sort of safety net underneath. It is evident that this is a most unstable situation. To be able to deal with peoples and not only with leaders, no matter how gifted these might be, and no matter how much they have been consciously built up precisely for this appointed role; to bridge the gap between the West and the peoples, not only unstably through leaders, but stably through winning at least the fear, if not also the respect and love, of the peoples; to have done with "hypocrisy" and "double-talk" —all this is visionary, unpractical, and therefore quite revolutionary these days.

22. As between the Communist realm (both Soviet and Chinese) on the one hand, and Western civilization on the other, the former enjoys distinct natural advantages—strategically, racially, economically, culturally, ideologically, and spiritually—over the latter in its dealings with the peoples of Asia and Africa. In the one case, there are relative kinships and continuities; in the other, there are relative discontinuities and differences. This cultural handicap must be faced and overcome. Because we are dealing here with natural affinities, the effort to overcome or counteract this handicap is so tremendous that it can only be revolutionary. Apart from reliance on the ordinary operations of diplomacy, economics, politics, and military matters—all of which are necessary— the West, to make itself acceptable to the peoples and cultures of Asia and Africa, is called upon to go much more deeply into itself than are the Communists. Books and literature are not exploited enough. Fundamental ideas are not adequately believed in nor put forward. Western propaganda is amateurish compared to that of the Communists. The great asset which the English language, as the chief *lingua franca* of the world, provides (at the Bandung Conference in 1955 nothing was more natural than for Asia and Africa to agree immediately that English was the official language of the Conference)

is not taken full advantage of; in fact, the Communists are taking more advantage of this fact for their own purposes than is the West, for the intellectuals of Asia and Africa have learned about communism far more through the medium of English than through any other medium. But nothing is half as important in this whole realm of overcoming natural handicaps and "making oneself acceptable" as faith, conviction, sincerity, depth, and the cultivation of mutual trust and respect. To speak from evident conviction and not mere interest; to believe in something that belongs to the depths of your being; to command the courage and ability to articulate it and stand for it; to appear and be absolutely sincere; and to think of and treat others on the basis of respect for their individuality and freedom, and therefore to develop an atmosphere of confidence between you and them—these are certainly revolutionary qualities in the complacent world of existence-as-usual where "depth," even if known, is scoffed at and ridiculed, and where, to be fair and modern and open-minded, you must not "believe" anything.

23. Suffering alone confirms and chastens. One important way of expressing the present distress is to say that significant sections of the West have not known real suffering—cultural, existential, fateful suffering. They have had it too easy all their life. This is why existence-as-usual is still the norm. The "beyond," the "above," the "other," is not revealed. Do we then have to wait until more suffering, real suffering, suffering "of the right kind," has supervened before salvation can come? *It is possible that this is the last word.* And yet one may be granted the grace of suffering even before he is actually made to suffer. This is voluntary suffering, which is when you give, not of your means or margin, but of your soul and substance. Dare the West give of its soul and substance? This is the question today, and the expected revolution depends precisely on the answer to this question. Not until in its homecoming the

West reaches such depths of love and understanding and daring that it knows and lives again the mystery of "whoever will save his life shall lose it" can light and salvation once more burst forth from it. The West will then be true to itself, and the meeting of the Communist menace will only be a by-product.

24. Entirely apart from any challenge coming from Marx or Lenin, Russia, China, or the East, the West owes it to itself to rediscover and reaffirm its fundamental values. If everyone else moved to Venus or Mars and Western civilization alone remained on this earth, it must still face the question: What do you make of man, reason, nature, destiny, and God? If these things were alien to it, it might perhaps afford to disregard them; but they are at the very base of its existence, stirring it to the depths. These issues have been more radically raised and pondered by this civilization than by any other. It can never forget them, because thereby it will forget itself, and self-forgetfulness is death. Thus, Pericles and Plato and Aristotle are alive; so are the order and universalism of Rome; so are Christ and Paul and the Apostles; so are the great Mediaevals—Christian, Jewish, and Moslem; so are the Fathers and saints; so are Leonardo and the Renaissance; so are Newton and Shakespeare and the seventeenth century; so is that wonderful modern creation of man—science; so is the great German thought; so is the great Russian literature. Ivan Karamazov was right in "falling upon the earth and kissing those stones and weeping over them" (and if not Ivan, certainly Alyosha would include many a stone in the Near East), but where he was wrong—where the whole of Soviet Russia is wrong today—is in supposing that those stones belong to a cemetery. Mediterranean-Western civilization is never a cemetery and will never be such. It has fallen upon hard days, but it will bounce back and recover. It has the secret of eternal life. Thus, there is love; there is suffering

that shatters and sweetens and deepens and makes humble; there is forgiveness; there is the active reason that orders and apprehends everything; there is the infinite freedom of the spirit; there is that creativity that simply creates; there is the inner joy that knows no bounds; there is certainty in the truth; there is real trust and hope; there are company and fun and fellowship and the giving of life by losing it; there is victory over the powers of darkness; there is the Divine Liturgy of Saint John Chrysostom; there is the Church, both the Church of the East and the Church of the West, the Universal Church; there is Christ; there is the resurrection from the dead; there is Easter morn. A civilization that contains these things will be saved by them, even if it should go through hell in the process. The reaffirmation of these things, the return of the West to itself—a reaffirmation and a return, not in words and thought alone, but in the family, in the school and university, in the market place, in industry, in literature, in the whole tone of culture, in political activity, in social existence, in the life of the spirit—this is the expected authentic revolution of the West. And the West owes it to itself, independently of any external challenge, to rise to the highest it already is and knows. This rise is simply a repentant homecoming, an authentic return to itself. For I repeat what I have said before: In a great revolutionary age, when everything is on the move, when everyone everywhere is awakening, when no level of existence is without its ferment—in such an age, for the West to exist-as-usual and *not* to develop its own distinctive revolution—this is the tragedy of the day.

25. In some respects there is already a glimmering of a revolutionary spirit in the West; this is evidenced by the momentous movement for European and Atlantic union, by the general awakening as to the nature and menace of communism, and by the interest in training guerrillas. But the fundamental transformation of the character of a whole civilization

is still a matter of the future. In the end, it is a question of faith in the values of freedom. If there are a hundred men, *well placed* in government, in the press, in industry, in labor, in the universities, and in the churches, one hundred men *who really work as a team,* who really see through the sham and vacuity of Communist existence, who really understand that it is now a matter of life and death for the highest and deepest they believe in, and who really believe that there is nothing like the values of the mind and spirit and man and God which have come down to Mediterranean-Western civilization from the last four thousand years—if there are one hundred such men, well placed and working as a team, then I believe we can rest; not because nationalism, change, and war are going to defeat communism, but because the revolution has started, because everyone will be called upon to do his part in it, and because the Communists are already on the run.

INDEX

Adenauer, Konrad, 185, 191
Aeschylus, 186
Africa, *xxiii,* 57, 185
    communism and, *xxxi,* 116, 141,
        145, 172, 189, 190, 192, 202,
        212
    nationalism of, 161
    new nations of, 80–81, 82, 92, 110,
        112, 135
    United Nations and, 79, 83, 100
    Western values and, *xxxvii-xxxviii,*
        xxxix, 187, 226–227
    see also specific countries
Albania, 132, 168, 210
Algeria, 81
American Association for the
    United Nations, 97 *n.*
American University, Washington,
    D.C., *xli*
Anselm, Saint, 186
Arabs, *xxi, xxxvii,* 158
    United Nations and, 68, 93, 102
Aristotle, 185, 188, 228
Arms:
    disarmament, 64, 73, 74, 92, 124,
        178
    nuclear:
        cold war parity, 174–178, 193,
            203, 205, 210–211
        Soviet, *xxxiii,* 130, 164
        war goals and, 198–201, 202–
            203
        Western, 145–146
    Russian counter-revolution, 171
    United Nations, 69, 80, 99
Asia, *xxiii,* 57
    communism in, *xxxi,* 116, 141,
        142, 145, 172, 189, 190, 192,
        194, 202, 212

Asia *(Continued)*
    India and, 102
    nationalism in, 161
    new nations of, 80–81, 82, 110,
        135
    United Nations and, 79, 100
    Western values and, *xxxvii-xxxviii,*
        xxxix, 187, 226–227
    see also specific countries
Atheism, *xv*
    communist, 130, 166–167, 202,
        214, 217–218
Athens, Greece, *xxi*
Atomic energy, 92, 199, 201
Atomic weapons. *See* Arms, nuclear
Augustine, Saint:
    on love, 47
    on pride, *xviii*
    as a Western value, 185, 186, 188
Augustine Synthesis, An (Przywara),
    47 *n.*
Austro-Hungarian empire, 160

Bach, Johann Sebastian, 186
Baldwin, Stanley, 181
Bandung Conference, 226
Beethoven, Ludwig van, 186
Being and Time (Heidegger), *x n.*
Belinsky, Vissarion Grigorievich,
    quoted, 219–220
Berdyaev, Nicholas, *xl,* 219, 221 *n.*
Berkeley, George, *bishop,* 4
Berlin, Germany, 75, 80, 145, 185
Bible, The:
    Dostoevski on, 222
    Jaspers on, *xliii*
    ontology and, *x-xiii, xv*
    parable of the Prodigal Son, 108
    see also specific Books

231